PARTNERSHIP WORKING

Policy and practice

Edited by Susan Balloch and Marilyn Taylor

The POLICY PRESS

First published in Great Britain in July 2001 by

The Policy Press
34 Tyndall's Park Road
Bristol BS8 1PY
UK

Tel +44 (0)117 954 6800
Fax +44 (0)117 973 7308
e-mail tpp-info@bristol.ac.uk
www.policypress.org.uk

Susan Balloch is Reader in Health and Social Care and **Marilyn Taylor** is Professor of Social Policy, both at the University of Brighton.

Cover design by Qube Design Associates, Bristol.

Contents

List of tables and figures   v

Notes on contributors   vi

Introduction   I
Susan Balloch and Marilyn Taylor

Part One: Regeneration and social exclusion

one   'Holism' and urban regeneration   17
             Peter Ambrose

two   Partnerships and power in community regeneration   39
             Marjorie Mayo and Marilyn Taylor

three   Local government, anti-poverty strategies and partnership   57
             working
             Sarah Pearson

four   Partnership and change in social housing   77
             Barbara Reid

five   Improving partnership working in housing and mental health   97
             Simon Northmore

Part Two: Partnerships in social care and health

six   The potential of project status to support partnerships   II7
             Valerie Williamson

seven   Promoting independence: a partnership approach to   143
             supporting older people in the community
             Helen Charnley

eight   Partnership between service users and statutory social   165
             services
             Michael Turner and Susan Balloch

nine   Partnership working in health promotion: the potential role   181
             of social capital in health development
             John Kenneth Davies

Part Three: Power, participation and place

ten   Partnership and power: the role of black and minority   203
        ethnic voluntary organisations in challenging racism
        Jabeer Butt

eleven Rounding up the 'usual suspects': police approaches to   223
        multiagency policing
        Peter Squires and Lynda Measor

twelve Partnership – participation – power: the meaning of   243
        empowerment in post-industrial society
        David Byrne

thirteen Spatial considerations in multiagency and multidisciplinary 261
        work
        Philip Haynes

Conclusion – can partnerships work?   283
Susan Balloch and Marilyn Taylor

Index   289

List of tables and figures

Tables

3.1   Anti-poverty and social inclusion initiatives in local government   60

3.2   Partners in generic and specific partnerships   63

4.1   Different levels at which partnership is defined in social housing   81

4.2   Types of partnership operating in social housing   83

4.3   A framework for understanding partnerships in social housing   92

5.1   Proportions of homeless people with mental health problems   102

Figures

1.1   Graphical representation of the service delivery system in a typical local authority area   19

5.1   A checklist for partnership working   108

6.1   Factors inhibiting partnership working   120

6.2   Prerequisites for partnership working   122

6.3   Management and operational structure of the Joint Continuing Care project   126

6.4   Management and operational structure of attachment project   128

6.5   Perceived strengths of Projects A and B   130

6.6   Perceived weaknesses of Projects A and B   133

7.1   Joint Continuing Care project: key players   149

13.1   Weston District Council: sketch map of key urban and rural areas   265

13.2   A multidisciplinary service location and its effect on users take-up   278

Notes on contributors

Peter Ambrose trained as a Geographer and holds degrees from London, McGill and Sussex Universities. He taught Geography, Urban Studies and Social Policy for 35 years at the University of Sussex before his retirement in 1998. He is now Visiting Professor in Housing Studies at the University of Brighton. He has carried out extensive research on housing systems in many east and west European countries but in recent years has concentrated on the relationship between housing conditions and health in a number of urban regeneration situations in several London boroughs and in Brighton and Hove.

Susan Balloch is Reader in Health and Social Care in the Health and Social Policy Research Centre (HSPRC) at the University of Brighton. Her research interests include community profiling, partnership working, the health and social care workforce and social inclusion. She is a co-editor of *Social services: Working under pressure* (The Policy Press, 1999). Previously she worked as Policy Director for the National Institute for Social Work.

Jabeer Butt is a Researcher and Consultant with the Race Equality Unit (REU). He has carried out research on various aspects of Britain's black and minority ethnic communities' experience of social care, including the work of voluntary organisations. Recently he has completed work on *Between ambition and achievement: Black young disabled people's views and experiences of independence and independent living,* written with Tracey Bignall (The Policy Press/Joseph Rowntree Foundation, 2000), and *Directing support* (2000), a report from a workshop on Direct Payments.

David Byrne is Reader in Sociology and Social Policy at the University of Durham. He has previously worked as Research Director of the North Tyneside Community Development Project in the 1970s and in Community Research in Northern Ireland. His publications include *Social exclusion* (Open University Press, 1999), *Complexity theory and the social sciences* (Routledge, 1998), *Beyond the inner city* (Open University Press, 1989) and *Understanding the urban* (Palgrave, 2001).

Helen Charnley is Senior Lecturer in Social Policy and Social Work at the University of Brighton. Her research interests in partnership span national and international boundaries and have focused on supporting older people, and children separated from their families. She has published in both areas.

John Kenneth Davies is Senior Lecturer in Health Promotion in the Faculty of Health, University of Brighton. He has served as Visiting Professor at the Research Centre in Health Promotion, University of Bergen, Norway. His interests focus on international, particularly European, aspects of health promotion development. He is Project Manager of the 15-country study funded by the European Commission to establish a European postgraduate programme in health promotion. He is Associate Editor of *Health Education Research:Theory & Practice* (Oxford University Press).

Philip Haynes is a Senior Lecturer at the University of Brighton. From 1984-91 he worked as a probation officer and multiagency project worker for those with substance misuse difficulties. He has completed a number of research evaluations for multiagency projects, including projects providing services for drug users, those with eating disorders and children with attachment disorders. He recently published a book entitled *Complex policy planning* (Ashgate, 1999) and is currently beginning work on a book about the management of complexity in the public services.

Marjorie Mayo is a Reader in Community Development at Goldsmiths, University of London. With colleagues at the Centre for Urban and Community Research, she is evaluating partnerships for regeneration and for health. Her previous publications include *Communities and caring: The mixed economy of welfare* (Macmillan, 1994), *Imagining tomorrow: Adult education for transformation* (NIACE, 1997) and *Cultures, communities, identities: Cultural strategies for participation and empowerment* (Palgrave, 2000).

Lynda Measor is a Senior Lecturer in the School of Applied Social Sciences at the University of Brighton. She completed undergraduate and postgraduate degrees at the University of Sussex and the London School of Economics. She was a Research Fellow at the Open University before her appointment at Brighton.

Simon Northmore is co-director of 'In Tandem', an independent consulting partnership which provides services to the voluntary sector. He has been Development Coordinator for the National Community Care Alliance and a Senior Lecturer in Social Policy at the University of Brighton. He is currently completing an MPhil on the health needs of families in temporary accommodation.

Barbara Reid is Principal Lecturer in Housing in the Faculty of the Built Environment at South Bank University.

Sarah Pearson is a Research Associate at the Centre for Regional Economic and Social Research (CRESR), Sheffield Hallam University. Her research interests are in policy responses to poverty and social exclusion.

Peter Squires is a Reader in Criminal Justice Research at the University of Brighton. His research interests lie in fields relating to policing, community safety and crime prevention, social theory and social control. He has recently published *Gun culture or gun control?* (Routledge, 2000) a study of firearms, violence and society, and, with Lynda Measor, *Young people and community safety* (Ashgate, 2000).

Marilyn Taylor is Professor of Social Policy at the Health and Social Policy Research Centre, University of Brighton. She has written widely for policy and practice audiences on community development, user involvement and relationships between government and the voluntary sector.

Michael Turner is an experienced writer and researcher on issues around disability and service users. He was the worker on the Citizens' Commission on the Future of the Welfare State and the co-author of its report *It's our welfare* (1997). He is currently the worker on the 'Shaping Our Lives' project which is developing user perspectives on outcomes.

Valerie Williamson is Principal Lecturer in Social Policy at the University of Brighton. Health authority membership stimulated an interest in researching relations between health professionals and service users but lately she has been studying the impact of 'special projects' on collaborative working.

Introduction

Susan Balloch and Marilyn Taylor

Partnership working is an increasingly central feature of all public services. It plays a pivotal role in the modernisation agenda, supported by financial incentives to bring potential partners together. In this book we explore the experience of partnerships in different policy fields, identifying the theoretical issues and the practical impediments to making partnership work. We concentrate primarily on the development of partnership working in England, although some chapters make use of comparative data from other countries. While acknowledging the importance of the private sector in partnerships, in this edited collection we focus mainly on the statutory, voluntary and community sectors as well as partnerships with service users.

In this Introduction, we outline the background to partnership working and the experience on which it can build. We then review key partnership initiatives in current policies and the wider context within which these policies must operate. We summarise the current debates about partnership and introduce the reader to the chapters that will follow and the main arguments that will be developed. Finally, in our conclusion, we review the implications of partnership for changing radically the current cultures of service provision and addressing the government's social exclusion agenda.

Does partnership makes sense?

Superficially, partnership makes a lot of sense. At one level it is a rational response to divisions within and between government departments and local authorities, within and between professions, and between those who deliver services and those who use them. It is also a necessary response to the fragmentation of services that the introduction of markets into welfare brought with them. It has the potential to make the delivery of services more coherent and hence more effective. If each partner stands to gain from the additional resources that other partners bring, from pooling ideas, knowledge and financial resources, then partnership 'adds value' for each participant. It can generate 'new insights or solutions' and provide a 'synergy' that offers more than the sum of its parts (Mackintosh, 1993). This is reflected in its policies for modernising local government, in a range of policies to tackle social exclusion by making money available to targeted areas on the basis of partnership working, and in its approach to service quality. Partnership can offer participants the opportunity to influence other agencies to operate in ways that help them to achieve their objectives more effectively and it has the potential to transform radically the culture of public service delivery, through compelling people to think in new ways. Ultimately, it has the potential to transform the governance of welfare at local level, in ways that have far-reaching implications for the local democratic system.

Partnership reflects ideals of participatory democracy and equality between partners. It assumes overarching common interests between different players and it can underplay the difficulties in bringing together different interests and different cultures. For this reason, it is important to bring a critical perspective to bear, to understand the expectations and assumptions that lie behind a term that commands such widespread support across the political spectrum and to be clear about its implications. Will it enhance services for the people who are supposed to benefit from them and transform the relationship between them and the professionals who deliver services? Will it really produce more efficient and effective systems? Or will it dissipate energies through the proliferation of new structures, which are ill-defined, inadequately resourced and which do not change the underlying power structures or cultures? Will it get stuck in considerations of structures, procedures and systems or will it really deliver changed outcomes? Will new partnerships exclude more vulnerable groups and communities and prove less rather than more accountable to those they are supposed to serve than previous institutions?

The background to partnership working

As several chapters in this volume emphasise, partnership is not a new phenomenon. Before the advent of the welfare state, local authorities worked alongside voluntary organisations to deliver welfare, and while in some policy areas statutory provision began to outstrip voluntary effort, in others statutory funders supported and encouraged the continued role of voluntary provision. The end of the 1960s saw a major drive to address deprivation in particular localities. The initiatives introduced then – Educational Priority Areas, the Urban Programme, the Community Development Projects, and the short-lived Comprehensive Community

Programme – combined a number of the features of current par[tnership]
initiatives, including interagency working, targeting those areas i[n]
need and community participation. Major reports from the Lords
Seebohm (on the social services, 1968) and Skeffington (on planning,
1969) emphasised in particular the need for consultation and support for
community initiatives.

With the introduction of markets into welfare in the Thatcher era, the
emphasis changed from coordination to contracts, from participation to
individual consumer choice, but elements of coordination remained, such
as joint planning in community care. At the same time, with the erosion
of local government responsibilities and the advent of a mixed economy
of care, the growing fragmentation of responsibility for services demanded
some form of action. An Audit Commission report in 1989 was highly
critical of the piecemeal approach of the Thatcher government to
regeneration and the deliberate exclusion of local government. This
eventually gave rise under the Major government to an emphasis on
partnerships in bidding for funds and a consolidation of Whitehall
responsibilities and budgets. While the impetus for the restructuring of
community care was largely financial, this too was characterised by an
emphasis on partnership, joint finance and joint planning between health
and social care agencies.

Current policy initiatives

The new Labour government elected in 1997 tied its colours firmly to
the partnership mast, announcing its intention to move from a contract
culture to a partnership culture. A national compact, for example, was
agreed between government and the voluntary and community sectors
to provide a framework for relationships between the sectors (1998).
Partnership initiatives across a number of fields were required to bid for
central government funds through multiagency partnership and in
consultation with communities and/or service users. This was a
requirement already inherited in the regeneration field from the previous
Conservative administration, but additional programmes were introduced
on a similar basis – for example, Sure Start, the programme jointly
sponsored by the Departments of Health and Education for children
under the age of four and their families, and the New Deal for Young
People. Early Years partnerships were set up at local authority level to
encourage joint working, while targeted Education and Health Education

Zones were introduced to do the same thing in areas facing particular disadvantages.

Joint working has also become a central plank of the National Strategy for Neighbourhood Renewal (Social Exclusion Unit, 2000, 2001), with its proposals for neighbourhood management and local strategic partnerships, the latter building on the experience of the Local Government Association's New Commitment to Regeneration Programme. The advance of partnerships under New Labour had threatened to become a victim of its own success, with the proliferation of partnerships and the sheer pace of change stretching agencies, service users and communities to their limits. But the intention is that the introduction of Local Strategic Partnerships will rationalise this, and while they were originally proposed as part of the neighbourhood renewal strategy, recent guidance on their introduction makes it clear that they will also take responsibility for the development of overall community strategies.

Local government

Modernising local government: In touch with the people (1998), the local government White Paper, argued that "effective local partnerships are fundamental to the success of the council's strategic role" (Chapter Eight). The importance of councils working with a wide range of agencies and organisations that operate locally, that is, local people, the local business community, voluntary groups, private organisations and public bodies, was reflected both in initiatives to give a bigger say to local people (local democracy) and to provide a better deal for local people through best value. New powers have provided scope for pooling or sharing resources, accommodation, IT and staff, and have encouraged the delegation of responsibility for decisions within an agreed framework.

Social services

The social services White Paper, *Modernising social services: Promoting independence, improving protection, raising standards* (1998), devoted the whole of Chapter Six to improving partnerships. This chapter covered better joint working to help people get the services they need, integrated health and social care, and better coordination of children's services. It argued (6.5) that government had made it one of the top priorities to bring down the 'Berlin Wall' that divides health and social services and to create a system of integrated care that puts users at the centre of service provision. What was most striking about this chapter, however, was the concluding five-line paragraph that mentioned, almost as an afterthought, the importance of public sector partnership with voluntary and community groups.

Further examples of initiatives to promote joint working between social services and other agencies have included: Better Services for Vulnerable People, Better Government for Older People, Promoting Independence Grants, the Long-Term Care Charter and the development of National Service Frameworks to cover mental health and care for older people. Particular recommendations have included pooled budgets, lead commissioning and integrated provision.

Health services

Here the aim to replace the internal market with a "system of integrated care based on partnership and driven by performance" has been reiterated in the White Papers *The New NHS: Modern, dependable* (1997) and *Our healthier nation: A contract for health* (1998a). Central to partnership are the Health Improvement Programmes, Health Action Zones, Primary Care Groups, and Joint Investment programmes. The 1999 NHS Act has laid down a duty of partnership requiring health authorities to work with local authorities on health improvement issues and supplemented this with circulars on the importance of Health Act partnership arrangements. In particular these stipulate improving services for users through pooled funds and the delegation of functions through lead commissioning and delegated provision.

The NHS Plan (Secretary of State, 2000) has defined financial incentives to encourage and reward joint working between primary care groups and trusts, NHS trusts and social services. Social services will get additional ring-fenced funds from April 2002 to reward improved joint working, focusing initially on intermediate care. The NHS Plan also makes it a requirement for the powers in the Health Act for pooled budgets, lead commissioning and integrated provision to be used in all areas. It is envisaged that there will be far greater joint working between social services and primary and community health care, often working from the same premises and with more joint assessments of patients. The NHS Plan (2000) has also proposed the creation of new 'Care Trusts' able to commission and deliver primary and community health care as well as social care for older people and other client groups. The first wave of these new care trusts could be in place as early as 2001 (p 73, paras 7.9-

7.12). Meanwhile, Herefordshire has become the first local authority to form a partnership with a health authority under the Health Act (White, 2000).

Types of partnership

Although this is a book about partnership working, we lay claim to no single definition or model of this popular concept. Variously identified as interagency, interprofessional, collaborative or joined-up working, joined-up thinking or a whole systems or holistic approach, that which we have chosen to call 'partnership working' exists along a broad continuum of theory and practice. The essence of this is captured by Pratt's model of a spectrum of commitment and working arrangements that extends from competition to cooperation, coordination and co-evolution (Pratt et al, 1998), with shared goals only a feature of the latter (a similar distinction – between cooperation, coordination and collaboration – is made by Mattesich and Monsey, 1994). The most important distinction here is between types of joining up where partners maintain their individual authority but cooperate on some issues (usually at the margins of their main 'business'), and types of joining up where partners pool authority. In a different vein, Mackintosh (1993) distinguishes three types of partnership according to what the partners want out of it: budget enlargement, added value or synergy. But this distinction also suggests different levels of commitment.

Within this range, partners may experience different types of relationships depending on the extent to which partnerships are based on market, hierarchical or network principles (Skelcher et al, 1996). They may also experience different partnership cultures. Lowndes and Skelcher (1998) suggest that the principles on which partnerships are based may change at different points in the life cycle. Partners may also experience different partnership cultures. Reid and Iqbal (1996, p 31) distinguish two such cultures. Their 'competitive' networks are entrepreneurial, flexible and opportunistic, but also exclusive, relying on organisations to secure their own entry. Conversely, their 'collaborative' networks are less exclusive and more concerned with legitimacy, but less entrepreneurial and may simply rubber-stamp decisions taken in more entrepreneurial networks. As such they often deliver much less than participants expect or than their energies and effort would appear to deserve.

Finally, as Hastings et al report (1996), partners come to the table with very different expectations of what the partnership is for. Rarely are these different expectations laid on the table and negotiated. They may revolve around the aims of the partnership: the level at which it will have influence (policy, agenda setting, policy implementation); the powers of different partners. In these circumstances, it is perhaps not surprising that some go away disappointed.

As the chapters in this book suggest, new approaches need to be based on clarity about the roles, powers, and accountability requirements of stakeholders at all levels. They also require an understanding of the different expectations different players bring to the partnership and the factors that support or create barriers to partnership working at different stages in the process. This needs to include attention to the expectations and support needs of communities, front-line staff and service users, as well as managers and politicians. All this needs to be set in the context of the wider political agenda (for example, regionalisation, modernising local government, best value) and the demands of central government.

As the above discussion suggests, partnership involves major tensions. This means that there can be no blueprint for successful partnerships. Rather each partnership needs to find its balance: between the flexibility that partnerships require if they are to break new ground and public accountability for public expenditure; between leadership, expertise and participation; between consensus and diversity. Finding that balance requires skills that are not always available – there is rarely a person specification for those who find themselves on a partnership board and the reasons that they come to be there may not equip them for the complexities of the task. This is especially true when it comes to finding the all-important 'chair'. Finding that balance also means that partnership involves both pain and gain. As such, it cannot remain at the margins but will require commitment and investment.

Current debates on partnerships: the potential and the pitfalls

Past research on partnership working suggests that it tends to take place at the margins of participating agencies, focusing on special initiatives (as in the case of regeneration or anti-poverty strategies) or special pots of money for specific objectives (joint finance in health and social care). While it has allowed progress to be made and supported innovatory projects and ways of working, it has failed to transform departmental and agency specific budgets and delivery mechanisms or to penetrate into the core of public service cultures (see, for example, 6 et al, 1999; Wilkinson and Appelbee,

9). Our earlier discussion of recent policy innovations suggests that is has been recognised in more recent policy innovations, particularly the National Strategy for Neighbourhood Renewal (see also PIU, 2000). The formation of local strategic partnerships with a responsibility for developing community strategies could provide the impetus to transform mainstream spending, and to bring together under one roof many of the more specific partnerships that have developed at local level.

Why has it been so difficult to address this agenda in the past? After all, while the current drive to partnership has distinctive features, interagency working and community/user participation have been around for some time. Research highlights problems at political, cultural and technical levels.

Firstly, partnership has largely left existing power relationships intact. Partnership working has too often been dominated by the more powerful partners and has not 'delivered', especially for the communities and service users who are now a required part of most partnerships. By and large, they have remained on the margins of processes where the rules of the game are determined by government partners, legitimating rather than making decisions. Power relationships are also reflected in the resources available to different partners. These can be very uneven. Smaller partners from the voluntary, community and business sectors simply do not have the resources to engage effectively in partnerships, especially if they are there to represent large and diverse communities. They do not have the back-up that other partners take for granted and the time spent at the partnership table takes them away from their constituency, their customers and the front line. Their infrastructure is fragile, insecure and stretched to capacity by the demands of partnership – it is rarely resourced to deliver what is required. In that sense, representatives from these sectors are 'set up to fail'. There are also issues about the funding relationship between different partners. Communities, small voluntary organisations and service users rarely have financial assets to bring to the table and many are dependent for their funding on their statutory partners. It is unlikely that they will feel that they are equal partners until they have access to independent support and assets of their own.

Secondly, public service cultures need to be transformed if agencies are to work effectively with each other and with those they are supposed to benefit. For example, under the heading 'Creating partnerships', the consultation document *A quality strategy for social care* (DoH, 1998b) noted (p 30):

Excellent social services departments will ensure that:

- local partnerships are actively used to explore and develop new ways of delivering services;
- priority is given to partnership and maximum use is made, for the benefit of the local community, of the new flexibilities in the Health Act;
- users' and carers' views are recorded, and feedback is given about action taken;
- users and carers are fully involved in the development of Long-Term Care Charters;
- local charters are both honest and challenging;
- children are listened to and their wishes and feelings respected;
- the views of the wider local community, including potential users and other stakeholders, are actively sought through a variety of means.

Partnership will require new incentive structures and people who can work with change – spreading rather than protecting knowledge, working creatively with diversity and conflict, learning to handle risk. Public service bureaucracies have not been designed for this in the past and public sector workers have not been rewarded for it. There are genuine difficulties involved in breaking down existing cultures and working in new ways, and this takes time and investment.

Thirdly, partnership also presents major structural, technical and managerial challenges, requiring new information and communication systems, new budgeting systems and new approaches to handling complex and multiple accountabilities. Boundaries are often not co-terminous between agencies and this hampers the pooling of budgets and information as well as responsibility. Physically, the location of partners in different buildings prevents that face-to-face communication on which a shared culture depends. Technically, the use of different computer systems slows down the exchange of information. Agencies are also protective of their own data sources and often, quite rightly, are concerned about breaching confidentiality in sharing information about clients.

Reading this book

The chapters in this book illustrate many of the issues outlined above as well as focusing on other significant topics such as accountability, user empowerment and social capital. Each may be read as a free-standing discussion but, where appropriate, has been cross-referenced with other contributions. The chapters have been grouped into three parts within which they are loosely related. The chapters in Part One look at different aspects of urban regeneration and local authority-based partnerships to combat social exclusion; those in Part Two are primarily concerned with social care and health; and those in Part Three with issues of power, participation and place.

In Part One, the first chapter by Peter Ambrose draws on a study of housing renewal in inner London and on a 'benchmarking' study in Brighton to demonstrate the need to view the regeneration of estates in the context of how all public services operate. It refutes the idea that public services are now successfully engaged in 'joined-up' thinking and action, and suggests innovative ways of moving closer to this central objective.

Chapter Two draws on the growing partnership literature to identify the issues and tensions that continue to haunt partnership initiatives in the UK and beyond. Drawing on evaluations of a range of regeneration initiatives, Marjorie Mayo and Marilyn Taylor consider how far the continuing barriers to partnership can be eroded and the tensions addressed. They explore the implications for community development work, both within communities and across the boundaries with statutory and other agencies.

Sarah Pearson, in Chapter Three, then reviews local authorities' experiences of partnership working as an element of strategies to combat poverty and social exclusion. She draws on research into local authority anti-poverty strategies to address the rationale behind anti-poverty partnerships, to examine the nature and extent of anti-poverty partnerships in the UK, and to assess their impact in promoting unitary and innovative policy responses to poverty and exclusion.

Barbara Reid discusses the place of social housing at the centre of social exclusion policy in Chapter Four. She considers organisational vehicles for advancing the regeneration agenda and responding to the immediate challenges of introducing the Best Value and Tenant Participation Compact regimes, and assesses the implications of different forms of institutional and organisational partnerships associated with local policy networks.

Linked closely to Chapter Four, Simon Northmore bases Chapter Five on evidence from three Joseph Rowntree Foundation-funded workshops aimed at partnership working. They were organised by the Royal Borough of Kingston Community Services Directorate in May and July 1998 for 45 housing and mental health staff from a wide variety of professional backgrounds, including nursing, social work, mental health and housing. The chapter examines the themes that emerged from the workshops, particularly focusing on the pressures facing the different types of staff.

In Part Two, Chapters Six to Nine explore aspects of partnership working related to social services and health. Through the medium of two special projects, one involving social services departments and the NHS in the care of older people and the other bringing together education and social services departments and the NHS to provide an intensive therapeutic regime for emotionally disturbed children and adolescents, Valerie Williamson explores the potential and limitations of project status. She evaluates the extent to which the pitfalls of collaborative working can be resolved and effective collaboration developed, and then goes on to argue that the benefits will ultimately be lost without the development of the internal collaborative capacities of the participating agencies.

Helen Charnley then addresses in Chapter Seven the contrasting pressures that have been brought to bear in establishing a range of policy measures aimed at reducing reliance on long-term residential care, and analyses recent practice initiatives designed specifically to support vulnerable older people to remain in the community. She argues the need for institutional learning to ensure that the main beneficiaries of interagency initiatives are, indeed, service users and carers.

Michael Turner and Susan Balloch follow on from this in Chapter Eight with consideration of strategies to develop partnerships with users of social services. They look first at examples of progress made towards user involvement and empowerment that support a more balanced partnership of equals, then at the partnership working required by direct payments, and finally at the significance of developing user-defined outcomes. They express concern at the reluctance of local authorities and professionals to share decision making, tokenistic gestures in the direction of user empowerment that fall far short of power sharing, and the temptation to rely on carers and proxies to understand what users want.

In Chapter Nine, John Davies reviews the significance of partnerships between organisations, and between organisations and communities, to maximise health gain. Global policies towards Health for All (WHO, 1999) and its key principles of participation, empowerment and equity have only belatedly been reflected in the ideology underpinning British government public health policy. These are discussed and their importance in developing social capital reviewed.

In Part Three, the last four chapters demonstrate how analysing partnership working is dependent on understanding the structural inequalities, discriminatory behaviour and spatial context of the wider society. Chapter Ten emphasises the importance of issues that affect black and ethnic minority communities, with Jabeer Butt reflecting on partnerships between black and ethnic minority voluntary organisations and local government over the past 30 years. His chapter reflects on the achievement of these partnerships and the lessons for the future that have come from them.

Peter Squires and Lynda Measor, in Chapter Eleven, evaluate partnership issues related to multiagency policing. Interagency working is presented as a political process in which agencies, particularly the police, pursue both their own narrow interests as well as other, wider, 'community interests'. Examples show how multiagency initiatives can often involve the pulling in of a familiar array of stakeholders and service representatives who are called upon to assist in the achievement of a variety of policing objectives.

Dave Byrne develops the discussion on 'empowerment' and 'partnership' in Chapter Twelve, using empowerment as a benchmark against which the claims of partnership will be tested. Partnership is evaluated according to whether it facilitates, is neutral towards, or has negative consequences for empowerment. The debate is focused on the Education Action Zone in west Newcastle but draws comparisons with Freire's account of the experience of communities in Brazil.

Finally, in Chapter Thirteen, Philip Haynes encourages readers to explore aspects of spatial location and emphasises how these relate to the development of new forms of organisation, combating social exclusion and improving the efficiency and cost effectiveness of services. He starts with an introduction to the relationship of space with welfare services, rejects the Marxist notion that human space is entirely defined by capitalism, social life and social relations, and supports the postmodern idea that geographical space itself can be one of the defining features of social life. His chapter provides a salutary reminder that spatial location and spatial operations are a crucial aspect of partnership working and have a major impact on multiagency and multidisciplinary service development.

References

6, P., Leat, D., Seltzer, K. and Stoker, G. (1999) *Governing in the round: Strategies for holistic government*, London: Demos.

Audit Commission (1989) *Urban regeneration and economic development: The local government dimension*, London: HMSO.

DoH (Department of Health) (1997) *The New NHS: Modern, dependable*, London: The Stationery Office.

DoH (1998a) *Our healthier nation: A contract for health*, London: The Stationery Office.

DoH (1998b) *A quality strategy for social care*, London: DoH.

DETR (Department of the Environment, Transport and the Regions) (1998) *Modernising local government: In touch with the people*, London: The Stationery Office.

Hastings, A., MacArthur, A. and MacGregor, A. (1996) *Less than equal? Community organisations and regeneration partnerships*, Bristol/York: The Policy Press/Joseph Rowntree Foundation.

Lowndes, V. and Skelcher, C. (1998) 'The dynamics of multi-organisational partnerships: an analysis of changing modes of governance', *Public Administration*, vol 76, pp 313-33.

Mattesich, P. and Monsey, B. (1994) *Collaboration: What makes it work?*, St Paul, MN: Amherst Wilder Foundation.

Mackintosh, M. (1993) 'Partnership: issues of policy and negotiation', *Local Economy*, vol 7, no 3, pp 210-24.

PIU (Performance and Innovation Unit) (2000) *Wiring it up: Whitehall's management of cross-cutting policies and services*, London: The Stationery Office.

Pratt, J., Gordon, P. and Plamping, D. (1998) *Working whole systems: Putting theory into practice in organisations*, London: King's Fund.

Reid, B. and Iqbal, B. (1996) 'Redefining housing practice: inter-organisational networks and local housing networks', in P. Malpass (ed) *The new governance of housing*, Harlow: Longman.

Secretary of State (1998) *Modernising social services: Promoting independence, improving protection, raising standards*, London: The Stationery Office.

Secretary of State (2000) *The NHS Plan: A plan for investment, a plan for reform*, Cm 4818-1, London: The Stationery Office.

Seebohm, F. (1968) *Report of the Committee on Local Authority and Allied Personal Social Services*, Cmnd 3791, London: HMSO.

Skeffington, A.M. (1969) *People and planning: Report of the Committee on Public Participation in Planning*, London: HMSO.

Skelcher, C., McCabe, A., Lowndes, V. and Nanton, P. (1996) *Community networks in urban regeneration: 'It all depends who you know!'*, Bristol/York: The Policy Press/Joseph Rowntree Foundation.

Social Exclusion Unit (2000) *National strategy for neighbourhood renewal: A framework for consultation*, London: Social Exclusion Unit.

Social Exclusion Unit (2001) *A new commitment to neighbourhood renewal: National strategy action plan*, London: Social Exclusion Unit.

White, M. (2000) 'Director to take up first join social services and health post', *Community Care*, 28 September-4 October.

Wilkinson, D. and Appelbee, E. (1999) *Implementing holistic government: Joined up action on the ground*, Bristol: The Policy Press.

Part One:
Regeneration and social exclusion

ONE

'Holism' and urban regeneration

Peter Ambrose

Context

As the Introduction makes clear, much recent thinking and policy formation is predicated on the need for better 'partnership working' in the form of 'interagency' and 'multiagency' cooperation both in the development of urban regeneration programmes and in the quality of services delivered. Other words and phrases frequently employed in this context include *synergy, holistic approaches* and, less elegantly, *joined-up thinking* (see Appendix to this chapter for glossary). In this chapter, which seeks to add some precision to the language being used and to draw on experience gained in working on several recent regeneration projects, the terms *holistic* and *holism* have been adopted to sum up the idea of multiagency approaches to regeneration and cooperation in service delivery. These terms have been preferred because they have an established dictionary meaning, carry positive general connotations and are also in current use in the relevant arenas of discussion.

The need to be more precise in defining terms and analysing process arises because:

- the central idea has lost some sharpness of meaning as a result of political sloganising;
- one key effect flowing from non-holistic working, the 'exporting of costs' across sectoral boundaries, has so far been insufficiently considered (but see the exploratory work of Barrow and Bachan, 1997);
- greater precision in the identification of investment flows and their effects will produce more systematic evidence concerning other forms of inefficiency in the use of resources;

• this in turn will assist in devising more cost-effective policies and practices.

Most of the ideas and arguments presented in this chapter arise from several years of foundation work on the Cost-effectiveness in Housing Investment (CEHI) programme based at the University of Sussex over the period 1993-97 (see Ambrose, 1996) and the various empirical studies of urban regeneration projects that have drawn on this foundation. These include the Central Stepney Single Regeneration Budget (SRB) 'Health Gain' study (Ambrose, 1997, 2000), a project on the quality of local housing advisory services carried out for Brighton and Hove unitary authority (Ambrose, 1998), a study of interagency working in the Holly Street renewal scheme undertaken for the London borough of Hackney (Ambrose and Randles, 1999), the 'benchmarking and baseline' project carried out as part of the delivery programme for the East Brighton New Deal for Communities programme (Ambrose and MacDonald, 2000) and research and advisory work currently in progress in relation to the Brighton and Hove SRB 7 bid due for submission in 2001.

Local service delivery systems

We can start with a graphical representation of the service delivery system in a typical local authority area (see Figure 1.1): the columns represent the various service-delivery agencies. As indicated, these agencies vary in a number of ways, for example in terms of:

• legislative frameworks defining powers and responsibilities;
• form of political accountability, especially in relation to the local electorate;
• funding regimes and the nature of financial accountability;
• agency norms, 'language' and career structures;
• the geographical areas of jurisdiction;
• data collection, management of information and indicators of progress.

These sets of characteristics are collectively referred to as *agency characteristics* (see Appendix).

Figure 1.1: Graphical representation of the service delivery system in a typical local authority area

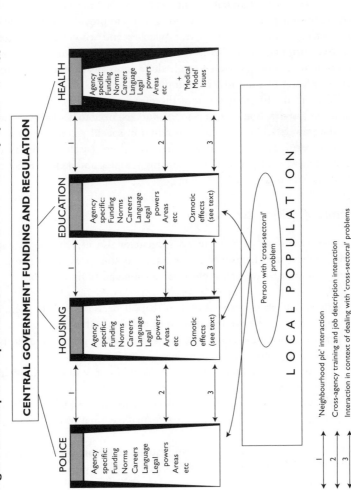

Agency characteristics

Legislative frameworks

The services identified in the diagram work in a complex legislative framework built up over a century or more. Public health legislation dates from the 1840s, the first important Housing Acts from the 1860s, the great Education Act from 1870 and much local government legislation from the closing decades of the 19th century. This legislation varies not only in its era of origin but also in its purpose and the extent to which it lays clear duties on departments and agencies to provide specific services. For example, the duty to provide primary and secondary educational services is much more clearly defined in law than the duty to provide housing of acceptable quality, while there is no clearly evident statutory duty to foster or support 'community development'.

Workers in different services therefore operate in quite different procedural styles. Some (such as social workers) need to be closely attentive to the powers and constraints laid down in specific sections of the key acts governing their conduct whereas others (such as community development workers) are much more free-ranging and perhaps innovative in their day-to-day work.

Forms of political accountability

As part of this set of characteristics, agencies also vary in the extent to which they are electorally accountable to the local population. In descending order of formal electoral accountability they can be:

- fully locally democratic (FLD) in that all decision makers hold, and can lose, office by the mechanism of universal suffrage;
- partly locally democratic (PLD) in that only some proportion of decision makers hold office by these means;
- central government appointed (GA) with or without some local representatives;
- voluntary and/or non-statutory (VNS) with local representatives who emerge by some self-selected or informal electoral process.

In addition to these forms of accountability much attention recently has been focused on the development of new 'delivery vehicles' set up, in most cases, as ad hoc mechanisms to deliver specific regeneration programmes (Taylor, 2000). These are at present too disparate and at too early a stage of development to categorise in terms of their electoral accountability.

There is an extremely significant issue of local democracy here. The more that budgetary and decision-making power is shifted from FLD agencies to agencies with other forms of accountability (as has clearly been the trend for several decades), the less the local population has power by means of the ballot box to place in office and remove those controlling events. The growth in power and public funding of quangos of various kinds has been very rapid since the early 1980s. In particular, in the context of east London, the London Docklands Development Corporation has had enormous effects (discussed for example in Ambrose, 1994; Brownill, 1990 and elsewhere) on the pattern of funding and development in important sections of three inner London boroughs. In the field of national housing policy the analagous trend has been to make non-FLD agencies such as housing associations (VNS bodies), supervised and funded by the Housing Corporation (a large quango), the main intended provider of 'social housing'.

These policy changes, whatever their virtues in other ways, amount to a loss in the power of the vote. This form of loss of electoral power has been less discussed by commentators and the general public than would have been a reduction in the power of the vote of similar magnitude but by a different means (say a period between General Elections of eight years rather than five). It seems paradoxical that the present government, like its predecessor, is simultaneously supporting power shifts away from FLD agencies towards less formally accountable forms of local decision-making agency while at the same time calling for more 'consultation and participation' from residents – and indeed making some funding programmes conditional upon demonstrating that such consultation and participation is happening. There seems to be a logical inconsistency in promoting policies that produce a systematic reduction of the power of the vote, which is easily accessible at no cost to virtually everyone, while depending more and more on 'participation' processes that many marginalised, or 'hard to reach', people find it difficult to participate in (because it may well cost them time and money) and which give no guarantee of reflecting the general weight of feeling in an area.

This is not to deny the apparent high degree of answerability to local wishes built into short-life ad hoc agencies such as SHADA (the Stepney Housing and Development Agency), which is managing the regeneration of a significant area of central Stepney. It is to raise the question of whether pragmatic solutions of this kind are to be seen as the norm in the future governance of this country.

Funding regimes and financial accountability

Agencies that differ in terms of their accountability tend to work, quite understandably, to different financial agendas. Local authority departments are democratically answerable to the chairs and councillors of various committees, and to the local voters that elected them, housing associations are answerable to their boards (which may have nationwide interests), police departments to their police committee and health agencies to their health authority.

Private sector organisations, that are increasingly being drawn into 'partnerships' with public and voluntary agencies, are sharply different in that they are legally and in practice responsible solely to their shareholders. The more they are funded by shareholders' funds the less it is proper for them to act primarily on 'social' or 'public interest' motivations. This is not to deny the very constructive effects flowing from the activities both of organisations such as Business in the Community and of the 'social' and 'public interest' activities of individual firms. But it does mean that the key prerequisite for attracting investment from private sources is to demonstrate that the economic regeneration of a previously rundown area carries potential commercial benefits, perhaps in terms of the growing disposable income and self-confidence of the local resident population. If this effect can be clearly demonstrated the objection that shareholders' capital should not be risked on 'non-profit' activities falls away and an important source of investment and expertise opens up.

One example of the confusion that arises is that the provision of better 'public transport' is often considered to be something within the power of public agencies. In fact, most 'public transport' is now privately owned and ultimately it is up to the shareholders to sanction investment. They will naturally want to judge any additional investment in regeneration areas in terms of profitability.

Agency norms, 'language' and career structures

As noted in the Introduction, different agencies tend to have different 'cultures'. The very language used, the extent to which a job-specific jargon is developed, the styles of meetings, the tacit political agendas, the dress codes and the overall degree of formality vary in ways that it is sometimes easier for an outside observer (such as a consultant engaged on cross-agency work) to see. In some service agencies management structures are much more hierarchical, and managers are far more 'protected' by junior staff, than in others. Important differences also exist in career structures, performance indicators and the extent to which external professional certification governs advancement. Clearly some professions (such as medicine) are much older than others (such as careers guidance) so professional certification and codes of guidance are at different stages of development.

The key difficulty from the point of view of moving towards better interagency working is that performance indicators are almost invariably service-specific and measure something internal to the service. The metropolitan authority that has adopted a cross-sector strategy and has specified the reduction in the rate of underweight babies as a performance indicator for its chief education officer is very much a pioneer in this field.

Geographical areas of jurisdiction

Over much of the country some services that have strong functional interconnections (such as housing and education) are delivered by agencies at different levels in the local government hierarchy (such as districts and counties). Planning issues are dealt with at both district and county level depending upon their significance. This potential impediment to holism does not exist in Greater London, where the boroughs are responsible for education, housing, social services and other closely related services, or in the new unitary authorities such as Brighton and Hove. While in theory the difficulties in these authorities should not be as severe as where closely related services are delivered by authorities at different tiers, it is quite evident that communication between departments is not all it might be.

In the case of London there are bewildering differences between the geographical areas of responsibility of, for example, the boroughs, the health authorities, the police divisions, the London Fire and Civil Defence Authority and the ambulance service. These carry with them a number of problems for a more holistic approach. They also complicate the task of identifying and measuring cross-sectoral cost effects because the various agencies collect data on the basis of areas that differ widely in size and have non-congruent boundaries. Policy moves to integrate services more closely in a defined local area may also have to consider the repercussions on the wider responsibilities of partner agencies' work, perhaps in geographical areas some distance removed.

One implication is that it might be more cost-effective if a high proportion of all service provision activity were delivered by unitary authorities. These might gradually begin to incorporate more of the 'mainstream' programmes, including health and policing, into one service delivery structure serving a clearly defined local area and run by neighbourhood managers. The obvious advantage is that it would be much easier to see the exported costs and to adjust agency budgets to compensate for them. Furthermore it might be argued, on grounds of the health of democracy, that such authorities and managers should be fully democratically answerable to the local electorate.

Clearly this concept is light-years away from the highly varied, multisectoral and pluralistic structure that currently, one might say increasingly, provides services in most areas. While postmodern pluralism may be a fertile source of energy and innovation in problem solving, this has to be balanced against the difficulties for holistic working that are inherent within it. The issue is not about waving imaginary magic wands to convert the system to this, or any other, particular scenario. That simply cannot be done. The issue is the direction that policy is taking in national political structures and the effects of this tendency for areas undergoing regeneration.

Data collection, management of information and indicators of progress

The DETR guidance for the identification of the 'baseline' situation for bids for New Deal for Communities funding requires that data on 67 specified variables be assembled for the small area identified for additional investment under the bid. A similar dataset is also required on the same variables for the local authority area in which the New Deal area falls and similar data again at the national scale (the latter mostly supplied in the guidance material).

The collection of the required data for the east Brighton New Deal area faced a number of difficulties that were no doubt also experienced in the other 16 New Deal 'Pathfinder' areas. The 67 variables were categorised under 12 main headings (Demographic, Income, Health, Education, Crime, Transport, and so on). To gather information on so disparate a range of variables it was necessary to consult with a broad range of public agencies and private organisations including several departments of the local authority itself, the police authority, the health authority, NHS trusts, private sector business organisations, the Benefits

Agency, national unemployment databases and voluntary sector organisations with specialist expertise in relation to, for example, the incidence of low incomes. Some of these collated their data by street address, some by postcode, some by enumeration district or ward and some (such as doctors' practices and schools) by catchment area.

The New Deal area identified in east Brighton was not co-terminous with wards but fell in parts of four wards. There was a need first to identify it as a set of streets, as a set of full postcodes and as a set of enumeration districts, so as to relate it to the various data collection areas used by the agencies providing information. Given the variety in the area bases used for information gathering it is extremely difficult for different agencies to compare information one with another. The problem is compounded by the variations in the frequency with which different agencies update the information they collect. There is also very little overlap between the indicators of progress used by different services, even when seeking to measure progress in very similar fields (such as educational achievement and health).

Rhetoric and reality in relation to holism

The agency columns in Figure 1.1 have been drawn with lines that are thicker at the top than at the bottom to convey the idea that the barriers to effective cooperation with other agencies in the set may be, in reality, more inhibiting at senior levels. This is at present a generalised hypothesis rather than a fully evidenced statement, but it is based on the empirical work in the three local authorities referred to. It reflects the frequently observed effect that as individuals work up though each agency, and acquire greater decision-making and budgetary power, they may well think more in terms of loyalty to the agency and less in terms of the cost-effectiveness of overall service delivery to a population who have, very often, 'cross-agency' needs.

This may be an over-simplistic assessment and the 'in reality' caveat should be noted. Senior members of local authority departments and agencies often appear at least as enthusiastic as anyone else in expressing the need for more holism in service delivery. This may reflect a genuine intention as well as a pragmatic response to the increasing significance of this form of working as a condition for some funding reward. But senior managers might see two different strategies for achieving greater holism in service delivery. These are:

(a) to work in cooperation with another agency to solve a particular problem;

(b) to develop in-house strategies to extend their field of operation so that they can provide more holistic answers to 'cross-agency' problems (and perhaps seek more resources to do so).

Many managers might instinctively veer towards strategy (b) since it poses less threat to service autonomy and raises no question of merging budgets or resources in any way. But (b) might induce further stress on staff both in terms of extra time taken on coordinating activities and in terms of stretching demands beyond staff expertise. So the strategy might be self-defeating, partly because there may be an *expertise diversion* effect (see Appendix). Clearly another local agency might be better set up in terms of resources and expertise to deal with the 'other' aspect of the cross-agency problem. Thus, it might be more cost-effective for both agencies to concentrate on the activities they do best and to combine to carry out strategy (a).

The vertical lines delimiting the health services in Figure 1.1 are drawn thicker than those of other agencies to signify graphically the widely encountered view that it is more difficult to enter into joint working with health service providers than with other service providers (the Introduction cites the analogy of a 'Berlin Wall' dividing health and social services). This is, of course, a *general* statement which lumps together very disparate groups of health workers from GPs to school nurses and from consultants to occupational therapists. It certainly implies no criticism of the many 'front-line' health workers who seek to cooperate, often very successfully, with colleagues in other fields of service provision. But there may be systemic impediments to the fuller development of this cooperation. These appear to include a set of factors ranging from the 'medical model' approach, incorporating at the extreme the 'God syndrome' exhibited by some doctors, to the very distinctive agency characteristics of health authorities and NHS trusts.

Types of additional cost flowing from lack of holism

The search for more holism in service delivery is not only about developing more sensitivity to user needs; it is simultaneously a search for better cost-effectiveness in service delivery.

Two types of additional cost may flow from a lack of holism – *structural* and *frictional*.

'Structural costs' arising from failure to account for exported costs

Over four years the CEHI programme (and other research) has given strong
indications that underinvestment in one sector produces *exported costs* (see
Appendix) to other sectors (Ambrose, 1997; Barrow and Bachan, 1997).
One example of a cost-exporting effect is revealed by a recent study of a
sample of 350 middle and secondary schools in England and Wales. This
found that 34% of children mention at least one extra-curricular factor
that is affecting their ability to do well at school (NHF/MORI Social
Research, 1998). Of the list of ten factors drawn up by the researchers,
eight were directly to do with housing conditions. One or more of these
reasons was mentioned by 33% of the children. The exported cost in this
case takes the form of a waste of a proportion of the funds invested in the
education system since a significant proportion of children are impeded
from making optimal use of the education provided as a direct result of
underinvestment in another sector.

These findings relate to the particular case of the relationship between
poor housing conditions and the exporting of costs to education. There
is similarly a mass of evidence relating poor housing and environmental
conditions to additional costs on health services (reviewed in Ambrose et
al, 1996). But there is no reason to see housing conditions as the only
source of exported costs. It is equally plausible that underinvestment in
policing exports costs to health (in terms of increased stress from fear of
crime), underinvestment in education exports costs to policing (in terms
of increased truancy), underinvestment in energy efficiency and advice
exports costs to health (in terms of illness related to cold and damp), and
underinvestment in job creation exports costs to more or less everything
(for a whole raft of reasons), and so on.

It would not be politically realistic to expect the cross-sectoral exported
costs, which in any event have not yet been adequately calibrated, to be
met by any voluntary budgetary concessions from either local agencies
or the national departments of government they relate to. Nor can one
expect simply more public sector investment overall. The issue is not so
much about the overall magnitude of the 'mainstream funding' cake. It is
more about the adequacy of the set of factors, and the levels of
understanding, that feed into the process of cutting it up in the public
spending review every financial year.

Decisions about mainstream funding regimes reflect inherited patterns
of national budget setting that are politically difficult to adjust. They are
also to some degree capricious. One source of capriciousness might be

the relative strength of personality of particular secretaries of state. Another, perhaps more ubiquitous, shortcoming in the process may well be that the mainstream funding allocations currently leave out an important generator of cost effects. *They do not yet take any systematic account of the cross-sectoral cost-exporting effects identified by recent research.* Perhaps it is reasonable to expect that future annual funding formulae might gradually begin to reflect what we are beginning to understand about cost-exporting effects. In other words the issue is about the gradual increase in sophistication of budgetary allocations rather than the ad hoc transference of existing funds from one hard pressed agency to another.

Compounding this analytical deficiency in the procedures for allocating spending is the perverse effect that the geographical pattern of mainstream funding can have on health and welfare provision in different local authority areas. Theoretically, mainstream spending programmes could be worked out so as to be 'progressive' (more is allocated to poorer areas), 'regressive' (more is allocated to better-off areas) or 'flat' (much the same is allocated to different areas regardless of how poor or rich they are).

A crucially important pilot study focusing on Brent, Liverpool and Nottingham by a research group led by Bramley (Bramley et al, 1998) has produced a number of key findings. They calculated that spending in the most deprived wards in these areas is on average about 45% more than spending in the least deprived wards – an apparently 'progressive' effect overall. But the pattern varied by type of service. For example, while certain categories of spending, such as means-tested social security benefits, were heavily skewed towards poorer areas the pattern in other categories, such as disability benefits and bus subsidies, was less markedly skewed. Some important services, for example health and secondary education, showed a virtually 'flat' pattern between richer and poorer areas. Some services again, such as higher education and rail subsidies, were actually skewed towards richer areas – a 'regressive' effect. These findings, although very partial and tentative at this stage, provide a significant insight into why some areas seem to stay poor from generation to generation (for example large tracts of the inner cities; see Ambrose, 2000, section 6, for a review of the 'regressive' factors at work in these areas).

'Frictional' costs at the service/user interface

These arise when a local resident experiences a problem that requires information, action or support from more than one local services agency. A difficulty might arise that crosses the boundaries between the areas of responsibility of different agencies and might, for example, require responses of some kind from some combination of housing, health, police and educational authorities. As is well known, there may well be frustrations and loss of time in accessing the correct parts of the agencies concerned, each may tend to direct prime responsibility towards the others, and even when this does not happen the agency characteristics may make a fully coordinated response difficult to achieve.

There are clear costs inherent in this situation that we can define as *frictional costs*. They may be felt by:

- the person or household with the cross-agency difficulty in terms of the time and money spent contacting several agencies and perhaps being directed back and forward between them. This process is in itself very stressful and may progressively reduce the capacity of the individual to deal with the next problem that occurs;
- professionals working in agencies who may experience an *energy diversion effect* when they spend time seeking to contact relevant colleagues in other agencies to cooperate on a cross-agency problem, or *an expertise diversion effect* when they themselves seek to deal with a problem for which their professional training has not equipped them (Ambrose, 1997, section 9.4).

The costs may be both monetary and measurable but also non-monetary in terms of stress, frustration and loss of time.

We can call these two types of cost *lack of holism costs* because it is reasonable to believe that if more holistic approaches could be introduced into agency funding formulae and service delivery practices the total impact of these costs would be reduced. At present we have little idea of the magnitude of the costs involved, but it is reasonable to believe that the total magnitude may be very significant. It is evident that the government also takes this view since it is placing increasing emphasis on more holistic approaches.

Some strategies for improving interagency working

Research carried out in recent years in both Tower Hamlets and Hackney, especially those parts of the work that have concentrated on interviewing service providers (see Ambrose, 1997, pp 83-98 and Ambrose and Randles, 1999), has identified a number of strategies that, singly or in combination, might lead to better interagency working. Five ideas are presented for consideration, listed in 'bottom-up' order (see Figure 1.1).

1. Retain the benefits of 'frontline-ness'

In a number of discussions held while carrying out one recent project (Ambrose and Randles, 1999) 'frontline' staff stressed that good service delivery and job satisfaction depend to a large extent on:

- a sense of personal engagement with and responsibility to the service user;
- being able to see whatever issue it is through to a conclusion;
- knowing the buck stops with them if things go wrong;
- working closely with colleagues in another service to achieve a good outcome.

These characteristics define 'frontline-ness' – they also call for close interagency working, especially if the situation is urgent in nature. But frontline-ness can be lost with progress up a 'hierarchy' and more senior policy and decision makers may thereby lose the key 'driver' to working with other agencies to achieve effective service delivery. This 'loss' effect seems not to be standard across services but to affect some more than others. For example, senior medical consultants still deal with patients and senior police officers still work on the streets whereas social services managers may never see a client and the government's Chief Inspector of Schools may not spend much time teaching classes.

Where senior staff moving up any hierarchy have lost or forgotten frontline-ness, policies might well be put in place for them to regain it and be kept in touch with it (perhaps 'frontline' experience two days a month or an actual caseload?).

2. 'Bottom-up' problem solving and 'osmotic' effects

One source of progress towards better cross-agency working might be the actions of local community leaders, advocates and housing managers who take up issues on behalf of local residents that by their nature require a 'cross-agency' response. The 'model' of this process is one particular frontline housing manager (JB) working in a high-profile local regeneration scheme (see Ambrose and Randles, 1999). It is instructive that this housing manager has no formal qualification in housing management.

When approached by a resident with a problem requiring cross-agency action she locates the individuals far enough up in each agency who have the competence to do something about it. She then discusses the issue with those individuals. If need be, she acts as a 'clearing house' in getting responses from several agencies and in cross-referring responses from one agency to another. The matter is pursued until either a solution is reached or clear and acceptable reasons are given as to why a solution cannot be reached.

By her actions in the context of the particular problem she does the 'joining up' between agencies rather than simply giving the resident several contact numbers and leaving her or him to deal with a sometimes confusing or contradictory set of responses. She takes care to see that her actions are empowering rather than the reverse because her aim is to assist the resident, and the agencies she contacts, to understand how the problem has arisen and how it might be resolved. One resident commented of this process that "problems were sorted out in front of me". This can be termed the 'JB effect'.

The benefits of the JB effect might be more pervasive than the achievement of limited, although welcome, outcomes for particular individuals. The repeated experience of cross-agency contact and cooperation in the addressing of particular difficulties for individuals might well contribute to a 'culture' of interagency contact and collaboration among the junior to middle managers in provider organisations who have been drawn into discussion of the problems. This then might seep 'upward' through hierarchies by a process of 'osmosis' or absorption and by carrying these habits of working 'upward' when promoted.

3. Job descriptions and training regimes and performance indicators

Many service providers and other professionals working in the fields of health, housing, policing and similar services stressed in interviews and focus group discussions that, although in their working lives they necessarily made contact and developed working relationships with colleagues in other statutory and voluntary services, the requirement to develop cooperation of this kind was rarely written into their job description or explicitly recognised in performance indicators. More holistic approaches had tended to be adopted as and when necessary instead of being a specified aspect of the job. It might be a helpful (and inexpensive) first step to make explicit in *all* job descriptions some reference to the need to develop working relationships with those in other services and organisations whenever such action might help to deliver a better service. Equally, activity of this kind could well be recognised in the performance indicators for the job.

This standard requirement to think in more holistic terms might be reinforced in training regimes. Statutory, voluntary and community organisations working in an area and seeking to deal with common problems might well consider reaching an agreement that all training courses, whether initial or in-service, include a period (a day, a week or as appropriate) working or 'sitting with Nellie' in other agencies or organisations. This would not only give some first-hand knowledge of other organisations' aims, policies, problems and procedures but would also thicken up the network of personal contacts between agency staff. The subsequent 'voice on the phone' would belong to someone one had spent a week working with and perhaps had a drink with.

4. The extra 10% question

During the CEHI programme round of interviews in the Stepney SRB area in 1996, service providers were asked:

> "If a 10% increase in funding to your organisation were available on condition that it be spent only on *another* agency's budget, with the aim of making your task easier, which other agency or agencies would you nominate?"

Many respondents found this question extremely interesting, but initially few could come up with an answer. This seemed to be partly because the idea of *any* budget increase tended to take respondents aback and partly because few staff had the time to spare from dealing with day-to-day pressures to think in cross-system terms. This lack of response is instructive and indicates some of the difficulties of engendering a greater degree of holism.

The question was also asked in a round of focus group discussions held for a variety of service providers in the context of a follow-up study of the Holly Street renewal project in Hackney. In this study most participants were able, following discussion of the issue, to identify three or so other services towards which they would direct such additional funding (Ambrose and Randles, 1999).

When using the question again in a round of service provider interviews relating to a project in Brighton and Hove (Ambrose and May, 1998) it was established that the probation service does actually implement a version of this strategy. Nationally, an extra 7% tranche of funding is available that cannot be spent by the service itself but can be distributed to other local service providers to smooth or reduce the demand for probation activity. One local branch of the service gave details of the way this extra 7% is allocated to a wide range of voluntary and private sector agencies working in the area (some of them housing provision agencies).

The systematic raising of this question, in a round of interviews with middle to senior managers in all relevant services in an area, might promote further consideration of costs 'imported' from shortfalls in other services, give valuable insights into the pattern of mutual dependencies between local services, and encourage 'cross-sectoral thinking' among managers.

5. The 'Neighbourhood plc' exercise

Another way of breaking through the barriers posed by 'departmental thinking' would be to approach the task of carrying out a regeneration programme in 'corporate' terms – to envisage it as a task to be handled by a private sector corporation ('Neighbourhood plc') managed by a board of directors with ultimate responsibility to the shareholders. The key intention is to get away from the 'if she wins I lose' syndrome – in other words to move beyond 'zero-sum game' thinking.

In this imaginary corporation each department has specific responsibilities for matters such as health, housing management, law and order, emergency services, and so on. Departmental heads within the corporation can certainly be expected to 'fight their corner' about resources and strategies but overriding this is a collective responsibility for optimal performance in relation to *all* the corporation's overall objectives and thus the maximisation of the 'dividend' (in reality the quality of life) to the shareholders and creditors (in reality local residents).

One way of 'modelling' this situation is to run a role-play simulation exercise. This might last for a full day. It would need to be directed by leaders professionally competent in the running of management games.

The simulation exercise

The roles would be those of the managing director and the directors of 'Neighbourhood plc'. Each director would have a specified area of responsibility such as housing management, the promotion of employment, health care, law enforcement, education and training, financial control, and so on. There might be six to eight such directors each with an executive assistant.

The players taking on these roles would be pairs of 'real life' participants in the administration of the area in question – for example two senior members each from education services, housing services, social services, the relevant police division, the energy efficiency services, the health authority, environmental health, the emergency services, and so on, plus a number of residents. But for the initial role-play exercise *the roles would be 'shuffled'* so that the pairs of participants would have to think their way into situations and tasks other than those carried out in real life. For example, the chief environmental health officer pair might take on the role of the head of the police division and the director of education might become the chief housing officer.

It would be an essential element in the exercise for the role-playing pairs to 'read themselves into' their roles and to prepare their positions for the first board meeting. This preparation might well take up an entire morning session. The set of 'briefing material' to be assimilated by each pair would include a short version of the mission statement and current strategies of the department or service for which they were now responsible, a budgetary allocation, outcome targets, reports and findings of recent surveys that have been carried out in the area, and it would also include key pieces of central government policy guidance for each service from the relevant departments of state.

The agenda for the afternoon 'board meeting' would be to an extent structured by the simulation controllers and should start with an item focusing on a consideration of corporation objectives, short, medium and long term, for the area. The aim would be to identify and agree a 'corporate strategy'. Precise departmental targets might need to be set (for example, concerning the number of residents gaining employment in a specified period, a specified level of improvement in GCSE levels in schools or a rate of crime reduction). The board would then need to address the problem of identifying optimal strategies to meet these objectives and targets. It would inevitably have to consider budgetary strategies both within departments and at the corporate level. This might mean considering possible transfers of funds between departments where shortfalls in one departmental budget could be seen to be generating heavy 'exported' costs on other budgets and inhibiting the achievement of overall corporate objectives.

Returning to real life

This initial exercise might be the first in a series of cross-departmental meetings (at perhaps three monthly intervals) as the regeneration programme proceeds. In these later meetings participants would 'play' their real-life roles. But hopefully they might have acquired a much clearer view of the agreed ultimate objectives for the regeneration process, of the complex way in which policies, initiatives, costs and benefits react upon each other, and of the necessity for seeing the viewpoints and *modus operandi* of other departments or interests.

'Neighbourhood plc' at other levels and in other contexts

It may well be that using the technique of role-play simulation, the shuffling of roles and the assimilation of briefing material relevant to other departments might be beneficial not just at senior management level but at all levels where the need for multiagency working arises or where special projects are initiated that require cooperation from a number of agencies.

Equally it might be beneficial to carry out the exercise as an 'icebreaker' and learning exercise for a partnership newly formed for implementing a regeneration scheme in the area.

Implications for regeneration programmes

It might help to achieve more holistic working in urban regeneration programmes if some of the concepts discussed in this chapter were fully considered and written into programme guidance. They include:

• Holism
• Lack of holism costs – structural and frictional
• Exporting costs across sectoral boundaries
• Energy and expertise diversion effects
• Osmotic effects
• FLD and non-FLD organisations
• Non-zero-sum situations.

Appendix: Glossary

Meanings derived from the *Concise Oxford Dictionary* are annotated COD. Others are the author's definition.

Agency characteristics – the set of characteristics that differentiate provision agencies including legislative framework, powers and responsibilities, degrees of electoral accountability, codes and practices, career paths, and so on.

Expertise diversion – the effect whereby the difficulties of interagency working are producing a situation where staff are seeking to deal with problems that fall outside their professional training and thus inhibiting their capacity to focus on areas of service provision in which they *are* fully competent (for example health service workers seeking to solve difficulties arising from poor housing).

Exported costs – the additional costs generated by the malfunctioning of a given sector (say housing) which are then felt in another (say healthcare).

FLD agencies – agencies such as local authorities whose decision-making body is elected, and can be turned out of office, by the local electorate.

Frictional costs – costs that arise for both agencies and users as a result of inadequate cooperation between provision agencies in the solution of specific problems.

Holism *(COD)* – the theory that certain wholes are to be regarded as more than the sum of their parts.

Lack of holism costs – the aggregate effect of frictional costs and structural costs.

Osmosis *(COD)* – any process by which something is acquired by absorption.

Structural costs – additional costs in providing services that arise because the central funding arrangements for a given sector have not reflected the exported costs felt by that sector.

Synergy (*COD*) – the combined effect of drugs, organs, and so on that exceeds the sum of their individual effects.

References

Ambrose, P. (1994) *Urban process and power*, London: Routledge.

Ambrose, P. (1996) *Bad housing: Counting the cost*, Brighton: Centre for Urban and Regional Research, University of Sussex.

Ambrose, P. (1997) *I mustn't laugh too much: Housing and health on the Limehouse Fields and Ocean Estates in Stepney*, Brighton: Centre for Urban and Regional Research, University of Sussex.

Ambrose, P. (1998) *Housing advisory services in Brighton and Hove: A 'best value' assessment*, Brighton: Centre for Urban and Regional Research, University of Sussex.

Ambrose, P. (2000) *A drop in the ocean: The health gain from the Central Stepney SRB in the context of national health inequalities*, Brighton: Health and Social Policy Research Centre, University of Brighton.

Ambrose, P. and MacDonald, D. (2000) *The Benchmarking and Focus Group Project: Final report*, Brighton: Health and Social Policy Research Centre, University of Brighton.

Ambrose, P. and May, J. (1998) *Customer service standards in the context of joint commissioning*, Brighton: Centre for Urban and Regional Research, University of Sussex.

Ambrose, P. and Randles, J. (1999) *Looking for the joins: A qualitative study of inter-agency working in Holly Street and Hackney*, London Borough of Hackney.

Ambrose, P., Barlow, J., Bonsey, A., Donkin, V., Pullin, M. and Randles, J. (1996) *The real cost of poor homes*, London: Royal Institution of Chartered Surveyors.

Barrow, M. and Bachan, R. (1997) *The real cost of poor homes: Footing the bill*, London: The Royal Institution of Chartered Surveyors.

Bramley, G., Lancaster, S., Lomax, D., McIntosh, S., Russell, J., Evans, M., Atkins, J., Shell, M. and Hatley, J. (1998) *Where does public spending go? Pilot study to analyse the flows of public expenditure into local areas*, London: DETR.

Brownill, S. (1990) *Developing London's Docklands: Another great planning disaster?*, London: Paul Chapman.

NHF (National Housing Federation)/MORI Social Research (1998) *School Omnibus Report*, London.

Taylor, M. (2000) *Top down meets bottom up: Neighbourhood management*, York: Joseph Rowntree Foundation.

TWO

Partnerships and power in community regeneration

Marjorie Mayo and Marilyn Taylor

Introduction

Partnership working, as the opening chapter argued, aims not only to promote 'joined-up government', but to reduce bureaucratic and professional power, promoting decentralisation and participation from the private, voluntary and community sectors as well as individual citizens. This chapter focuses on the challenges inherent in partnership working with communities and service users, and on questions of power and power imbalances in partnerships for regeneration. It discusses some of the practical steps that need to be taken to strengthen partnership working in policy making, service delivery, consultation and training.

Despite the rhetoric of official support for community participation in partnerships for regeneration and development, both in Britain and beyond, the reality has been problematic. 'Partnership' as a term has a positive resonance and implies a measure of equality or at least balance and reciprocity between partners. But partnerships for regeneration – like any other type of partnership including marriage – are by no means necessarily equal (Hastings et al, 1996; Mayo, 1997a). And they can, and all too often do, become increasingly unequal as time goes by and partners settle back into role. The most powerful partners are in a position to determine the time frames and set the agendas, too often failing to provide communities with the resources to challenge these, let alone to develop their own agendas to meet social as well as economic needs based on their own definition of need (Taylor, 1997). Despite mission statement commitments to the contrary, regeneration partnerships can have the effect of actually reinforcing the unequal distribution of social capital

(Taylor, 2000a). Thus, power imbalances apply to the relations between partners – from the public, private, voluntary and community sectors. However they can also apply to relations within the sectors engaged in partnerships – between one grouping within a community and another, between representatives and those they are supposed to be representing, between majority groups and minority interests, between those with the most extensive networks and those with the least extensive. Regeneration partnerships impact upon these power imbalances in varying ways.

This chapter will first unpack different definitions and perspectives on power and empowerment. It will then summarise the literature on community participation in regeneration partnerships, drawing upon research in Britain and the authors' own research (Hastings et al, 1996; Mackintosh, 1993; Taylor, 1995, 1997; Mayo, 1997a; Anastacio et al, 2000) and research elsewhere (including a case study of partnerships for development in Zimbabwe – Johnson and Wilson, 1999 – which illustrates comparable issues and dilemmas in the development context). This will set the framework for the discussion of strategies for change, which can challenge existing power imbalances within partnerships, and work towards enhancing community empowerment.

Power, capacity building and social capital

The case for partnership working has been developed, at least in part, within the context of strategies to counteract bureaucratic and professional power. The aim is to reduce excessive 'producer' power by sharing or giving power to communities. The most visible aspect of power is probably the power to shape outcomes. In the context of regeneration partnerships, this aspect is relatively easy to track – the power that can be exercised by a particular group with a significant majority on the board, such as a majority of councillors representing the dominant political party in the locality.

But power, like an iceberg, is not only to be delineated in terms of what can be seen. The dimensions of power that are not so directly evident may be just as, if not more, significant (Lukes, 1974). Lukes' approach to the study of power was developed over a quarter of a century ago, but it continues to provide insights that are relevant to the study of power in regeneration partnerships, as this chapter aims to demonstrate. Lukes argued that the decision-making aspects of power represented only the most visible elements. Beneath this first dimension lay two further dimensions. Lukes' second dimension of power was described as 'non-decision making' or the ability to limit the range of alternatives to be considered. This is the power to shape the agenda or conversely to ensure that some issues never emerge on the agenda at all. Powerful partners such as government departments or major private sector stakeholders can influence outcomes through setting partnership agendas, determining what is – and what is not – up for consideration, and within what time frames. Resources may be made available but only for specific types of initiative. Governments can also define certain policy solutions (such as policies involving significant increases in public spending) as off limits, professionals can control the agendas of users of their services, and private sector developers can refuse to consider the possibility of less profitable land-use planning options for key development sites.

Lukes' third dimension of power is wider still. It includes the power to shape people's desires, to define the terms within which public debates take place. It enshrines the 'common-sense' assumptions which tend to go unchallenged. And this dimension of power can define particular issues and agendas as beyond the realms of the possible or even the desirable (Lukes, 1974). Lukes' third dimension of power can be located within wider debates about ideology and hegemony, the power of ruling interests in society to shape the framework of debate, the generally accepted 'common-sense' view of what is and what is not 'thinkable' (Forgacs, 1988; Habermas, 1976). There is not the space here to develop these theoretical discussions in detail, simply to note that, here again, partnerships for regeneration provide ample contemporary illustrations.

Thus, the role of private sector interests and the requirements of profitability, for example, tend to be perceived as beyond the need for justification. Similarly, at least until relatively recently, assumptions about children and young people have tended to go unchallenged: young people have too often simply been assumed to be potential trouble, while children have too often been assumed to be incapable of participating in any significant way. Until very recently, to suggest that even relatively young children have the capacity to make valuable contributions to planning the regeneration of their neighbourhoods would have been to think the unthinkable – despite mounting evidence to the contrary (Fitzpatrick et al, 1998).

The relevance of Lukes' analysis of the three dimensions of power to regeneration partnerships can be illustrated through exploring some of the tensions involved in addressing issues of housing and homelessness within a particular regeneration programme, focused in a strategic urban development site (Anastacio et al, 2000). Here the wider framework of government housing policies and private sector development agendas effectively ruled community demands for more affordable housing as being off limits. From the outset, partners on the board seemed to assume that this was simply the way things were and community activists who challenged this view found themselves effectively frozen out of the first round of discussions. The third dimension of power is also demonstrated in the ways that communities engaged in partnerships across the country scale down their expectations and may declare themselves satisfied with outcomes that in no sense match up to their original aspirations (Hastings et al, 1996; Stewart and Taylor, 1995).

The experience of not being listened to – effectively being ruled out of order – has given rise to much frustration. Whether regeneration partnerships are empowering or disempowering depends at least in part upon whose interests are at stake – which group's demands can be accommodated and which are being defined as non-negotiable. This also defines who is recognised as representative (the community 'stars', the community 'godmothers' and 'godfathers'). Those who are accepted into the frame are most likely to be those whose demands can be relatively easily accommodated and who learn to speak the same language as the power holders. Others are marginalised still further as a result of these processes, except when it is in the interests of power holders to use their continued exclusion to support accusations that those who have been allowed into the policy process are unrepresentative.

Empowerment, capacity building and social capital

This raises two further aspects of debates on power and empowerment. How do definitions of empowerment vary (depending upon differing theoretical approaches to the definition of power) and how do these in their turn relate to contemporary preoccupations with capacity-building and the development of social capital?

If power is conceptualised in 'zero-sum' or 'constant-sum' terms, the empowerment of some implies the potential disempowerment of others. If the relatively less powerful are to increase their power, and use the power that they already have more effectively, then those with more power will face challenges. If power is conceptualised in variable terms, this implies that there is potentially plenty of power out there in society for the taking. Everyone can become empowered (Craig and Mayo, 1995; Mayo and Anastacio, 1999). Indeed, analysts of power who believe that power is a fluid rather than a fixed concept, argue that power is constantly reproduced through our day-to-day activities and interactions. In this view individuals are not necessarily the pawns of capital, but are capable of redefining the rules of the game (Healey, 1997). However, it is still arguable that those who come to the power game with most power and resources will go away with most.

Both views of power, therefore, imply an approach to capacity building that goes beyond the simple assumption that training residents in the rules of the regeneration game will create an improved balance of power. Firstly, they imply that those partners who are relatively more powerful, including professionals and decision makers, are as much, if not more in need of capacity building, to develop the capacity to work with less powerful partners in new and less dominating ways.

Secondly, the different partners will need to recognise the wider structural constraints implied by Lukes' analysis of power as the basis for developing strategies for change. Capacity building, from this perspective, includes building the capacity effectively to challenge, as much as to understand, the rules of the regeneration game as currently constituted and to change existing assumptions not only about power, but about the nature of knowledge – a challenge to which we shall return.

The concept of social capital has been applied in varying ways in this context (see also John Davies' discussion in Chapter Nine). 'Social capital' is itself a contested term, with differing views on the extent to which it can be measured, let alone built effectively, through public policy interventions (Putnam, 1993; Gittell and Vidal, 1998; Burns and Taylor, 1998). In relation to partnerships for regeneration there are two aspects with particular relevance, the conceptualisation of social capital as networks and relationships of trust *within* communities and its conceptualisation as networks and *relationships with external organisations and agencies (bridging capital)*. In the context of regeneration partnerships both aspects are crucial: the first emphasising solidarity rather than division between different interests within areas and the second emphasising the networks needed to access resources from elsewhere, including resources from the public, private and not-for-profit sectors.

Strengthening social capital has often been presented as relatively unproblematic in principle, a generally desirable goal. As Bourdieu's work (1984) has demonstrated, however, those who have capital to start with have the potential to increase this, whether the capital in question is of the economic, social or cultural variety. Conversely, those who initially lack social capital may paradoxically face increasing marginalisation, as a direct result of capacity-building policy interventions. As some individuals and groups build upon their existing knowledge and skills – including skills as community entrepreneurs – others may feel more and more excluded. Policies to promote capacity building and empowerment can therefore result in further polarisation in the voluntary and community sectors.

Partnerships and power: experiences in practice

The previous section summarised some alternative perspectives on power and empowerment. Whatever the perspective there would seem to be widespread agreement that power in regeneration partnerships is all too often problematic. Partners do not typically come from positions of equal power. Power relationships can take varying forms at different levels and these relationships can become more rather than less unequal over time.

The continuing and inherent imbalance in power relationships is not a uniquely British experience. On the contrary, similar issues have emerged from studies of regeneration in the USA (for example Gitell and Vidal, 1998) and in development contexts in the South. The literature on participatory approaches to development comes replete with 'health warnings' about the dangers inherent in disregarding the impact of power differences (Chambers, 1997; Holland and Blackburn, 1998; Gujit and Shah, 1998). Johnson and Wilson have argued, on the basis of their research in Zimbabwe, that unless deep social inequalities and power imbalances are openly acknowledged and actively addressed, then partnerships for development are unlikely to be sustainable let alone to meet the needs of the most marginal and deprived groups in society (Johnson and Wilson, 1999).

Policies in Britain have shifted in recent years, however, and current guidelines place far greater emphasis on active participation together with increasing emphasis on capacity building to facilitate this (for example in guidelines for recent rounds of the Single Regeneration Budget). This creates new opportunities to address imbalances of power. Despite this, however, the literature on participation in regeneration partnerships provides depressing evidence to demonstrate the continuing size of the gap between rhetoric and reality (Hastings et al, 1996; Anastacio et al, 2000). Evaluations of regeneration partnerships have tended to focus upon the extent to which outputs have been achieved. Evaluations based upon participants' own perceptions of their experiences have been considerably less common, let alone evaluations of their perceptions of the overall outcomes in terms of the relative powers of the different stakeholders (Clapham, 1996). How far do communities feel they have been empowered and how far have they felt disempowered as a result of their experiences of partnerships for regeneration?

Illustrations from area regeneration partnerships in Britain

This section draws on two research studies. The authors have both been engaged in differing aspects of a research project to explore participants' own perspectives on their experiences of partnerships (Anastacio et al, 2000; Burns and Taylor, 2000). This is referred to below as the main study. This chapter also draws on a parallel study in a further regeneration partnership, not yet published and referred to below as the second study (see Taylor, 2000b for more discussion of the second study). How far in these studies have community representatives been listened to as partners and how have they themselves been accountable to those that they represent? What do they consider to be the lessons for developing more equal partnerships in future and how might they play a more active role in monitoring and evaluating the processes and outcomes as well as the outputs of regeneration partnerships?

In the main study, interviews and focus group discussions with some 150 stakeholders in four different localities (Barnsley, Birmingham, Kings Cross and the Waterfront in southeast London) identified a number of related issues. There were significant differences between the four areas studied (with fewer examples of good practice in some than others) and there were differences over time (sometimes for the better, other times not). But despite these differences there were a number of common threads. These commonalities are reinforced by the second study cited above.

In each area of the main study, participants reflected that power inequalities were evident even before the regeneration programme's launch. Agendas had already been determined to a considerable extent through the process of bidding for and obtaining funding, in accordance with government determined guidelines. Tight time frames (also determined by government) reinforced these initial power imbalances. There was too little time to begin to consider alternative approaches. In the words of one community representative, participants felt "saddled with outputs which exclude community concern". In the second study, an extended initial process of negotiation between local authority (as accountable body), the regional office and the European funder meant that, despite an intended emphasis on capacity building in the programme and some initial involvement of selected voluntary sector participants, representatives from local communities came on board when key decisions had been made, and initial meetings were dominated by discussions on structure. There were no resources for community development and little time was left, once the parameters of the local programme had been agreed, for developing an action plan or an applications process that fully involved community representatives, let alone a shared vision:

> "It's about someone else's agenda. They just want you to tinker with this bit or that bit. You are never actually asked to set the priorities."

These initial sources of power imbalance were reinforced in a number of cases. Being a community representative on a partnership board – or even on an associated community forum – was for some a profoundly disempowering experience (as if being in a small minority is not problematic enough) and was compounded by the failure to provide any kind of induction and a subsequent lack of training, mentoring or technical support (despite the masses of papers to be digested). In addition, community representatives in both studies complained of specific problems due to inadequate notice of meetings, inadequate minuting and confusion about which decisions were being made, by whom and with what possibilities for alternatives. This can mean that community participants are bound into decisions for which they have been inadequately prepared and where discussion has been limited:

> "... the action plan went through in the last 20 minutes of a crowded agenda."

The sheer complexity of procedures means that paid officers from the accountable body – often a statutory body – exercise a great deal of power as interpreters of the rules and as those with most time and energy to devote to the process, even if they in turn feel disempowered by decision making further up the hierarchy.

There were some examples of good practice in these respects. Some community representatives in the second study said that they had learnt an enormous amount, even if the learning curve was steep, demanding and sometimes painful. There were cases in the main study where community representatives and their organisations had received excellent support (including technical support such as planning aid), with training tailored to meet their learning needs as they themselves defined these. There were examples of effective mentoring schemes and community-based exchanges to enable communities to learn from sharing the experiences of others and reflecting upon these, but these tended to be the exceptions rather than the rule.

Patchy training and support

Overall, the provision of training and support emerged as patchy, and in some cases actually counterproductive (when external trainers were parachuted in, without sufficient consultation, so that the training provided was experienced as inappropriate and sometimes worse – patronising lectures of marginal relevance). There were particular criticisms of the use of consultants who were being paid "large sums to tell people what they knew already" (Anastacio et al, 2000). In both studies, training was often low down the agenda and late in the process, at a point when residents had already, as it were, learnt on their feet. Community representatives and activists made a range of forceful points about these aspects of their experiences.

The issue of affordable housing has already been raised. Both community representatives and the professionals who were working with them reflected on the contradictions here: developing imaginative outreach programmes to consult homeless people; working with community groups to ensure that homeless people's issues were genuinely included; and then finding that there was no way in which the policy implications were going to be included on local (let alone national) regeneration agendas. As one community representative expressed this:

> ... there seems to be a consensus that the quantity of housing is no
> longer an issue – that only improvements of existing housing is needed.
> (Anastacio et al, 2000)

Effectively, she concluded, "housing is off the agenda" in terms of social housing. And there were no effective channels for feeding local views on this back to government at regional and national levels. Even if there had been channels, it was suggested, government would not have been willing to listen, given the parameters of policy on social housing and on public expenditure. In addition, in the specific situation in Kings Cross, the regeneration agenda had already been shaped by the interest of private property development – for more up-market uses.

Community participation in regeneration partnerships could be (and often was) experienced, then, as disempowering. Community partners tended to be in a minority, reacting to agendas that had already been predetermined to a considerable extent. Key community issues were being defined as 'off limits', out of the frame, beyond the regeneration pale. Each of Lukes' dimensions of power was potentially problematic.

The role of community representatives emerged as a particular problem. This was described as a stressful role, squeezed between the hopes and aspirations of those people whom the representatives were supposed to be representing and those on the board who might have preferred not to hear them; "stuck in the middle" as one community professional explained it, potentially viewed by other parts of the community "as part of the problem rather than as part of the solution". Many regeneration programmes hit the local press early on in the regeneration process with the promise of lots of money. This hype can place impossible expectations on community representatives, while promoting conflict between different groups with the focus on 'getting a piece of the action' rather than on a larger vision of what needs to be achieved in the area (Taylor, 2000a, p 1028). Community representatives are accused of only being involved for the money they can get for their own projects. This may be true of a minority, but it does not do justice to the time and energy put in by many representatives with little support, or address the conflicts of interest that they have to unravel.

In addition, representatives find themselves in an increasing number of forums, wearing a bewildering number of hats. The most powerful interests are able to define who is to become a 'community star' and those who become stars are then deluged with invitations to further meetings, each with associated bundles of papers to be digested. Conversely, those whose demands and/or demeanor are defined as less acceptable tend to become labelled as 'unrepresentative' and are excluded from further influence.

Problems of representing differing interests

There are undoubtedly important issues to be resolved around representation and accountability. None of the communities studied was homogeneous: each was characterised by differences and potential divisions. The most evident were divisions of race, ethnicity, gender, disability, age, social class, sexual orientation and housing tenure.

Community stars were faced with the problem of how to represent these differing interests to boards that seemed to prefer simple rather than complex answers – 'the community view' rather than the variety of differing and sometimes competing 'community views'.

Regeneration partnerships can and sometimes do exacerbate these differences, enabling some individuals and groups to participate, developing their 'social capital' and their access to scarce resources, while leaving others feeling even more marginalised as a result. The complexity of partnership processes means that smaller groups without paid staff can rarely afford to engage or indeed to apply for partnership funds or to carry out the complex monitoring and accounting procedures. They are thus effectively excluded from benefiting. This is particularly true of black and ethnic minority groups (see Chapter Ten). A number of black respondents expressed the view that these processes were by no means accidental: their increasing marginalisation was the result of deep-rooted institutional racism. "Local black groups don't even know that the board is giving money, let alone know how to access it," one respondent commented.

In the second study, an attempt was made to address this problem by bringing representatives of communities of interest onto the board alongside locality representatives. However, it did not prove easy to fill these positions – there were no channels for representation and accountability comparable to the community forms to which locality representatives reported and there was some tension at the outset between locality representatives and those representing communities of interest.

Despite all this potential for increasing polarisation and further fragmentation in the community, the findings were by no means all negative. There were examples of good practice. These included case studies of successful struggles for inclusion, waged by relatively powerless groups (such as young Bangladeshi women and men in Birmingham) who achieved these breakthroughs as a result of their own determination, along with the backing of supportive community professionals. In the second study, some communities of interest were able to gain access to decision making and funding through this process and to raise their profile with other parts of the community. There were, as we have already suggested, cases where individuals and groups clearly felt empowered as a result of their experiences, developing knowledge and skills that were shared in solidarity in their communities and beyond. Networks were developing to facilitate these processes.

But these positive outcomes cannot be expected to emerge

spontaneously. There are powerful forces driving towards increasing polarisation. If regeneration partnerships are to be empowering rather than disempowering for the most marginalised individuals and groups, then there needs to be continuing support. This includes the need for community development facilitation and infrastructure support as well as the need for training – to meet the learning needs of communities as they themselves define these. It also includes the need to support participative monitoring and evaluation – to identify appropriate benchmarks and to monitor and evaluate processes as well as outputs, including monitoring the independence, strength and solidarity of the community sector itself.

Challenging power imbalances within regeneration partnerships

So what steps might be taken to challenge power imbalances in regeneration partnerships? How might communities be empowered to participate more effectively? From whichever perspective power is analysed, knowledge and critical understanding emerge as potentially key ingredients – Foucault's view of knowledge as power has relevance here, with his analysis of knowledge and critical understanding as the basis for challenge and change. If power is conceptualised in variable and fluid terms, then increased knowledge and critical understanding could enable participants to gain the power that is there, becoming more equal partners in the process. As we have already seen, Healey (1997), building on Giddens (1984) and Habermas (1976), underlines the potential, through dialogue, of structuring power in new ways.

There is an increasing emphasis, among popular commentators in the UK and elsewhere, on the 'knowledge economy'. Leadbeater (1999), for example, discusses the importance of tacit knowledge in economic and social progress. Local communities have a great deal of tacit knowledge to bring to the partnership table: knowledge of what local residents see as priorities and how problems are experienced; knowledge of what is likely to work and what is not; ideas about new ways of tackling problems and using local assets (see Wilkinson and Appelbee, 1999, for a development of this argument). But this knowledge needs to be validated from above and below – respected and acknowledged by the power holders and recognised as a basis for empowerment by communities. Freire's seminal work on conscientisation in the 1970s showed how building on knowledge from below, rather than accepting the received view, allowed poor people in Latin America to develop their own analysis of power in society, which could be used as the foundation for political action (Freire, 1972) (see also Chapter Twelve).

The more complex the notion of power, the more crucial the role of knowledge and critical understanding may become. Lukes' third dimension of power, for example, would seem to imply the need for correspondingly greater degrees of knowledge and critical understanding, to enable participants to unpack the underlying interests and structural constraints, the in-built biases and unspoken assumptions, which need to be challenged in regeneration partnerships. This is not about training, in the relatively limited sense of information giving. It is about active learning processes for groups and organisations as well as for the individuals concerned. Armed with this learning, communities can maximise whatever power and influence they do have within partnerships, in the short-term, going on to develop strategies for longer-term change, if they so decide. These learning processes need also to be developed across sectors, bringing professionals, policy makers and community representatives together in a 'vertical slice' to share their frames of reference and learn together.

'Power mapping'

One example of a practical step to facilitate this type of learning can be provided through 'power mapping'. Power mapping has been developed as part of participatory approaches to development in the South (Fals-Borda and Rahman, 1991; Gaventa, 1991; Estrella and Gaventa, 1998) as well as to regeneration in the North (Mayo, 1997b). Through drawing diagrams to represent power and power relations, participants can work together to develop shared perspectives on how to build effective strategies and alliances. As the discussion of Lukes' approach has already demonstrated, the power to shape agendas is not necessarily readily visible. For example, as it has already been suggested, the interests of private developers may fundamentally constrain the scope of regeneration agendas in prime development sites, whether or not local community participants are fully aware of these constraints. The use of power maps has the potential to disentangle these underlying interests. Through drawing the map (using local materials, flip charts or even laptop computers) participants explore their varying perceptions of where power actually resides, in its different dimensions, setting the context within which to explore what needs to change. As the previous section has already suggested, power relations are inherently dynamic and partnerships develop and change in any case – whether to become more or less unequal. Mapping power is a continuing process rather than a one-off exercise.

Power mapping is but one example of active learning processes with potential relevance as part of strategies to develop less unequal partnerships. Active learning processes need to be available throughout, before, during and after the life of regeneration partnerships – for professionals and decision makers as well as for community representatives.

Posing questions about processes and outcomes

One of the ways in which regeneration remains framed firmly in the understanding of government partners is in the ways that programmes are monitored and audited. This paper has already referred to the complexity of the processes for monitoring and accounting:

> The whole process seemed to be so unwieldy ... community reps had
> to grapple with this huge bureaucratic process.

Participants and those they represent in local communities need to be actively involved in monitoring and evaluating regeneration partnerships in terms of processes and outcomes as well as in terms of outputs. In the 1990s, the Scottish Community Development Centre produced indicators for community development for the Northern Ireland Office. More recently studies funded by the Joseph Rowntree Foundation have approached this issue from two directions, on the one hand developing benchmarks for community involvement and on the other a set of audit tools (Burns and Taylor, 2000), which identify key questions that partners need to pose about processes and outcomes as well as inputs and outputs. These provide a practical means by which communities and agencies can work together to address key questions about processes, outcomes and outputs that put community involvement at the centre of the regeneration process and enable communities to gain more effective control within the processes of partnership working.

Finally, communities could also build upon existing experiences of networking and exchanges, to support each other both in audit processes and in exchanges of learning more generally. The importance of networking has already been firmly established, both for the benefit of individuals and groups and for the potential development of alliances and solidarity around shared interests and concerns within the community sector more generally (Gilchrist and Taylor, 1997). Formal structures have an important role to play, especially when large sums of money are being spent. However there are many other ways of involving people if leadership is to be balanced with participation and public accountability with flexibility. Community development must be concerned with supporting and developing a variety of interlocking networks that cut across community divisions and with supporting those that already exist. Crucially, these need to operate at the informal as well as the formal level so that they can engage people in different and fluid ways (Burns and Taylor, 1998). Networks also need to be developed across sectors, linking communities into government at a variety of different levels, both formally and informally, so that they can be quick on their feet and respond to changing circumstances, rather than creating bureaucratic bottlenecks.

Working towards genuine partnerships

Power maps, audit tools, joint learning events, community networks – none of these provide an easy means of enabling communities to become more equal partners. And the use which communities make of them will depend on their own perspectives and agendas. Whatever perspective is adopted, however, the implications for community development are long-term. Partnerships are no more homogeneous than communities, and like communities they are dynamic rather than static, characterised by flux and change. This means that community development support needs to be made available on a continuing, flexible, and long-term basis, rather than in short-term 'special initiatives', together with access to independent technical advice and training. While this would not of itself guarantee greater equality within partnerships, of course, it could at least begin to redress some of the current patterns of inequality and effective exclusion.

References

Anastacio, J., Gidley, B., Hart, L., Keith, M., Mayo, M. and Kowarzik, V. (2000) *Reflecting realities: Participants' perspectives on integrated communities and sustainable development*, Bristol/York: The Policy Press/Joseph Rowntree Foundation.

Burns, D. and Taylor, M. (1998) *Mutual aid and self-help: Coping strategies for excluded communities*, Bristol/York: The Policy Press/Joseph Rowntree Foundation.

Burns, D. and Taylor, M. (2000) *Auditing community participation: An assessment handbook*, Bristol/York: The Policy Press/Joseph Rowntree Foundation.

Bourdieu, P. (1984) *Distinction*, London: Harvard University Press and Routledge and Kegan Paul (first published 1979).

Chambers, R. (1997) *Whose reality counts?*, London: Intermediate Technology.

Clapham, D. (1996) *Residents' attitudes and perceptions: Position paper, Area Regeneration Programme*, York: Joseph Rowntree Foundation.

Craig, G. and Mayo, M. (1995) *Community empowerment: A reader in participation and development*, London: Zed.

Estrella, M. and Gaventa, J. (1998) *Who counts reality? Participatory monitoring and evaluation: A literature review*, Brighton: Institute of Development Studies, University of Sussex.

Fals-Borda, O. and Rahman, M. (eds) (1991) *Action and knowledge*, London: Intermediate Technology.

Fitzpatrick, S., Hastings, A. and Kintrea, K. (1998) *Including young people in urban regeneration: A lot to learn?*, Bristol/York: The Policy Press/Joseph Rowntree Foundation.

Forgacs, D. (ed) (1988) *A Gramsci Reader*, London: Lawrence and Wishart.

Freire, P. (1972) *Pedagogy of the oppressed*, Harmondsworth: Penguin.

Gaventa, J. (1991) 'Towards a knowledge democracy: viewpoints on participatory research in North America', in O. Fals-Borda and M. Rahman (eds) *Action and knowledge*, London: Intermediate Technology, pp 121-31.

Giddens, A. (1984) *The construction of society*, Cambridge: Polity Press.

Gilchrist, A. and Taylor, M. (1997) 'Community networking: developing strength through diversity', in P. Hoggett (ed) *Contested communities: Experiences, struggles, policies*, Bristol: The Policy Press.

Gitell, R. and Vidal, A. (1998) *Community organising: Building social capital as a development strategy*, London: Sage Publications.

Gujit, I. and Shah, M. (eds) (1998) *The myth of community: Gender issues in participatory development*, London: Intermediate Technology.

Habermas, J. (1976) *Legitimation crisis* (translated by Thomas McCarthy), London: Heinemann Educational.

Hastings, A., McArthur, A. and McGregor, A. (1996) *Less than equal?: Community organisations and estate regeneration partnerships*, Bristol/York:The Policy Press/Joseph Rowntree Foundation.

Healey, P. (1997) *Collaborative planning: Shaping places in fragmented societies*, Basingstoke: Macmillan.

Holland, J. and Blackburn, J. (eds) (1998) *Whose voice?*, London: Intermediate Technology.

Johnson, H. and Wilson, G. (1999) 'Institutional sustainability as learning', *Development in Practice*, vol 9, no 1, pp 43-55.

Leadbeater, C. (1999*) Living on thin air: The new economy*, London: Viking.

Lukes, S. (1974) *Power: A radical view*, London: Macmillan.

Mackintosh, M. (1993) 'Partnership: issues of policy and negotiation', *Local Economy*, vol 7, no 3, pp 210-24.

Mayo, M. (1997a) 'Partnerships for regeneration and community development', *Critical Social Policy*, vol 17, no 3, pp 3-26.

Mayo, M. (1997b) *Imagining tomorrow: Adult education for transformation*, Leicester: NIACE.

Mayo, M. and Anastacio, J. (1999) 'Welfare models and approaches to empowerment: competing perspectives from area regeneration programmes', *Policy Studies*, no 1, March, pp 5-21.

Putnam, R. (1993) *Making democracy work*, Princeton, NJ: Princeton University Press.

Stewart, M. and Taylor, M. (1995) *Empowerment and estate regeneration: A critical review*, Bristol:The Policy Press.

Taylor, M. (1995) *Unleashing the potential*, York: Joseph Rowntree Foundation.

Taylor, M. (1997) *The best of both worlds: Local government and the voluntary sector*,York: Joseph Rowntree Foundation.

Taylor, M. (2000a) 'Communities in the lead: power, organisational capacity and social capital', *Urban Studies*, vol 37, nos 5-6, pp 1019-35.

Taylor, M. (2000b) 'Partnership: insiders and outsiders', in M. Harris and C. Rochester (eds) *Voluntary organisations and social policy in Britain: Perspectives on change and choice*, London: Macmillan.

Wilkinson, D. and Appelbee, E. (1999) *Implementing holistic government: Joined up action on the ground*, Bristol: The Policy Press.

THREE

Local government, anti-poverty strategies and partnership working

Sarah Pearson

Introduction

The Labour government has placed increasing emphasis on partnership working as the key mechanism for the delivery of policies to combat poverty, promote social inclusion and revitalise democratic citizenship. This focus on partnership working between individuals and agencies reflects the multidimensional nature of exclusion and deprivation. It also acknowledges the limitations of single agency approaches to tackling these enduring social problems.

In local government, a significant number of local authorities have sought to address issues of poverty and deprivation through anti-poverty and social inclusion strategies. A majority of these authorities have developed strategies on the premise that, working in isolation, local government has only limited capacities to impact in positive ways on the lives of people living in disadvantaged communities. Anti-poverty and social inclusion partnerships have therefore aimed to harness the resources and expertise of key stakeholders within the statutory, voluntary and community sectors.

This chapter assesses partnership working as a mechanism for the development and delivery of anti-poverty and social exclusion strategies in local authorities in England and Wales. It begins by charting the development of anti-poverty strategies in local government. Drawing on research into local authority anti-poverty strategies[1], it then addresses the rationale behind anti-poverty partnerships, examines the nature and extent of partnership structures and assesses their impact in promoting innovative policy responses to poverty and exclusion. Finally, the chapter highlights some issues for the future development of these partnerships including the fact that, in general, local authorities have not included people living in poverty in these arrangements.

Local government anti-poverty strategies

In their Introduction to this volume, Balloch and Taylor have outlined the main developments that have contributed to the emergence of partnership as a central component of local government activity. These developments have given rise to new kinds of local government services designed to meet the changing needs of local populations. Local authorities have sought to garner the resources and expertise of other agencies to enable them to deliver a growing array of policies and service programmes (Gregory, 1998).

Local authorities have also developed partnership working in response to growing levels of poverty and social exclusion. Anti-poverty and social inclusion partnerships have been one of the key mechanisms through which local government has sought to combat the effects of poverty and exclusion in local communities.

The origins of anti-poverty strategies in local government can be traced to the Community Development Projects and Urban Programme of the 1960s and 1970s. As Balloch and Taylor point out, these programmes also signified the beginnings of partnership working for local government when it began to develop relationships with other organisations through initiatives that aimed to address local poverty. In some authorities these initiatives were carried over into mainstream service delivery programmes when central government funding for projects ended.

Anti-poverty work has also been influenced by the activities of what was termed the 'new urban left' (see Atkinson and Moon, 1994, p 205) in the GLC, inner London boroughs, Sheffield and Liverpool in the early 1980s. These Labour-controlled authorities implemented a range of local initiatives (one of the most notorious of which was the GLC's 'Fares Fair' scheme to subsidise public transport) as part of their attempts to establish an alternative model of local government around the concept of municipal socialism (Cochrane, 1986) and in explicit protest against the policies of Conservative governments that combined to reduce public spending through, and by, local government. As an experiment in the transformation of local politics, the activities of the new urban left proved ethereal. A more lasting legacy, however, was that their commitment to special provision for disadvantaged groups contributed to the development of anti-poverty work. Anti-poverty initiatives established in opposition to Conservative government policies took on increasing significance as urban authorities attempted to cope with the havoc wreaked on communities by economic restructuring, a task made particularly difficult by governmental refusal to admit the existence of poverty in the UK, let alone address it as a policy issue (see, for example, Moore, 1989).

Throughout the 1980s and into the early 1990s many more local authorities, faced with evidence of increasing levels of poverty among local communities and the withdrawal of central government from local anti-poverty work, expanded service commitments to poor local citizens and established corporate strategies to combat local poverty (Alcock et al, 1995; Balloch and Jones, 1990). During this period, anti-poverty policies moved beyond the confines of the more radical left-wing urban authorities to be taken up by others from across the political spectrum (although only a small minority of Conservative-controlled local authorities would have admitted during this period to undertaking anything that they would define as anti-poverty work) and representing all the various forms of local administration.

Poverty and social exclusion are examples of what has been described as local government's 'wicked issues' (Wilkinson and Appelbee, 1999). Mirroring in many ways the cross-cutting issues affecting policy development in central government, local government's wicked issues cut across departmental boundaries and affect the development, delivery and impact of a wide range of services. Addressing these issues requires those working in local authorities to look beyond the boundaries of their departmental priorities and seek to work corporately, strategically and innovatively both within the authority and with others outside it who can provide expertise and resources (Stewart et al, 1999). Through anti-poverty strategies local authorities have, in effect, been pursuing 'joined-up thinking' for many years. A model anti-poverty strategy, therefore, has focused:

internally – on the structures and policies that are required for anti-poverty issues to inform budgetary and service planning mechanisms and on the continual review of policy; and
externally – on working in partnership with other agencies and local people.

As discussed above, anti-poverty strategies were largely developed in a climate of financial restraint. They have therefore focused largely on bending mainstream services and resources to meet the needs of disadvantaged people. Mainstream services occupy a key role in the effort to combat deprivation, and are likely to be those that impact most significantly on the lives of poor people. This latter point has been recognised in the National Strategy for Neighbourhood Renewal through the Report of Policy Action Team 17, which argues that mainstream services are at least as important as area-based initiatives in effecting long-term change (DETR, 2000, p 55). Some authorities also developed specific anti-poverty initiatives. Table 3.1 provides examples of initiatives commonly developed through anti-poverty and strategies.

By the end of the 1990s, anti-poverty strategies were a significant feature of the local government landscape. A survey of local authorities in England and Wales conducted in 1997 obtained responses from 180 of the 412[2]; 161 indicated that they were active in undertaking anti-poverty work and 47% of these had a corporate anti-poverty strategy (see Pearson et al, 1997; Alcock et al, 1999). In these authorities, those responsible for the development of anti-poverty strategies recognised that, working alone, their abilities to combat poverty were limited. Partnership with other organisations and with local people has therefore been a crucial mechanism in many local authorities for the achievement of anti-poverty objectives.

Table 3.1: Anti-poverty and social inclusion initiatives in local government

Area of work	Anti-poverty initiatives
Income maintenance	Welfare rights; charging policies; debt-collection policies; benefits administration policies; debt and money advice services; credit unions
Health	Food cooperatives; exercise on prescription schemes; food distribution schemes; public health partnerships
Access to services	Citizens' cards and leisure cards; service decentralisation; one-stop shops; community transport and concessionary fares
Energy efficiency programmes	Fuel poverty campaigns; energy efficiency advice and grants; administration of the Home Energy Efficiency Scheme
Community and economic development	LETS (Local Exchange Trading Systems); community economic development projects; community businesses

Government focus on poverty and deprivation

Since the election of the Labour government in 1997, the political and policy context for local authority anti-poverty work has changed substantially. One of the most fundamental, and positive, changes has been the government's focus on tackling poverty and deprivation. In this context, local authorities with a commitment to anti-poverty work have found themselves working with the broad direction of government policy, rather than against it as they had often been previously. The government's determination to widen the policy agenda beyond issues of material poverty, and also to address the multiple and interrelated difficulties faced by people experiencing social exclusion, means that there are now many opportunities for local authorities to work with central government and other agencies in formulating and implementing the various policy interventions aimed at promoting social inclusion. Some local authorities have developed social inclusion strategies in recognition of this changing, and broadening, agenda.

The problem of social exclusion has been the subject of considerable academic debate, both in the UK and in the wider European policy arena from which the term originated (for further reading see Oppenheim, 1998; Room, 1995). Social exclusion has been taken by academics and policy makers to mean many things, from a euphemism for poverty, to the experience of disadvantage as a denial of citizenship rights. The concept of social exclusion that informs the current UK policy agenda is one that has a strong emphasis on issues linked to welfare dependency and spatial concentrations of disadvantage. This has led to a policy focus on initiatives that target excluded individuals and communities, and on work as a route to social inclusion.

It is unclear whether these initiatives will make any impact on the structures and processes which 'cause' exclusion (Geddes and Root, 2000) or how they will improve the lives of those for whom paid work is not an option (Levitas, 1998). It is also unclear how many of these initiatives will interact with anti-poverty strategies. There has been little consideration, for instance, of the contribution of anti-poverty strategies to the National Strategy for Neighbourhood Renewal (Social Exclusion Unit, 1998). Experiences from local authorities that have undertaken anti-poverty work provide some important contributions to the debate. Poverty and social exclusion are not the same, but there is a strong correlation between them and it is important that the experience of anti-poverty work is not lost within the rush of policy initiatives to tackle social exclusion. The emphasis that anti-poverty strategies have placed on bending mainstream resources has highlighted the importance of these in addressing deprivation; targeted initiatives are only part of the solution. Similarly, in focusing on corporate processes and structures within local authorities, anti-poverty strategies have revealed how the well-intentioned actions of individuals, departments and partnerships can interact to impact negatively on the lives of local citizens. Crucially, also, anti-poverty strategies have considered the role of local services in ameliorating the effects of poverty for those who do not work, or experience low-paid and insecure employment.

The focus on partnership as a vehicle for addressing social exclusion means that there are also some important lessons to be drawn from local authorities' experiences of partnership working to address issues of poverty and deprivation. The remainder of this chapter addresses partnership working as a key element of anti-poverty strategies.

The extent of anti-poverty partnership working

The 1997 survey of local authorities in England and Wales explored the extent and nature of joint working undertaken through anti-poverty strategies. Over 90% of the 161 authorities undertaking anti-poverty work also indicated that this included joint working with other agencies. Anti-poverty partnerships are prevalent across all types of council: 100% of responding metropolitan and county authorities reported that they had developed anti-poverty partnerships, as did over 80% of other types of responding local authority (London borough, district and unitary).

The survey asked local authorities to indicate which of a range of organisations they engaged with in partnership working on anti-poverty issues. Local voluntary and community organisations were the most popular choice of partner followed in order by: health authorities, other local authorities, national voluntary organisations, police authorities and (in a minority of cases) the Benefits Agency, central government departments and the local offices of central government departments.

There is an important distinction, however, between strategic level partnerships that develop and review policy, and those that are concerned solely with operation and service delivery. Participation in strategic partnerships requires different rules of engagement and a different distribution of power among the organisations concerned (Mayo, 1997; Taylor, 1995). Respondents were also asked, therefore, to differentiate between their involvement with partners in arrangements concerning

Table 3.2: Partners in generic and specific partnerships

Partner agency	% of responding authorities working in partnership arrangements		
	Specific	Generic	Both
Other local authorities	35	10	15
Central government departments	17	5	3
Health authorities	45	11	16
Benefits Agency	24	10	3
Police authorities	24	7	8
Local employer	16	7	7
National voluntary organisation	23	11	9
Local voluntary or community group	46	11	22
Local office of central government department	26	8	3

either the delivery and implementation of specific anti-poverty initiatives ('specific partnerships') or in arrangements concerned with strategic development and service planning ('generic partnerships').

Local authorities have engaged most often with voluntary and community organisations in partnership arrangements for the delivery of specific initiatives; over 45% of responding authorities indicated involvement in such joint working arrangements. This is a reflection of the key role that voluntary agencies occupy, both in service delivery and in work with deprived and excluded communities (Taylor, 1997). Health authorities were also frequently involved in specific partnerships, reflecting the strong associations between poverty and ill health and the potential that local authorities have to impact on public health issues. It also reflects the fact that many local authorities have existing relationships with health authorities through statutory responsibilities for the organisation of community care services.

Much lower numbers of respondents reported being engaged in generic (or strategic) partnership arrangements. Around 10% or 11% of the respondents were working in such a manner with other local authorities, the Benefits Agency, national voluntary organisations and local voluntary and community groups. Central government departments featured in only a small number of these arrangements. This is a legacy, perhaps, of the fact that most anti-poverty strategies were developed in opposition to central government policy.

Low level of business community involvement

Few responding authorities reported that they worked in partnership with local employers. Given the well-established causal links between unemployment, poverty and social exclusion, this is perhaps surprising. However, other research has highlighted the business community's low level of involvement in anti-poverty issues (Alcock et al, 1998; Roberts et al, 1995). There are a number of reasons why this might be the case, but perhaps of most relevant here is the fact that in many local authorities economic development strategies and anti-poverty strategies have been developed and implemented in isolation from each other, often by different departments. Partnership working with the business community has generally been focused primarily on economic development, and less on social issues. There are signs that this is changing, however, not least because the guidelines for submission of bids to most regeneration funding streams now stress the importance of fusing economic regeneration with social gain. It has proved important within this context for local authorities to develop appropriate structures for the inclusion of the business community in strategy development, and to find the language through which to develop discourse on anti-poverty and social issues.

The business community does not always sit easily within partnership structures that comprise, in the main, individuals and agencies whose focus is on social issues and the delivery of social care services. There are examples of the business community participating in anti-poverty partnerships but this has generally been around specific initiatives. One of the most significant examples of joint working between local authorities and the private sector is around discount cards. These offer discounts on service charges (often leisure related) to people living in the borough, those in receipt of low income, or those falling into certain priority groups (for instance students, children or retired people). In many local authorities, private sector agencies participate in these schemes by offering discounted charges for their goods and services.

Variety of anti-poverty partnerships

Perhaps the most overriding feature of anti-poverty partnerships is that of variety. In addition to the categories of agencies listed above, local authorities that responded to the survey also reported working in partnership with church and faith organisations, schools, further education colleges, universities, the armed forces, fire and rescue services, rural community councils, the Rural Development Commission (now defunct, the RDC merged with the Countryside Commission in 1999 to form the Countryside Agency), the probation service, residents' associations, utilities companies, trade union associations, chambers of commerce and the Forestry Commission (some of these agencies could perhaps be included in the categories above but were listed separately by responding authorities). The gains that local authorities have sought from anti-poverty partnerships, the form that partnerships have taken, the agencies that have been involved, and in what capacities, have differed greatly. The remainder of this chapter reviews a number of features of anti-poverty partnership working in local government. These are:

- partnership development;
- partnership organisation and management;
- community representation;
- the impact of local authority anti-poverty and social inclusion partnerships.

Partnership development

The most important reason for the development of anti-poverty and social inclusion partnerships in local government has been the desire on the part of elected members and local authority officers to maximise the potential of local authorities to impact in positive ways on the lives of those living in disadvantaged communities. They have also secured a range of more tangible benefits from working in partnership with other agencies and individuals. These have included:

- the incorporation of the wider experience of other agencies working in, and with, deprived communities;
- the establishment of contacts with external organisations and networks;
- the opportunity to pool and share resources and expertise (this is especially important in light of the fact that most anti-poverty strategies do not attract additional resources, a point which is discussed further below);
- information sharing to support the appropriate targeting of programmes and initiatives;
- sharing of best practice;
- avoiding duplication of effort;

- coordinating work and promoting joined-up solutions and thinking; and
- maximising outcomes for communities.

Partnership organisation and management

It is clear from the evidence presented in Table 3.2 that anti-poverty and social inclusion strategies have been driven primarily by local authorities and that other partners have been largely involved in the implementation of specific initiatives rather than in devising strategy or formulating policy. In some local authorities officers and members have been of the opinion that multiagency working at the development stage of anti-poverty strategies introduces mixed agendas that can impede progression (Alcock et al, 1995). The emphasis in these authorities has been on the need to develop clear vision and objectives internally before involving external agencies.

The failure of these authorities to engage external agencies in strategy development has, to some extent, been caused by difficulties in opening up intricate corporate planning processes to other partners. But there has been another factor. Other agencies have sometimes wanted to hold themselves at a distance, both politically and organisationally, from the work of the local authority. This has been particularly true of some agencies in the voluntary sector. Relationships between voluntary organisations and local authorities vary enormously; they tend to be most developed where the local authority has had a social service responsibility and there has been a history of grant aid to voluntary agencies concerned with the delivery of social services. Not unreasonably, most voluntary sector agencies seek to participate in partnership on equal terms with others, and some have perceived a potential conflict of interest between the formation of anti-poverty strategy and the withdrawal of funding to voluntary agencies. In cases where funding to the voluntary sector has been under review, these agencies have perceived difficulties negotiating on equal terms with their funder when there has also been a possibility that funding could be withdrawn (Roberts et al, 1995).

In other authorities the benefits of engaging partners at an early stage in strategy development have outweighed the difficulties involved in negotiating the boundaries of relationships between the statutory and voluntary sector. Anti-poverty officers in these authorities have sought from the outset to engage a wide variety of stakeholders in strategy development in order to encourage shared ownership of the strategy throughout the borough. One of the most common approaches to the engagement of a wide range of stakeholders has been borough-wide anti-poverty conferences or workshops. These have been organised as platforms to announce the intention to develop a new anti-poverty strategy, to launch a strategy, or to review the progress of an existing strategy. Attendees at conferences have been invited to form broad-based anti-poverty partnerships to oversee the development and implementation of strategies and to act as consultation and sounding boards for the local authority.

This approach has a number of advantages. Firstly, it encourages inclusiveness. All those who wish to participate in the partnership are able to do so (although there may be some difficulties with agencies and individuals omitted from conference invitation lists). It is also likely to result in the bringing together of a useful range of individual and organisational perspectives to inform anti-poverty work. There is a greater likelihood, too, that local authorities' anti-poverty messages will reach their target audiences in deprived communities, as agencies that are in regular contact with these communities are more likely to be involved. This kind of approach also lends itself to bringing a range of agencies together at intervals (annually, for instance) to review the overall progress of strategies and to reassess the needs of communities as a basis for agreeing priorities for future anti-poverty and social inclusion work.

Partnership structures of this magnitude present a number of difficulties. They can be unwieldy, and in some cases it has proved difficult for partnerships to coalesce a wide range of perspectives and agendas to achieve consensus. There is also the issue of legitimacy, and what role there may be for agencies whose remit is not directly related to the local authority's anti-poverty strategy. There is evidence, both from research into local government anti-poverty strategies and from the much wider body of research relating to the proliferation of partnerships concerned with the delivery of regeneration programmes, that although structures of this kind are useful forums for information sharing, they run the risk of becoming little more than talking shops (Hastings, 1996; Lowndes et al, 1997). In these instances, participating agencies and individuals can feel disempowered and experience partnership 'fatigue' if other avenues are not available through which to pursue more direct action.

It has been for these reasons that many local authorities have participated in partnership working through smaller groups and have focused on strategic working around specific anti-poverty and social inclusion issues.

These structures have been likely to include small numbers of local authority officers and representatives of statutory agencies and non-governmental organisations with a remit for policy delivery around the issues concerned. In only a very small minority of cases have these arrangements also included people experiencing poverty and exclusion, a point which is discussed further below.

In almost all anti-poverty and social inclusion partnerships, local authorities have been the principal partner, despite the fact that joint working with others is crucial to their success in achieving objectives. Again, there are advantages and disadvantages to this approach. Local authorities are well placed to take the lead in anti-poverty work by virtue of their resources, remit and expertise. They bring democratic accountability to partnerships, have knowledge of local needs and capacities, and are likely to be able to devote resources and administrative support, both to the partnership itself and to projects and initiatives that are developed.

The key role occupied by local authorities does, however, highlight the issue of power balances within anti-poverty and social inclusion partnerships. Local authorities have tended to act as host and chair for partnership meetings because they have generally been the driving force behind the development of strategies. Councils have often perceived their role to be administrative, and have held the responsibility for organisation and management of partnership activities. This approach is not necessarily wrong, although rotation of the chair and the hosting of some, or all, partnership meetings outside of the local authority might help to redress balances of power. But there are three potential difficulties that arise when local authorities hold control over partnership arrangements.

Local authority control: potential difficulties

The first of these difficulties relates to the fact that local government tends to be dominated by the demands of funding and bureaucracy. Work that aims to tackle poverty and exclusion requires long-term commitment, but the dictates of annual budgeting cycles often limit what local authorities can achieve. Very few anti-poverty strategies have carried their own budgets and, unlike many regeneration partnerships, the agencies participating in anti-poverty and social inclusion partnerships are unlikely to have come together with a view to attracting additional resources with which to achieve their objectives. This has been a potential source of conflict between local authorities and other agencies, particularly if these are not in a position to commit resources to anti-poverty work.

The second issue relates to the nature of participation. Partners have sometimes felt that because local authorities have taken the lead on the development of anti-poverty strategies, the framework and boundaries for anti-poverty work are set outside of partnership structures. To some extent this has been true, as almost all anti-poverty strategies have been managed within local authorities by working groups of officers and/or members. To achieve a corporate focus to anti-poverty work, individual officers serving on anti-poverty and social inclusion partnerships are often co-opted as departmental representatives. Representation can change, or disappear, if other service and policy priorities take over. It is important therefore, for anti-poverty strategies to have departmental champions who are committed to them and who see working with the partnership as a core element of their role. This can help to ensure consistency, that discussions do not need to be repeated, and that other partners are confident that their priorities are being taken seriously elsewhere within the authority. In this latter context it is also important that structures are in place to feed back between partnerships and departments, and that local authority staff are empowered, and resourced, to act on the recommendations of partner agencies.

Finally, there is the issue of political change. It is increasingly common for the balance of political power within local authorities to change significantly at each local election. Despite the current policy emphasis on addressing social exclusion and the duty on local authorities to promote the economic, social and environmental well-being of communities, there is no statutory obligation on them to undertake anti-poverty and social inclusion work. Anti-poverty strategies have inevitably been concerned with some statutory commitments for service delivery in relation to benefit administration, education and social services but in some authorities, anti-poverty and social inclusion work has been vulnerable to changes in political priorities. It can be difficult for partners to commit their energies and resources to anti-poverty work when there is little or no long-term political commitment to the work within the authority.

Community representation

As discussed above, a wide variety of partners have been involved in joint arrangements for the delivery of anti-poverty and social inclusion work. Poverty impacts on many aspects of the lives of those who experience it, and it is crucial therefore that many different agencies are involved in initiatives to combat it. Despite this comprehensive approach, however, few anti-poverty partnerships have succeeded in including all relevant local actors. For instance, agencies representing churches and faith communities, those operating in the housing field, and those working with very excluded groups such as drug and alcohol misusers have been notable by their absence from most anti-poverty and social inclusion partnerships.

Many of these partnerships have also failed to incorporate adequate representation from deprived spatial communities, and from those communities of interest that are vulnerable to poverty and exclusion. Anti-poverty and social inclusion partnerships have been unlikely, for instance, to have included representation from all local minority ethnic groups, people with disabilities, older people, or gay and lesbian groups.

As highlighted by the data in Table 3.2, only a relatively small number of local authorities have succeeded in engaging local people (as individuals, or through their representative agencies in the voluntary and community sector) in strategic anti-poverty partnerships. There is a large body of academic and policy literature highlighting the need to involve local people in regeneration initiatives (for example, Fordham, 1995; Taylor, 1995; Thake, 1995) and there is now a general consensus, both in the literature and among policy makers, that in order to ensure that anti-poverty and social inclusion initiatives are appropriate to local needs, and sustainable, local authorities and regeneration practitioners must develop structures to facilitate the participation of local people, not only in project implementation, but also in policy development and direction through strategic partnerships (Pearson and Craig, 2001).

Some local authorities have, in fact, gone to considerable lengths to develop structures to include voluntary and community groups in policy development. They have employed a range of strategies for harnessing community opinion, including community forums, open consultation meetings, citizens' juries and focus groups. This practice is likely to continue, and increase, not least because of the duty on local authorities to consult local people through the best value process. But these structures have largely been limited to consultation, they have not allowed local people to participate on equal terms with other agencies in partnerships that determine strategic priorities for the local authority, and where there is some control over the distribution of resources.

In the previous chapter, Mayo and Taylor discussed some of the power imbalances in partnerships for regeneration and illustrated the limited involvement of people living in poor communities in strategic anti-poverty and social inclusion partnerships. They confirmed that some communities have lacked the capacity to participate on equal terms. This has been especially true in communities where large numbers of the population are living in poverty. Ensuring that local communities are empowered to participate in strategic partnerships requires, among other things, that local authorities and their partners provide the resources to develop local capacity (Thomas and Duncan, 2000). Anti-poverty and social inclusion partnerships have not usually had the resources to provide funding for capacity building in communities or to facilitate the active participation of voluntary and community groups. As a consequence, their participation has been limited.

This is likely to have been particularly true for the most excluded groups, such as black and minority ethnic communities, and women. Equal opportunities are an important dimension to anti-poverty work, but there has been little or no research that addresses the experiences of particularly excluded groups participating in anti-poverty partnerships. Evidence in the literature relating to participation in regeneration initiatives suggests, however, that although these groups are frequently living in the most deprived circumstances, their involvement in policy development and planning has been limited (Cook, 1995; Skelcher et al, 1996; Brownill and Darke, 1998) (see also Chapter Nine). Particular issues have arisen where there are not significant concentrations of black and minority ethnic groups. In some instances local authorities (and other policy makers) have argued that their scarcity negates the need for a coherent policy response (Craig, 1999).

There has similarly been little research that addresses the participation of the most vulnerable minority communities – those made up of refugees and asylum seekers. The more generalised exclusion experienced by many of these communities suggests, however, that their capacity to participate in anti-poverty partnerships will be limited.

The impact of local authority anti-poverty and social inclusion partnerships

As discussed above, few anti-poverty and social inclusion partnerships in local government have attracted substantial resources with which to undertake new work. A small minority of anti-poverty strategies have included limited budgets for the development of new initiatives but these have been rare, given that many of these strategies have been developed within an overall climate of resource constraint. Many of the causes of poverty and social exclusion are beyond the control of local government and most anti-poverty strategies have aimed to utilise mainstream resources, and some marginal spending. It is within this context that the impact of anti-poverty and social inclusion partnerships should be judged.

Local government anti-poverty and social inclusion partnerships have had some success in bringing together those agencies and individuals involved in efforts to combat poverty. This approach has gleaned important benefits for anti-poverty work. Partnerships have brought it legitimacy through networking and liaison between agencies; they have provided resources and expertise to local authorities in support of the achievement of their anti-poverty objectives; and the wider involvement of stakeholders has gone some way to ensuring the sustainability of anti-poverty work in a climate of financial and political uncertainty. In many local authorities, partnership working through anti-poverty strategies has resulted in some innovative projects. It is unlikely that many of the initiatives listed in Table 3.1 would have been achieved by local authorities working in isolation. While it is unlikely that any anti-poverty and social inclusion partnerships could claim that their impact has been the eradication of local poverty, there are a great many which have succeeded in utilising the scarce resources available to make substantial impacts on poor and excluded communities.

Without additional resources, however, the impact of these partnerships has inevitably been limited. Without the unifying focus of a budget for project development, some partnerships have experienced a lack of clarity over aims. Where this has also resulted in a lack of tangible outcomes, the enthusiasm and commitment of partners has waned, and some partnerships have achieved very little.

Conclusions and issues for future anti-poverty and social inclusion partnerships in local government

The Labour government has made commitments to regenerate areas of deprivation and to eradicate child poverty within a generation. General elections notwithstanding, issues of poverty and exclusion are therefore likely to inform the policy agenda for some time to come. Partnership working is also likely to prevail, as most current and foreseeable policy directions continue to stress the importance of partnership working as a mechanism for policy development and delivery. Local authorities are likely, therefore, to continue to be involved in anti-poverty and social inclusion partnerships and it is important within this context to draw some lessons from their experiences so far.

The discussion in this chapter has highlighted some of the benefits, and difficulties that have arisen from working in partnership to undertake anti-poverty and social inclusion work in local government. We can conclude that:

• local authorities have achieved some innovative policy outcomes through working in partnership around the delivery of anti-poverty and social inclusion services. These have resulted, in many cases, in significant positive impacts on the lives of those living in poverty;
• in some partnerships, the achievement of objectives has been stalled by a lack of financial resources and a lack of political commitment to anti-poverty and social inclusion work within the authority;
• few local authorities have been successful in incorporating all the relevant agencies and individuals affected by anti-poverty and social inclusion issues. In the future, partnerships will need to seek ways to combine an inclusive approach with mechanisms for setting and achieving objectives;
• many local authorities have failed to engage partners in the development of strategy;
• there has been only very limited involvement of poor and marginalised people. Resourcing of anti-poverty and social inclusion partnerships needs to incorporate budgets that can be used to develop capacity in deprived communities, and allow those living there to participate effectively in partnership arrangements.

Notes

[1] This chapter draws on evidence from a number of research projects that examined local government anti-poverty and social inclusion strategies between 1997 and 2000. The research directors were Professor Pete Alcock (now at the University of Birmingham) and Professor Gary Craig (now at the University of Hull). Other members of the research team included the author, Cathy Barnes at the University of Lincolnshire and Humberside, and Adrian Harvey, until recently at the Improvement and Development Agency for Local Government (IDeA). The views represented in this chapter are the author's own and do not necessarily reflect those of other members of the research team.

[2] This survey was carried out as part of a research project to develop tools for the monitoring and evaluation of anti-poverty and social inclusion work in local

government. It was administered by the Anti-Poverty Unit at the IDeA. Full results of the research are available in Alcock, P., Barnes, C., Craig, G., Harvey, A. and Pearson, S. (1999), *What counts? What works? Evaluating anti-poverty and social inclusion work in local government*, London: Improvement and Development Agency.

References

Alcock, P., Barnes, C., Craig, G., Harvey, A. and Pearson, S. (1999) *What counts? What works? Evaluating anti-poverty and social inclusion work in local government*, London: Improvement and Development Agency.

Alcock, P., Craig, G., Lawless, P., Pearson, S. and Robinson, D. (1998) *Inclusive regeneration*, Sheffield/Hull: Sheffield Hallam University/ University of Lincolnshire and Humberside.

Alcock. P., Craig, G., Dalgleish, K. and Pearson, S. (1995) *Combating local poverty*, London: Local Government Management Board.

Atkinson, R. and Moon, G. (1994) *Urban policy in Britain*, London: Macmillan.

Balloch, S. and Jones, B. (1990) *Poverty and anti-poverty strategy: The local government response*, London: Association of Metropolitan Authorities.

Brownill, S. and Darke, J. (1998) *'Rich mix': Inclusive strategies for urban regeneration*, Bristol/York: The Policy Press/Joseph Rowntree Foundation.

Cochrane, A. (1986) 'Local employment initiatives: towards a new municipal socialism?', in P. Lawless, and C. Raban, (eds) *The contemporary British city*, London: Harper & Row.

Cook, J. (1995) *Invisible partners: The impact of SRB on black communities*, London: Black Training and Enterprise Group.

Craig, G. (1999) '"Race", poverty and social security', in J. Ditch (ed) *Poverty and social security*, London: Routledge.

DETR (Department of the Environment, Transport and the Regions) (2000) *Joining it up locally, national strategy for neighbourhood renewal, Report of Policy Action Team 17*, London: The Stationery Office.

Fordham, G. (1995) *Made to last: Creating sustainable neighbourhood and estate regeneration*, York: Joseph Rowntree Foundation.

Geddes, M. and Root, A. (2000) 'Social exclusion – new language, new challenges for local authorities', *Public Money and Management*, April-June.

Gregory, S. (1998) *Transforming local services: Partnership in action*, York: Joseph Rowntree Foundation.

Hastings, A. (1996) 'Unravelling the process of "partnership" in urban regeneration policy', *Urban Studies*, vol 33, no 2, pp 253-68.

Levitas, R. (1998) *The inclusive society? Social exclusion and new labour*, London: Macmillan.

Lowndes, V., Skelcher, C., Nanton, P. and McCabe, A. (1997) 'Networks, partnerships and urban regeneration', *Local Economy*, February, pp 333-42.

Mayo, M. (1997) 'Partnerships for regeneration and community development: some opportunities, challenges and constraints', *Critical Social Policy 52*, vol 17, pp 3-26.

Moore, J. (1989) 'The end of the line for poverty', Speech to Greater London Area CPC, 11 May.

Oppenheim, C. (ed) (1998) *An inclusive society: Strategies for tackling poverty*, London: Institute of Public Policy Research.

Pearson, S. and Craig, G. (2001) 'Community participation in strategic partnerships', in J. Pierson, and J. Smith, (eds) *Rethinking community: The policy and practice of urban regeneration*, London: Macmillan.

Pearson, S., Kirkpatrick, A. and Barnes, C. (1997) *Local poverty, local responses*, Sheffield/Hull: Sheffield Hallam University/University of Lincolnshire and Humberside.

Roberts, V., Russell, H., Harding, M. and Parkinson, M. (1995) *Public/private/voluntary partnerships in local government*, Draft report to the Local Government Management Board, Liverpool John Moores University.

Room, G. (ed) (1995) *Beyond the threshold: The management and analysis of social exclusion*, Bristol: The Policy Press.

Skelcher, C., McCabe, A., Lowndes, V. and Nanton, P. (1996) *Community networks in urban regeneration: 'It all depends who you know...!'*, Bristol/York: The Policy Press/Joseph Rowntree Foundation.

Social Exclusion Unit (1998) *Bringing Britain together: A national strategy for neighbourhood renewal*, London: SEU.

Stewart, M., Goss, S., Gillanders, G., Clarke, R., Rowe, J. and Shaftoe, H. (1999) *Cross-cutting issues affecting local government*, London: DETR.

Taylor, M. (1997) *The best of both worlds: The voluntary sector and local government*, York: York Publishing Services.

Taylor, M. (1995) *Unleashing the potential: Bringing residents to the centre of regeneration*, York: Joseph Rowntree Foundation.

Thake, S. (1995) *Staying the course: The roles and structures of community regeneration organisations*, York: Joseph Rowntree Foundation.

Thomas, S. and Duncan, P. (2000) *Neighbourhood regeneration: Resourcing community involvement*, Bristol/York: The Policy Press/Joseph Rowntree Foundation.

Wilkinson, D. and Appelbee, E. (1999) *Implementing holistic government: Joined up action on the ground*, Bristol: The Policy Press.

FOUR

Partnership and change in social housing

Barbara Reid

Introduction

In recent years, the notion of partnership has become a cornerstone of social housing and of the institutional arrangements that underpin the provision of social housing services. Partnerships of many different kinds now provide the organisational and institutional 'glue' for housing policy implementation, for the delivery of local social housing services, and for incorporating end-users in decision making, evaluation and regulation. As Malpass (1997) observes, this 'new governance' of housing reflects the climate of fundamental institutional, organisational and managerial change in local government and the public sector as a whole (see also Stoker, 1997a, 1997b).

This chapter explores partnership activity in social housing at an operational level. It discusses definitions of partnership in social housing and sets out the policy context for the development of operational partnerships, before highlighting the key themes in this area of partnership activity in social housing. It then draws on recent research[1] to focus on five main areas of operational partnership activity, looking at patterns of activity in each of these areas. It concludes with an assessment of the prospects for the development of operational partnerships and the place of partnership activity in housing service delivery.

The place of partnership in social housing

The term 'partnership' is used in a number of different ways in housing policy and practice. 'Partnership' and 'working with partners' is presented both at national policy level and at local project level as a necessary part of the implementation and service delivery process. For example, the Housing Green Paper, *Quality and choice: A decent home for all* (DETR, 2000) declares that tenants, residents, housing associations, private sector landlords, housebuilders, voluntary sector agencies, black and minority ethnic community representatives, parish and town councils, planning departments, health authorities, social services and the police should be seen as the 'key partners' of local authority housing services in the development of local housing policies (DETR, 2000). There is also an expectation that housing services will work increasingly in cross-functional partnerships in order to tackle the more complex and intractable challenges presented by socio-economic disadvantage and 'problem' housing estates. Thus, the Green Paper stresses the importance of housing services being part of, among others, Crime and Disorder Partnerships, Health Improvement Partnerships, Supporting People Partnerships, Connexions Partnerships for young people, the work of the Regional Development Agencies, Single Regeneration Budget Challenge Fund projects, the New Deal for Communities, and so on.

Partnership activity such as this has provided the operational underpinning for major structural change in the British housing system from the 1980s onwards, and the Green Paper reinforces this role. It has been used as a vehicle for introducing greater consumer choice, providing a greater role for markets, introducing performance-centred operating cultures, for diversifying tenure and housing provision, and deregulating housing finance (Hamnett, 1993). As the Introduction has emphasised, partnership working is now seen as a vehicle for delivering modernised services, of framing intervention on regeneration and of tackling social exclusion. The present policy role for partnership in housing is therefore a twin one, which has direct operational ramifications: first, as a mechanism for delivering improved housing services; and second, as a mechanism for delivering cross-cutting or joint approaches for tackling disadvantage of a more complex nature.

The policy context for partnership

Partnership throughout the 1980s and 1990s has changed alongside the general restructuring of housing in the public sector, influenced in particular by two main waves of policy change. The first wave is associated with the former Conservative government's policies of privatisation, marketisation, and the reduction of the size and role of the local authority social rented sector; the second wave can be said to be associated with the present Labour government's modernisation 'project' (DETR, 1998a).

The first wave

Up until the beginning of the 1980s, local authorities were directly responsible for the provision and management of social housing. By the early 1990s, as Goodlad (1997) has described, privatisation policy and the new public management set out new parameters for indirect intervention, which de-emphasised the role of local authorities and focused on a wider range of other agencies, including financial and regulatory bodies such as the Housing Corporation and the Audit Commission, housing providers particularly housing associations, and tenant management and voluntary organisations.

These changes were intended to reorientate housing organisations' patterns of activity and foster the development of contractual partnerships. There was provision, for example, for housing organisations to contract out parts of their housing services on a voluntary basis prior to the introduction of compulsory market testing through compulsory competitive tendering and to transfer ownership of parts of their stock in order to access private funding. The new arrangements did lead to the development of a more competitive market-oriented business culture in social housing, though housing organisations often felt compelled to work in partnerships simply to capture the resources needed to fulfil basic policy and service delivery obligations.

The second wave

At present, the shape of partnership activity continues to change. With the election of the Labour government, the spotlight in housing policy implementation remains focused on partnership as a means of assembling 'policy chains', generating private finance, improving standards in the construction sector, protecting tenants' rights to decent-quality housing, improving housing services, involving tenants in decision making, regulating the housing market, and providing help for vulnerable people (DETR, 2000).

At the same time, the notion of partnership is used in a more abstract and nebulous way, as a doctrinal component of the new social policy and regeneration agenda. This is seen in the work of the Social Exclusion Unit, and in particular its work in relation to 'problem estates', where there is a focus on 'joined-up' forms of intervention to tackle crime, unemployment, low educational attainment, poor health, poor housing, drug abuse and poverty (Policy Action Team 17, 2000; Social Exclusion Unit, 2000). A key feature of the approach is the notion of partnership with local communities as a kind of social compact. In social housing, two initiatives, the Best Value regulatory regime and Tenant Participation Compacts, were both introduced in 2000 into the local authority sector, with parallel provisions being developed in the housing association sector. Both of these develop this aspect of partnership by, for example, requiring housing organisations to engage tenants in decision making, with the aim of fostering a 'fluid and evolving dialogue' between partners in the service delivery process (DETR, 1998b).

Partnership of different kinds – 'top-down' and 'bottom-up', on the policy chain model and the social compact model, focused on housing services alone and cross-cutting, market-led and modernising – has therefore come to play an enduring role in social housing. The chapter now goes on to look at different levels of partnership in more detail.

Levels of partnership

In a changing political, institutional and organisational environment, partnership and partnership arrangements have come to be used as bridges, in order to initiate policy dialogue between sectors or social partners, to change policy emphases, link organisations, or establish capabilities (DETR, 1998a; Benyon and Edwards, 1999). Partnership in social housing can refer to loose, informal linkages involving, for example, institutional partners, social partners or financial partners, and it can also refer to the tighter organisational arrangements put in place by groups of organisations or agencies that come together formally to work on a particular project. Housing organisations have come to see partnership as an operational arrangement that gives them a measure of control in situations where service delivery expertise and capacity have become fragmented locally. On the concrete or operational level, partnership involves diverse working practices and norms: it incorporates competitive and collaborative organisational behaviour, task-centredness and open-endedness, defensive coalitions and complementary competencies (Reid, 1995, 1999).

Table 4.1 sets out the detailed 'levels' at which partnership can be said to operate in social housing, from the abstract level through to the concrete or operational level.

Table 4.1: Different levels at which partnership is defined in social housing

Level of usage	Purpose	The scope of partnership at the different levels
1. Ideological Partnership as ideology or rhetoric	Creating new policy rhetoric and shifting ideologies	Partnership as a means of promoting major cultural or ideological change, eg promoting privatisation, promoting modernisation of the public services
2. Structural Partnership as an established approach to implementation in the sector	Policy change within the sector; extending partnership to new areas of policy and practice	Partnership as a means of shifting the focus of policy, eg using partnership to promote consumer choice, markets, performance /best value culture, tenure diversification, housing provision, housing finance, participative decision making
3. Mechanisms Partnership as value-adding chains or networks	Sectoral capacity building/ system integration	Partnership as a means of re-engineering capacity through cross-functional initiatives, multiagency projects, integrated approaches, eg local authorities building houses in partnership with housing associations or private developers
4. Mechanisms Partnership as an operational necessity	System integration; 'joining up' at project level	Partnership as a means of pursuing cross-cutting, integrated activity, eg joint approaches to area regeneration through SRB (now SRB Challenge Fund) Budget or New Deal
5. Mechanisms Partnership as an organisation	Favouring the establishment of organisational vehicles (partnerships)	Partnerships as an organised group of various partners implementing an agreed project or plan, eg local development consortia of groups of housing associations, joint local registration and allocations procedures

Table 4.1 distinguishes five levels at which partnership operates in housing, identifying for each the purpose of partnership in policy and practice terms and giving examples of the nature of the partnership activity that flows from each. The chapter now goes on to discuss the organisational responses to partnership, by reviewing some of the main themes in operational partnership activity, or how organisations 'do' partnership.

Partnership in practice: organisational responses

One of the difficulties of reviewing organisational responses to partnership formation in social housing in recent years is its extreme diversity. Partnerships, networks, and interorganisational arrangements often possess differing degrees of formality, they can be sectorally or non-sectorally based, they can have spatial or territorial aspects, and they can be thematic or issue based. They can also have a 'defensive' dimension or they can be capacity building in nature; they can be market oriented and behave competitively in organisational terms, or they can be collaborative in style. While many factors influence the local development and character of partnerships, the local 'propensity' to grow effective partnerships also has a cultural dimension that is bound up in past practice, conventions, and 'how things have traditionally been done'. Another important influence is the interplay between 'top-down' central government promoted initiatives, leading *directly* to specific local projects coordinated by local organisations that receive direct support from government funding programmes, and 'bottom-up' responses, which are an *indirect* result of these same processes but result in organisations adapting and modifying their behaviour to fit the new conditions.

This part of the chapter focuses on present partnership activity at the operational level of policy implementation, much of which is nonetheless coloured by the more abstract rhetoric around partnership. Table 4.2 presents an organising framework for locating the different types of operational partnership found within social housing.

The table focuses on partnership as it is expressed at the level of partner organisations, whether they are traditional, hierarchical organisations, or they are quasi-market and market oriented, or they can be said to be 'modernising' as this relates to the government's modernisation agenda. It sets out seven key features of partnership, from the way in which the policy chain is perceived, through to the way in which tenants and residents are seen by the partners. The discussion which follows draws out these features. Five operational themes or important 'clusters' of partnership

Table 4.2: Types of partnership operating in social housing

Partnership features	Type of organisation or partnership		
	Traditional	**Quasi-market**	**Modernising**
Policy chain	Direct, vertically integrated	Indirect, vertically integrated	Indirect, horizontally articulated
Organisational delivery infrastructure	Single agency, single function, integrated hierarchically	Pluri-agency, fragmented functions, integrated hierarchically or through markets	Pluri-agency, dispersed functions, integrated through forms of network
Examples of primary organisational vehicles	Local authority, housing association, private developer, etc	Contracted/sub-contracted organisation or arm's-length agency	Locally based implementation agencies, based on interorganisational project team model
Role of the local authority	Policy maker and implementer	'Enabler'	Strategic authority
Examples of policy initiative	Direct provision and maintenance of social rented housing stock	Private finance for social housing, CCT, HATs, City Challenge, early SRB	Later phases of City Challenge and SRB (now SRB Challenge Fund), Housing Plus, New Deal, Social Exclusion/Regeneration linked projects
Style of partnership	Undeveloped: hierarchical, dyadic (2 partner-agreements)	Market driven: based on sub-contracting/external decentralisation based on price/cost factors	Capacity augmenting: based on assembling partners needed to tackle complex problems
Position of tenants and residents groups as service beneficiaries	Service recipient model: relationship based on meeting the needs of a mass of 'deserving poor'	Customer-citizen mimicry model: relationship based on presenting bounded and limited choices, information and rights to redress	Participant-pro-user model: relationship based on securing involvement in institutional decision making, project implementation and in the regulation cycle

activity are examined. These comprise strategy development and design; system integration; development and regeneration; tenant participation and consultation; and services for vulnerable people. Each of these is discussed in turn.

Strategy design and development

The government is committed to encouraging local authorities to develop local housing strategy in collaboration with 'key partners' (DETR, 1998a, 2000), and a majority now report that they consult with a range of organisations and interest groups when developing their housing strategies. Key partners in this process are housing associations and the Housing Corporation, tenants and tenants' groups, voluntary sector groups, the health authority or social services, private landlords, residents' groups, and black and minority ethnic groups. Other reported examples of partners include housing cooperatives, estate and lettings agents, builders, leaseholders and owner-occupiers, and the police. Partnership in the strategy process sees local authorities relating to organisations and formal groups, as well as to individuals and loose coalitions of interest.

The partnership-building techniques employed by organisations are typically of a 'brief' nature, comprising community meetings and forums, surveys or focus groups, and conferences or seminars (Reid and Hickman, 2001: forthcoming). Local authorities further report that the main areas of strategy influenced by this type of partnership consultation are the housing strategy as a whole, anti-social behaviour and crime, regeneration and the management of private sector stock, and homelessness.

System integration

The challenge of delivering smoothly operating integrated local housing services is another important focus for the development of service delivery partnerships. Examples include local joint allocations schemes or common housing registers, and systems for providing aids and adaptations in the homes of people with special needs. Both these areas are governed by protocols and entail partnership between specified agencies with a clear division of labour. Partnerships are typically underwritten by a formal agreement, usually with a lead agency providing the gateway to the service being provided. In the case of allocations, a basic-level partnership already exists in the nominations agreements which all local authorities establish with housing associations and through that they nominate social housing applicants for housing association accommodation.

Common housing registers are underpinned by more sophisticated partnerships. The scheme operating in Bristol, for example, brings the council together with 22 housing associations. The initiatives involve local authorities and selected housing association partners operating common allocations policies or adopting a common housing register for a given local area. Some schemes combine the common register with existing nomination arrangements. Information and communications technology has been an important factor in helping partners to pool information and registration data, and carry out initial matching of applicants to properties. Partnerships of this kind rely on formal contractual obligations and commitments, which include provision for review and performance auditing. Though common housing registers are not yet universal, they are widely believed to increase accessibility to the social housing allocations process, particularly for groups at risk of exclusion.

With systems for providing aids and adaptations in the home, different models of partnership exist, giving rise to different service delivery systems. The key partners include housing services and social services staff within local authorities, occupational therapists who are involved in the assessment process (and who may be based within social services units or in other agencies), technical officers (including environmental health, and surveyors), housing associations, and 'care and repair' agencies. However, the needs of different households call for different combinations of professional and technical intervention, and at the same time, this expertise may be distributed differently across organisations in different local areas. Examples of the methods used to obtain system integration in this context include the development of joint service plans and agreed protocols, in the form of service delivery standards or targets; one-stop shops as a point of entry to the service; and the creation of joint and arm's-length agencies to carry out adaptation works. Fully unified services are provided in some authorities, with the adaptations service and the processing of Disabled Facilities Grant applications being handled by the same team.

Development and regeneration

It is this area of work that has received the greatest boost from present government policy and this is reflected in the range and scope of present partnership activity. The Urban Task Force (DETR, 1999) has put forward recommendations for more sustainable patterns of development, and in the Housing Green Paper local authorities are exhorted to maximise the full range of opportunities that exist locally to swell the supply of affordable housing, not only by encouraging new building, but also by ensuring that existing buildings, as far as possible, are brought back into use (DETR, 2000). The present focus on integrated approaches to tackling social exclusion and the tilt within national regeneration strategy away from economic to social regeneration places housing at the centre of the strategic arena of providing holistic solutions to neighbourhood regeneration (Prescott, 1998; Wilkinson and Appelbee, 1999), as discussed by Ambrose in Chapter One.

It has been acknowledged by housing agencies and professionals alike that there is a need for more comprehensive approaches to building stable communities on the one hand, and maintaining sustainable income streams from rents on the other. For example, with projects funded through the Single Regeneration Budget Challenge Fund (SRBCF), housing agencies have combined their 'traditional' role managing estates with broader approaches to tenant and resident consultation. Historically, this was aided by the community consultation strategies first required as part of the provisions of the former City Challenge initiative, and also by the guidance provided on community consultation within the framework of earlier phases of the Single Regeneration Budget programme, which once again highlighted the importance of building partnerships with local community groups. In a slightly different vein, in the housing association sector 'housing plus' approaches that were pioneered from the mid-1990s on, with an emphasis on training for employment and small business development, made inroads on the problem of unemployment with cross-cutting training and business development initiatives in local areas. Some housing associations set up new agencies to handle this work, while others mainstreamed it into their activity, changing their traditional single-function status. For many associations, 'housing plus' approaches provided the template for the 'joined-up' activity on the ground that has become a feature of the present approach to dealing with social exclusion.

The present social policy and regeneration agenda, then, provides huge scope for the development of partnerships at neighbourhood or community level (Social Exclusion Unit, 2000). Selective transfer of stock and management responsibilities, for example, already provides local authorities and housing associations with a means of creating opportunities for community-based groups and housing associations to take responsibility for managing their housing and local community facilities, where a 'parent' housing association acts as 'mentor' for the arrangement.

Meanwhile, traditional partnerships between local authorities and housing associations continue to be important to the delivery of social housing services, underpinning, for example, tenure diversification projects involving forms of low-cost and conventional home ownership, and joint approaches to estate improvement. Housing also has a role to play in regeneration partnerships, such as New Deal or SRBCF-funded projects, which bring together a wider range of social partners, including different local authority departments, local residents and community groups, voluntary sector organisations, the police, local employers, and other local commercial and service providers. These more complex projects reverberate on the cultures of housing participants, in that the 'joined-up' working requires corporate working through an organisational network coordinating strategic issues, direction, decision making, implementation monitoring and review, accountability, and control of spending.

Multiagency working is not without its problems where housing organisations are concerned. It fundamentally challenges the traditional 'norm' of direct, single agency-led provision of single-function services, which has been the trademark of 'traditional' housing service provision and which persists despite major sectoral change. Housing staff more familiar with the 'process functions' associated with the traditional working environment experience practical and cultural difficulties operating in a multiprofessional, multiorganisational context, and multiagency projects as a result appear to emphasise a growing split within the housing profession, between process functions, such as lettings and repairs management, and social entrepreneurial and project management functions.

Tenant participation and consultation

Tenant participation is a key concern for the present government in the delivery and regulation of housing services, echoing the theme of participation in institutional decision making and the objective of 'democratic renewal' within the government's modernisation agenda. In 2000, the government required local authorities to introduce Tenant Participation Compacts into their housing operations. These compacts require local authorities to agree with their tenants a range of service delivery standards against which their performance can be reviewed (DETR, 1998c).

The importance of the arrangements lies in the requirement that tenants play a role in the process on a collective basis, through representative organisations or consultative groups. The compact also requires local authorities to consult with tenants over the scope and content of the agreement and set up a cycle of 'target-setting/review/target redesign' on which they are required to work with tenants as partners. In due course it is anticipated that through such processes tenants will have a stronger part to play in influencing the design, delivery and review of services that they receive from their landlord. It is too early to tell what the longer-term impacts of compacts might be, and some tenants' groups are already critical of them on the grounds that they have not yet resulted in any substantial shift in the distribution of power.

The policy rhetoric of working 'in partnership with tenants' can obscure a range of different working arrangements (Cole et al, 1999a, 1999b). The benefits of tenant participation rest on the principle that if tenants are involved at an early stage in decision making about the services they receive or that affect their house and neighbourhood, they are more likely to feel a sense of ownership over the decisions made, and 'accept' change. For the landlord, working in partnership with tenants in this way, the existence of participation offers the prospect of more effective service delivery decisions, because they can be more closely aligned with local expectations. The nature of the partnerships built on this principle varies, from those where housing organisations simply provide information to their tenants, to those where tenants are represented on boards of management, to those where tenants have devolved responsibility for decisions in a number of areas.

A recent report by Cole, Hickman and Reid (1999a) emphasised how landlords 'scope' the partnerships that they develop with tenants by first establishing parameters for any participation project. This effectively sets out the limits for partnership, by taking account of such issues as the landlord's experience of working with tenant participation, the extent to which there is a developed tenant participation infrastructure locally, the perceived extent of flexibility existing around the implementation of a particular project, or the impact of the organisation's strategic concerns on its sense of needing to 'control' a project.

Organisations' agendas can include other 'scoping' factors that influence the nature of the partnership that develops with tenants. The way in which organisations choose, for example, to deal organisationally with their tenants can vary. Firstly, some see tenants as collections of individuals or 'citizens', where the nature of the partnership is more akin to a consultative set of arrangements, while others see tenants primarily as groups of customers, or collective consumers, where the emphasis is on identifying collective views. Secondly, organisations' understanding of the costs and benefits of working with tenants can also shape patterns of partnership. They may rule out, for example, tenant-led decision making on certain aspects of housing improvement work where they believe that the consequences of doing this will add to the longer-term maintenance responsibility facing the organisation, or they may structure decision-making processes to ensure that wider implementation schedules can be met, by, for example, using menu-based choice or decision-making options.

A third issue concerns those organisations that are confident with forms of innovation and tend to be less defensive about 'core functions', and the need to adhere to standardised services. They are alert to factors such as the marketability of project successes, they put a premium on new approaches, and they are able to support differential approaches, one-offs, and experiments. While standardisation has an important place in service development in that it enables good practice to become inculcated across an organisation, it is also perceived as a limiting factor where an organisation is called upon to be flexible and develop new approaches in dealing with local projects. Patterns of partnership in the area of tenant participation reflect these organisational development factors.

Services involving vulnerable people

This area of intervention and service provision carries with it some difficulties of definition. Local authorities primarily see their service delivery role here in terms of groups of households and individuals whose needs fall within the area of responsibility of local social services authorities, for example, people in need of supported accommodation, including those with disabilities and learning difficulties, rough sleepers and other homeless groups, people leaving care and other institutions, and survivors of violence.

The government in the recent policy and funding proposals of its 'Supporting People' initiative has addressed the support needs of all these and a wider range of groups, including families on low incomes, the frail elderly, the disabled and chronically sick, and the mentally ill (see Chapter Five). Their primary concerns are with the funding implications of providing support services in terms of the impact on benefits spending, and with the scope of the protection that is available to vulnerable people, for example to victims of harassment, or in the area of home security provision. Both perspectives on meeting the needs of 'vulnerable people' assume that 'packages' of services will be tailored to meet the needs of individuals, building on the community care model. Partnership in service provision is therefore built into the framework.

Nonetheless, the present scope of intervention to support vulnerable people already goes further than this and includes 'parallel' actions designed to tackle the underlying problems that provide the backdrop for the crises experienced by vulnerable individuals and households. Some partnerships of this kind are 'owned' and coordinated by housing organisations, though the lead agency may be another service team, or the arrangements may involve forms of interorganisational project team where all the partner organisations are involved.

These parallel actions centre mainly on partnerships involving in particular housing organisations, social services authorities, the probation service, and the police service in the areas of crime and disorder, community safety, antisocial behaviour, and vandalism. Other examples include partnerships with health authorities to work on housing and health issues, health promotion, and drugs education, and another cluster of activity around employment, 'welfare-to-work', education and training, and youth outreach work that brings education authorities and local employers into partnership.

Partnerships of this kind differ from the now relatively well-established community care model – which is based on clear divisions of labour and service responsibility – in that they blur the boundaries between the traditional functions and responsibilities of housing authorities, housing organisations and their partners. This places new demands on organisations and staff. Recent research on the education and training needs of housing employers, for example, reported that among housing employers who were working with these types of partnership, there was seen to be an increasing need for generic managerial skills among their staff, as well as knowledge and understanding of the policy and practice context outside the field of mainstream social housing services (Reid et al, 2000). A shortage of appropriate project management understanding was also reported. Other interesting evidence suggests that where departments other than housing, typically those of chief executives, were leading 'parallel actions', the housing 'department' was sometimes perceived as having become marginalised as an implementing agency. The role for the housing partner in such cases was tending to revert to one of 'monitor', drawing out the impacts that the project was having on existing housing problems. In such cases, 'parallel action' partnerships can be seen in terms of other agencies effectively contributing to the generation of housing outputs.

What is the significance of partnership working in the social housing sector?

Table 4.3 summarises the array of issues around operational partnership activity that have been discussed here in terms of its key focus, the broad approach adopted, the primary and secondary participants, and the techniques typically employed.

On an operational level, the expansion of partnerships in social housing reflects broader changes in the way in which government sees its responsibilities towards society and the role, therefore, of government intervention in creating conditions to allow individuals and communities to flourish.

The differing ideological approaches of different governments, however, are reflected in the current pattern of partnership formation across social housing. The Conservative government's attempts to 'marketise' social housing services enabled private sector organisations, particularly financiers, to play a more substantial role in local social housing services provision through public-private partnerships. The result was a redistribution of responsibilities, with the contractual nature of partnerships leaving the vertically integrated nature of the policy implementation chain virtually unchanged. Under Labour, this model of partnership is still important, but it has not generated substantial sectoral and organisational restructuring where the 'traditional' social housing organisations – local housing authorities and housing associations – are concerned. There has been some redistribution of social housing responsibilities in recent years, along with a redistribution of finance and subsidy, and there is presently pressure for more organisational change, in the form of large-scale voluntary transfers of local authority stock to new housing associations. However, the present institutional framework is still predicated on the *transfer* of social housing responsibilities, rather than a fundamental restructuring that might lead to forms of 'intermediate' organisations or hybrids.

There is acknowledgement that the task currently facing social housing providers and providers of allied services has become more complex (Mullins et al, forthcoming). This is because policy makers and their partners have to be more aware of the interconnections between housing and other aspects of the lived-in environment. Many of the present government's new initiatives, as well as some locally based 'bottom-up' initiatives, are founded on these 'everyday life' connections. This shift towards integrated intervention means that traditional single-function

Table 4.3: A framework for understanding partnerships in social housing

Partnership field	Key focus	Participants	Approach	Techniques
Strategy	Housing strategy; antisocial behaviour; crime; private sector stock; homelessness	• Primary: HAs/LAs; tenants, and tenants and residents groups; voluntary sector groups; health authority and social services; private sector landlords; BEM groups • Secondary: co-ops; estate agents; lease-holders/owner-occupiers; policy community	'Brief techniques'	Community meetings and forums; surveys; focus groups; conferences and seminars
System integration	Allocations; adaptations	• Primary: LAs (housing); HAs • Secondary: LAs (social services, environmental health, technical staff); health authority	Joint planning and service delivery; unified services	Contracts; joint service plans; protocols
Development and regeneration	Integrated regeneration projects; house building	• Primary: LAs; HAs; developers • Secondary: community and tenants groups	Joint projects often named as 'partnerships'	Contracts; output-driven strategic projects
Tenant participation and consultation	Tenant participation as component of good practice	• Primary: LAs; HAs; tenants' groups; individual tenants • Secondary: other residents; tenants federations; consultants	Structured 'participation opportunities'; dealing with tenants and residents as individuals and groups	Information and consultation exercises; market research; joint/ shared decision making; devolved decision making
Vulnerable people	Support for members of designated groups (older people, people with disabilities, low income households, mentally ill, etc)	• Primary: LAs (social services, education, health promotion, youth services); health authority; benefits agency • Secondary: police; probation service; local employers	Personalised support services packages	Diagnostic personal service plans; strategic initiatives

agencies, such as social housing organisations, are being challenged to find new ways of responding operationally (Mullins, 1997a).

Boundaries are beginning to break down. Because single-function agencies need to bridge gaps in professional expertise, organisational competence, functional responsibility and sectoral allegiance in order to generate and sustain partnership activity, partnership infrastructure has developed accordingly. Local interorganisational networks provide the basis of this infrastructure, providing local coordinative capacity. Networks allow organisations to be creative and pursue active 'mission creep' in a way that present regulatory frameworks do not yet actively encourage. Interorganisational project teams are an example of networks' ability to throw up new organisational forms in response to a project 'problem'. Though they cannot be considered to be 'housing organisations' like local authorities or housing associations, they behave nonetheless as implementing organisations, and allow one final observation on the partnership phenomenon and its significance.

In the context of privatisation, partnership can be interpreted as an innovative response to managing market-oriented supplier relationships (Best, 1990). In the context of modernisation, the attempts of partnerships, local housing networks, and interorganisational project teams to provide different organisational responses to differently defined housing 'problems', are reconfiguring the local housing service infrastructure.

This review of partnership activity suggests that sectoral realignment may already be beginning to occur through the vehicle of partnership. The present government's approach to regulating social housing is undergoing a fundamental rethink (Mullins, 1997b; Housing Corporation, 1999), while new regulatory regimes are fulfilling a central role in encouraging innovation (Walker and Jeanes, 2001: forthcoming). The combined effects of these challenges to social housing organisations, in terms of the extent to which they hasten partnership formation and sectoral restructuring in social housing, will be interesting to observe in coming years.

Note

[1] The main projects are first, a review of 1999 Housing Investment Programme: Operational Information Sections 2-4 for all English local authorities. The baseline review was carried out by Sheffield Hallam University for the DETR and additional analysis on partnership themes was carried out by the author. The second main body of work referred to is a project for the DETR on Good Practice

in Tenant Participation carried out by a team at Sheffield Hallam University, of which the author was a member; and a project for the Joseph Rowntree Foundation on the Costs and Benefits of Tenant Involvement in Modernisation Work, also carried out by a research team at Sheffield Hallam University, of which the author was a member.

References

Benyon, J. and Edwards, A. (1999) 'Partnership, crime prevention and community governance' in G. Stoker (ed) *The new management of British local governance*, Basingstoke: Macmillan.

Best, M.H. (1990) *The new competition: Institutions of industrial restructuring*, Oxford: Polity Press.

Cole, I., Hickman, P. and Reid, B. (1999a) *Accounting for the uncountable: Tenant participation in housing modernisation*, Coventry: Chartered Institute of Housing/Joseph Rowntree Foundation.

Cole, I., Hickman, P., Millward, L. and Reid, B. (1999b) *Developing good practice in tenant participation*, London: DETR.

DETR (Department of the Environment, Transport and the Regions) (1998a) *Modern local government: In touch with the people*, London: DETR.

DETR (1998b) *New Deal for Communities, Phase 1 Proposals: Guidance for Pathfinder applicants*, London: DETR.

DETR (1998c) *Tenant Participation Compacts*, London: DETR.

DETR and Lord Rogers of Riverside (1999) *Towards an urban renaissance: Report of the Urban Task Force*, London: DETR.

DETR (2000) *Quality and choice: A decent home for all*, Housing Green Paper, London: DETR/DSS.

Goodlad, R. (1997) 'Local authorities and the new governance of housing', in P. Malpass (ed) *Ownership, control and accountability: The new governance of housing*, Coventry: Chartered Institute of Housing.

Hamnett, C. (1993) 'Running housing policy and the British housing system', in R. Maidment and G. Thompson, (eds) *Managing the United Kingdom*, London: Sage Publications, pp 139-65.

Housing Corporation (1999) *Regulating diversity*, London: The Housing Corporation.

Malpass, P. (1997) (ed) *Ownership, control and accountability: The new governance of housing*, Coventry: Chartered Institute of Housing.

Mullins, D. (1997a) 'Housing responses in a changing environment', in D. Mullins and M. Riseborough, *Changing with the times*, Occasional Paper 12, Birmingham: School of Public Policy, University of Birmingham.

Mullins, D. (1997b) 'From regulatory capture to regulated competition', *Housing Studies*, vol 12, pp 301-19.

Mullins, D., Reid, B. and Walker, R.M. (2001: forthcoming) 'Modernisation and change in social housing', *Public Administration*.

Policy Action Team 17 (2000) *Joining it up locally, National Strategy for Neighbourhood Renewal*, London.

Prescott, J. (1998) *Housing and regeneration policy*, London: DETR.

Reid, B. (1995) 'Interorganisational networks and the delivery of housing services', *Housing Studies*, vol 10, no 2, pp 133-49.

Reid, B. (1999) 'Reframing the delivery of local housing services', in G. Stoker (ed) *The new management of local governance*, Basingstoke: Macmillan, pp 128-44.

Reid, B. and Hickman, P. (2001: forthcoming) 'Are housing organisations learning organisations? Lessons from organisational practice on tenant involvement in modernisation and improvement projects', *Housing Studies*.

Reid, B., Hills, S. and Kane, S. (2000) *Learning new tricks: Education and training for organisational development in housing*, Coventry: Key Potential UK/Chartered Institute of Housing.

Social Exclusion Unit (2000) *National strategy for neighbourhood renewal: Policy Action Team Reports*, London: DETR.

Stoker, G. (1997a) 'Local government in Europe after Thatcher', in J. Erik-Lane (ed) *Public sector reform*, London: Sage Publications.

Stoker, G. (1997b) 'The new forms of local governance', in M. Chisholm, R. Hales and D. Thomas (eds) *A fresh start for local government*, London: CIPFA.

Walker, R.M. and Jeanes, E. (2001: forthcoming) 'Innovation in a regulated service: the case of English housing associations', *Public Management*.

Wilkinson, D. and Appelbee, E. (1999) *Implementing holistic government: Joined-up action on the ground*, Bristol: The Policy Press.

FIVE

Improving partnership working in housing and mental health

Simon Northmore

Introduction

In 1998 the Joseph Rowntree Foundation funded three workshops organised by the Royal Borough of Kingston Community Services Directorate, aimed at improving partnership working. The workshops took place in May to July. Forty-five staff attended, from a wide variety of professional backgrounds, including nursing, social work, mental health and housing. This chapter explores the background to partnerships in housing and mental health, examines themes that emerged from the workshops and discusses the implications of the lack of direct input from voluntary and community organisations and service users.

Mental ill health is so common that at any time around one in six people of working age has a mental health problem, most often anxiety or depression. However, there are significant numbers of more severe and enduring cases. In addition, some 50% of people with mental health problems also have significant physical ill health. Nevertheless, over 90% of those who consult their GP with a mental health problem will never be referred to specialist services (Poxton, 1999). Not only are most people with mental health problems cared for by their GP and primary care team, that is what the majority prefer (DoH, 1999a). The aim of supporting people in the community therefore depends crucially on an integrated approach between health, social services and housing authorities.

Since 1997 the government has developed a range of policies for modernising health and social services, making primary care and partnership working central to the NHS and emphasising 'best value' in social services (DoH, 1997, 1998a). For mental health services these policies are underpinned by *Modernising mental health services* (DoH, 1998b), which identified the main problems as: inadequate care and support for people with common and severe mental health problems; some users with complex health and social care needs being socially isolated and difficult to engage; inadequate systems, poor management of resources and underfunding; overburdened families and carers; problems in recruiting and retaining staff and poor staff morale; an outdated legal framework, which has failed to support effective treatment outside hospital (Davidson, 2000).

The government's current mental health strategy is driven by the National Service Framework for Mental Health. This sets out a series of national standards to help shape local mental health service delivery and to improve the quality of mental health services for service users and their carers. It also aims to remove the wide variations in provision nationally.

Ten guiding values and principles underpin the National Service Framework. People with mental health problems should expect that services will:

1. Involve service users and their carers in the planning and delivery of care.
2. Deliver high-quality treatment and care that is known to be effective and acceptable.
3. Be well suited to those who use them and be non-discriminatory.
4. Be accessible so that help can be obtained when and where it is needed.
5. Promote their safety and that of their carers, staff and the wider public.
6. Offer choices that promote independence.
7. Be well coordinated between all staff and agencies.
8. Deliver continuity of care for as long as this is needed.
9. Empower and support staff.
10. Be properly accountable to the public, service users and carers.

The strategy for mental health includes new, earmarked funding; a focus on integrated services, including service user and carer involvement; and a review of the legislative framework contained in the Mental Health Act. Service changes are expected to provide greater consistency across the country based on measurable performance indicators; encourage services that support independence and work with service users, their families and carers; and protect both the public and vulnerable individuals.

In achieving these changes there is a recognition that effective mental health services will require "new patterns of local partnership, with mental health a cross cutting priority for all NHS and social care organisations and their partners" (DoH, 1999a, p 6).

While these developments are welcome, the Labour government's parallel attempts to establish compulsory treatment in the community for people with mental health problems and to introduce stronger powers to control the behaviour of 'bad' tenants represent an altogether different approach. The danger is that instead of providing support at an early stage to prevent mental health crises, people who are unable to get services when they first need them will reach crisis point before their needs are recognised (Mental Health Foundation, 1997). The National Service Framework has also been criticised for 'missed opportunities', particularly in tackling problems of social inclusion and discrimination (Davidson, 2000). Nevertheless, it does present a major challenge to mental health service providers to overcome the historical barriers between primary health, community health and social services, which "have developed in different structural, financial, contractual and cultural settings. They were not designed to work together" (Poxton, 1999, p 24).

Barriers to partnership

The consistent theme of government policy for mental health over the last 30 years has been the closure of large institutions and the creation of community-based services. However, the development of integrated community-based services has been patchy, with little attention given to how mental health fits with the broader community care agenda (Greatley and Peck, 1999). As mental health services have shifted from a model of hospital care to more community-focused services, the split between health and social care has become increasingly evident.

The Sainsbury Centre for Mental Health has identified some of the difficulties of partnership working in mental health as: different cultures, attitudes and mind sets – practitioners do not understand each others' objectives and models; different statutory responsibilities, political accountabilities and priorities; different procedural systems – for example, the Care Programme Approach in mental health and care management in social services; perverse incentives – different agencies subject to different financial incentives that undermine continuous care packages; lack of co-terminosity; instability – a reliance on personalities or prevailing local politics for effective joint working (Sainsbury Centre for Mental Health, 1998).

In response to some of these problems, the 1999 Health Act has created greater flexibility for pooling budgets; giving one agency the lead responsibility for commissioning some or all services; and developing integrated service provision. There remain outstanding questions of how this will work in practice, but the new flexibility should allow integrated services to develop more quickly where there is a commitment to do so.

Partnership and housing

Despite the much-quoted dictum from *Caring for people* that "housing is a vital component of community care and is often the key to independent living" (DoH, 1989), considerably more attention has been given to the problems of partnerships between health and social services. While many changes have taken place and there are positive examples of good practice, interagency collaboration between housing, health and social care agencies has been difficult to achieve (Arblaster et al, 1996). The Joseph Rowntree Foundation's Housing and Community Care programme has consistently highlighted the gap between policy and practice (Watson, 1997) and the role of housing in community care, as discussed in the previous chapter, has remained largely at the level of exhortation (Fletcher, 1998).

In the initial preparations for the implementation of community care there was a clear expectation that health and social services should plan together, backed up by the threat of withholding of Department of Health funding. However, it was not until 1992 that the Department of Environment and Department of Health produced a joint circular on housing and community care. This reflected fundamental policy differences. The Department of Health emphasised health gain through the provision of health care and preventative work, and keeping down the cost of the social care bill. The Department of the Environment's priority was to improve housing and increase owner occupation (Mental Health Foundation, 1997). Despite the joint circular, the responsibility for integrating housing and community care was left with local and health authorities. In practice, joint commissioning arrangements did not involve agencies other than health and social services (Lund and Foord, 1997).

Five years after the introduction of community care, the Audit Commission's report on the role of housing in community care concluded that "too many people fall through the net because of poor collaboration between housing, social services and health authorities" (Audit Commission, 1998). The main conclusions of the report showed how little progress had been made. It re-emphasised the need for a strategic approach to identifying and assessing needs; mapping local provision; consulting with service users and carers; and integrating housing and support services. The report also highlighted the need to improve the early identification of tenancy problems for people with mental health problems (Fletcher, 1998).

Why is housing important?

The growing recognition of the links between health and environmental factors, including housing (DoH, 1999b), represents an important shift in emphasis in health policy towards health promotion and prevention (see also Chapter Nine).

Nevertheless, while everyone needs a secure place to live, people with severe mental health problems have an even greater need for stability and are likely to need active support to secure and sustain adequate and appropriate housing. Supported housing schemes increasingly need staff with the skills to manage the complex and demanding needs of a diverse range of individuals (Jenkins, 1999). Partnerships with other specialist agencies are vital to maintaining that support.

The connection between housing and mental health is clear. Assessments of the prevalence of mental illness among homeless people range between 8 and 50 times the level among the general population, with figures typically in the range 30% to 40%. Half of young homeless people have a treatable psychiatric disorder. Behind these figures often lie complex and multiple problems, with high morbidity and high mortality levels (Mental Health Foundation, 1997).

While appropriate housing is important, it is not enough on its own. The mismatch between housing and care support can create additional problems. A study by the Royal College of Psychiatrists in 1995 found that a third of London's psychiatric admission beds were 'blocked' by patients needing long-term care. A census of acute and low-level secure psychiatric beds in the North and South Thames Regional Health Authorities in 1994 showed that 23% no longer needed hospital care. Of these, 45% could have been discharged if there had been suitable accommodation in the community.

However, social housing is also failing people with mental health problems. Thirty-six per cent of homeless people with mental health problems in central London became homeless when their social housing tenancy broke

Table 5.1: Proportions of homeless people with mental health problems

%	Description
34	People using day centres for homeless in London
29-43	Surveys of single homeless people in 10 local authority areas in England
33	People begging in central London
35	Hostel residents with a neurotic disorder (2.5 times the rate in private households)
25	Prevalence of schizophrenia among homeless people
60	Night shelter and day centre users with GHQ12 scores of 4 or more
8	Psychosis estimate among hostel residents

Source: Mental Health Foundation (1997)

down, while only 2% had ever been long-stay hospital patients (Mental Health Foundation, 1997). A survey by the Sainsbury Centre for Mental Health for the London borough of Merton found that nearly a fifth of all local residents with mental health problems were receiving housing and support services inappropriate for their current needs (Warner et al, 1998). These figures clearly show how important it is to tackle housing and care needs together. Yet the shared problems and interests of housing and mental health agencies have not been reflected in effective interagency working and strategic planning.

The Royal Borough of Kingston workshops

Recognising that findings from research studies are not easy for practitioners to translate into practical exploration of the problems that can be implemented at local level, the Joseph Rowntree Foundation decided to fund a short series of workshops for staff in the Royal Borough of Kingston. The focus was on bringing housing and mental health professionals together, as the provision of care and support for people with mental health problems was acknowledged as being particularly complex and there was widespread concern that care needs were not being adequately met. Three workshops were planned through Kingston Community Services Department for community services and community health trust staff. The workshops took place between May and July 1998.

The local context

Kingston's Community Services Department incorporates both housing and community care services staff. The 45 participants who attended the workshops came from a wide range of professional backgrounds, including nursing, social work, mental health and housing. They were based in a variety of geographical locations: Kingston has three community mental health teams in different parts of the borough and housing staff may be in estate-based, decentralised offices or located centrally in a number of different roles, such as allocations, resettlement, housing advice.

The organisational environment in which both housing and mental health professionals operate is complex. It encompasses not only other professionals and external agencies involved in the care and support of people who are vulnerable through homelessness, substance misuse, severe mental illness or other social problems, each with their own particular responsibilities and priorities, but also carers, relatives, advocates, voluntary and community organisations, service users groups and local councillors.

The aims of the workshops, therefore, were to provide an opportunity for staff to look at each others' roles; to examine problems of overlaps and constraints; to increase mutual understanding; and to consider opportunities for improving partnership working.

Needs of staff

It is important to recognise the different perspectives of housing and mental health staff. For mental health practitioners housing is important because service users themselves put housing problems high on their list of priorities, and because homelessness contributes to mental health problems, physical health risk, accidental injury and violent attacks. From the housing perspective there are different issues. Mental illness is seen as a frequent cause of tenancy problems and tenancy breakdown. New tenants are frequently referred with no information provided about current or past mental illness. Housing staff report that they are not taken seriously when calling for help with clients whose mental health they see as deteriorating (Mental Health Foundation, 1997).

In exploring what they wanted from the workshops, participants in all three expressed similar needs. These centred around: improving knowledge and understanding of each other's roles, understanding the different legal frameworks within which others work, and improving communication.

Improving knowledge and understanding

What participants shared in common was a strong commitment to putting the individual client's needs first and, as one said, "knowing the system" on behalf of their clients. However, several participants said they did not feel they understood the roles of their colleagues in other agencies/ departments. The feeling was prevalent that this lack of understanding led to an intolerance of the problems others face in their work and undermined good collaboration. As one participant put it, she wanted to "stop feeling lumbered" when she could not get a response and to deal with problems in a more constructive way.

The difficulty for many was not knowing what they could realistically expect from their housing or mental health colleagues. Lack of understanding of the constraints on others led to a concentration on problems rather than building on positive examples of good practice.

Understanding the different legal frameworks

Related to this was a need to have a better understanding of the legal frameworks within which housing and mental health workers operate. Mental health staff, in particular, felt they had little understanding of housing legislation and how the housing allocation system worked. Each of the workshops included presentations by senior managers on the working of the Housing and Mental Health Acts, which were highly valued by the participants.

Improving communication

Perhaps even more important to those attending the workshops was the chance to meet staff from other agencies and departments. As one participant said, "meeting people I have only spoken to on the phone or written to makes it possible to break barriers down". The importance of 'putting names to faces' cannot be underestimated and was confirmed by responses in the workshop evaluations as a significant factor in developing greater understanding of the respective roles of housing and mental health services and in creating a climate for better joint working. One mental health worker said:"Meeting with colleagues from different agencies means I'll feel more able to approach and communicate with Housing".

Key themes

A number of significant issues were raised in the course of the workshops. It was not possible to resolve these fully at the time but they serve to highlight some important themes. Key issues were: definitions of 'vulnerability'; sharing confidential information; fragmentation of services; bureaucratic delays; limited resources.

Definitions of vulnerability

A major area of discussion in the workshops focused on trying to clarify different understandings of 'vulnerability'. Frustration with what were seen initially as simply different professional perspectives did ease. For housing staff, better understanding of the provisions of the 1983 Mental Health Act proved useful in recognising the constraints within which mental health staff were working. Nevertheless, housing officers managing properties on estates felt that they were often ill-equipped to deal with tenants with severe behavioural problems who were not seen as the responsibility of mental health services. Particular issues arose with people suffering from 'personality disorder', frequently judged to be untreatable. Housing staff felt this should be a Mental Health responsibility.

Sharing confidential information

Many participants felt that, while recognising the importance of confidentiality, it could inhibit the sharing of legitimate information about individual clients that would assist in making decisions in the individual's best interest. At one level this was seen as a matter of trust. Some information would be more readily shared if staff knew each other and had developed better communication. At an organisational level a significant problem was the lack of an integrated information system. A single system would allow access to shared 'front sheet' client information while retaining confidential information to specific departments or staff where appropriate.

Fragmentation of services

Related to this was what participants experienced as the increasing fragmentation of services as a result of changes in local and health authorities over a period of years. Even within departments it was felt that staff did not always share knowledge and information. In a complex service like Housing, different parts of the same service may not have close working contact. Similarly, some mental health staff pointed to the important role of voluntary agencies in supporting people in the community but felt that they were not given sufficient priority.

Bureaucratic delays

Another problem housing staff identified was getting formal approval from managers for decisions on individual cases, resulting in delays to statutory enquiries, delays in rehousing and having to deal with frustrated clients. Not only did this create practical difficulties, it left staff feeling unsupported and unvalued.

Limited resources

Some participants strongly felt that the emphasis on improving joint working was misplaced and that the original ideals of community care were being undermined by lack of resources. They pointed to the basic problem that Kingston has too little suitable housing and too many people in need. From this perspective, the problems discussed above result, primarily, not from different priorities, organisational arrangements and professional cultures, but from long-term resource constraints.

Ideas for improving partnership working

Nevertheless, the majority of participants in the workshops were positive about improving partnership working and several practical ideas emerged. These might not be cost free but the benefits, in terms of improving services to individual users and sustaining the morale and effectiveness of staff, could be significant. Suggestions came under three headings: communication, training, and assessment.

Communication

A key point was to achieve more face-to-face or direct contact. An example was the admission of one participant that she regularly left her answerphone on even when she was in the office. A colleague who had experienced frequent difficulty contacting her was horrified. Solutions ranged from 'get rid of answering machines' to developing duty officer systems. Other ideas were to place more emphasis on liaison, perhaps having named individuals with this responsibility.

Sharing appropriate client information through an integrated computer system with a common 'front sheet' for all staff working with a particular individual was seen as vital. This would also allow appointments and follow-up to be better coordinated.

Other ideas included making available organisational charts explaining the roles of staff in different departments or agencies; specific written policy guidance on joint working; and ensuring that senior managers were more accessible to front-line staff. This could be simply 'touching base' or, for example, joining in training courses with staff.

Training

Joint training was seen as central, including updating knowledge of legislation and procedures, team-building, and workshops on specific topics. Participants felt that training events should involve more senior managers, both to give front-line staff the sense that there was positive support for partnership working at all levels in the organisation and to draw on their knowledge and experience.

At a more informal level, regular meetings between housing and mental health staff were suggested. While occasional meetings were arranged, they were often not at suitable times for staff. (Lunchtimes were often seen as a good time by managers but most workshop participants found this difficult.)

Opportunities for 'job-shadowing' or 'shadow days' in other agencies or departments were also seen as useful ways of developing understanding and encouraging better partnership working.

Assessment

Finally, participants felt that there should be more emphasis on an interagency approach to identifying unmet needs. Specifically, some housing staff thought that they could play a greater role in assessment. This might include a monitoring role for estates managers or making referrals when concerned about a tenant. A further suggestion was that, where appropriate, housing officers could be invited to attend mental health review meetings.

From the workshops a checklist for joint working was produced, as shown in Figure 5.1:

Figure 5.1: A checklist for partnership working

For all staff	✓ Follow through requests and give colleagues feedback
	✓ Be honest: if you can't help, say so, or direct them to someone who can
	✓ Stick to time commitments
	✓ Don't create artificial barriers – turn off the answering machine!
	✓ Make an effort to meet colleagues you do not normally see face to face
For senior managers	✓ Be accessible: 'touch base' with frontline staff regularly
	✓ Support staff in developing informal and formal links with colleagues in other agencies
	✓ Create opportunities for joint training – and attend training sessions yourself
For all agencies	✓ Develop shared information systems – internal and interagency
	✓ Agree joint guidance for staff on interagency working
	✓ Give more emphasis to an interagency approach in planning and assessment

Partnership with voluntary organisations and service users

As noted in the Introduction, the Kingston workshops were specifically aimed at Royal Borough of Kingston and community health trust staff, which meant that there was no structured opportunity for direct input from service users or voluntary and community organisations. Nevertheless, the needs and perspectives of service users should be central. They are both the effective 'link' between agencies and what gives real meaning to partnership. While the workshop participants were clearly committed to improving the services they provide to their clients, the workshops highlighted the fact that professional and organisational pressures dominated their concerns, resulting in a limited notion of partnership. Professional collaboration was emphasised but little attention given to including service users, or the voluntary or private sectors. Given the central role played by the voluntary sector in providing accommodation and support for people with mental health problems, and the importance of users' own views of their experience of services to finding ways of overcoming some of the barriers to joint working, this is an important omission.

Voluntary organisations

Voluntary organisations are a key element in the development of partnerships both directly and indirectly. Their activities address social exclusion and offer employment and other opportunities to people locally. More broadly, a voluntary sector perspective can help to create a balanced and informed approach to economic, social and environmental priorities (NCVO, 2000). The process of developing voluntary sector involvement in these new structures, and partnership in service provision, is slow and difficult for several reasons. First, the voluntary sector is heterogeneous, ranging from large national, regional, and county organisations with paid staff to small community groups reliant almost exclusively on volunteers. Second, structures within which voluntary organisations have worked in the past are being dismantled and replaced but with little guidance on ways of involving the wide range of stakeholder interests. Third, voluntary and community organisations encompass a wide range of values, traditions and styles of operating, all of which create problems of legitimacy and representation (Taylor, 1997). In addition, the voluntary sector at local level embraces a variety of services, including advocacy, facilitating and developing community projects and services, and the provision of direct services to individuals.

In their introduction to this volume, Balloch and Taylor argue that when partner agencies are not working together, it is the user that suffers. Yet in commenting on Chapter Six of the White Paper *Modernising social services* (DoH, 1998a), they point out that: "What is most striking about this chapter ... is the concluding five-line paragraph that mentions, almost as an afterthought, the importance of public sector partnership with voluntary and community groups". They also highlight differences in power relationships and the difficulties smaller voluntary, community and business organisations have in creating the necessary resources and infrastructure to engage effectively in partnerships.

The need for greater support to voluntary and community organisations to enable them to make an equal contribution to partnership working emerges in several recent studies. The National Tracker Survey of Primary Care Groups and Trusts (PCGs/PCTs) notes that "voluntary organisations ... had made relatively little contribution to policy formulation and service development" (Wilkin et al, 1999, p 14). It concludes that PCGs/PCTs will have to develop more effective strategies to involve stakeholders but makes no specific recommendations. A study of eight Regional Development Agencies (RDAs) in England found that voluntary and community groups had exerted only marginal influence on RDA strategies. It concluded that voluntary bodies and community groups needed greater support to enable them to contribute effectively to policy development (Robson et al, 2000). Another concern (see Chapter Ten) is that black and minority ethnic groups are under-represented in regeneration partnerships (Chahal, 2000).

Service users

A King's Fund study of mental health priorities for primary care (Greatley and Peck, 1999) identifies some possible solutions suggested by service users to the problems they experienced with primary care services. While these do not encompass housing needs or specialist mental health services, they give an indication of the perspectives of service users and contain ideas that could be adapted to different contexts. Suggestions included:

- more flexible services that trust service users to indicate what they need;
- telephone consultations, which might be more appropriate for some issues, but with the possibility of calling on someone for assistance directly if this is appropriate;
- clear written material for carers and families as well as users;
- staff to receive mental health 'awareness' training;
- regular liaison arrangements to ensure services are up to date on individual plans and on the general arrangements for users to access services;
- proper attention to the physical ill health of people with mental health problems;
- specialist support to primary care which gives up-to-date information on medication and the full range of other therapies available;
- information for staff about the voluntary sector. (adapted from Greatley and Peck, 1999)

Flexible arrangements for accessing services, better communication and consultation with service users, good information for both users and carers, *and* all those involved in providing mental health services, are not new ideas. As more people with serious mental health problems live in the community, partnership working, with its aim of creating flexible, responsive, needs-led services, must also give proper attention to developing partnerships with service users.

Conclusion

In its current reforms, central government has created new flexibility aimed at addressing health inequalities, developing primary and community care, and encouraging joint commissioning of specialist locality services. Primary care groups and primary care trusts will have a key role in identifying mental health needs, collaborating with other agencies in the production of Health Improvement Programmes (HImPs) and planning mental health services. These structural changes are fundamental to tackling the financial, organisational and professional barriers to partnership working (Hannigan, 1999). Nevertheless, the unrelenting nature of organisational change will require careful management if practitioners are not to focus more on organisational preoccupations than on the needs of service users (Hiscock and Pearson, 1999).

The barriers to partnership and the problems for professional groups working in mental health services that emerge from the Kingston workshops are not dissimilar to those found elsewhere (for example, Camp, 1998; Greatley and Peck, 1999; Hannigan, 1999), but there are some clear messages.

Firstly, that structural change does not in itself reduce the problems of interagency collaboration. Continuing organisational change needs to be carefully managed. Whether it delivers improvements in partnership working will depend crucially on the quality of the management and support of staff, in particular their need for effective communication systems and opportunities for joint training and development.

Secondly, that 'little things make a difference'. While the needs of individuals and the operational procedures of organisations may be complex, small changes to *how* things are done, and appropriate management support for those changes, is crucial. Joint working "is determined by a complex combination of factors which can only be addressed at a very local level" (Hudson, 1999).

Finally, that professionals working in mental health services need to have a broader vision of partnership that includes partnership with service users and voluntary and community organisations. The Kingston workshops were useful in identifying ways of breaking down professional barriers. However, they also highlighted the ways in which day-to-day pressures on staff can result in a limited notion of partnership.

Voluntary agencies and mental health service users/survivors organisations have been in the forefront in developing their own alternative services, based on a holistic approach to needs, including out-of-hours support services, helplines and peer counselling schemes. Though still small scale, these voluntary sector and user-led initiatives need to be recognised as having equal status in the development of partnership working. Mental health service users emphasise user-led, non-medicalised support services as an alternative to the medical model that tends to dominate mental health policy and practice (Beresford, 2000). Partnership approaches that do not include the perspectives of service users and voluntary organisations are likely to remain within professional and public sector agency cultures that are experienced by many mental health service users as insensitive and even discriminatory.

Service providers need to use the opportunities available in current plans for mental health services to go beyond professional collaboration and develop partnerships with users of mental health services and voluntary organisations, based on user definitions of need and supporting user-led alternatives.

References

Arblaster, L., Conway, J., Foreman. A. and Hawtin, M. (1996) *Asking the impossible? Inter-agency working to address the housing, health and social care needs of people in ordinary housing*, Bristol/York: The Policy Press/Joseph Rowntree Foundation.

Audit Commission (1998) *Home alone: The role of housing in community care*, London: Audit Commission

Beresford, P. (2000) *Our voice in our future: Mental health services*, London: Shaping Our Lives/National Institute for Social Work.

Camp, T. (1998) 'Developing a strategic approach to meeting the housing needs of people with a severe and enduring mental illness', *The Mental Health Review*, vol 3, no 3, pp 23-5.

Chahal, K. (2000) *Foundations report: Ethnic diversity, neighbourhoods and housing*, York: Joseph Rowntree Foundation.

Davidson, D. (2000) 'The National Service Framework for Mental Health', *Managing Community Care*, vol 8, no 1, pp 5-10.

DoH (Department of Health) (1989) *Caring for people: Community care in the next decade and beyond*, London: HMSO.

DoH (1997) *The New NHS: Modern, dependable*, London: The Stationery Office.

DoH (1998a) *Modernising social services*, London: The Stationery Office.

DoH (1998b) *Modernising mental health services: Safe, sound, supportive*, London: The Stationery Office.

DoH (1999a) *National Service Framework for Mental Health: Modern standards and service models*, London: The Stationery Office.

DoH (1999b) *Saving lives: Our healthier nation*, London: The Stationery Office.

Fletcher, P. (1998) 'Care comes into focus', *Housing Today*, vol 85.

Greatley, A. and Peck, E. (1999) *Mental health priorities for primary care: Essential steps for practices and primary care groups*, London: King's Fund.

Hannigan, B. (1999) 'Joint working in community mental health: prospects and challenges', *Health and Social Care in the Community*, vol 7, no 1, pp 25-31.

Hiscock, J. and Pearson, M. (1999) 'Looking inwards, looking outwards: dismantling the "Berlin Wall" between health and social services?', *Social Policy & Administration*, vol 33, no 2, pp 150-63.

Hudson, B. (1999) 'Joint commissioning across the primary health care-social care boundary: can it work?', *Health and Social Care in the Community*, vol 7, no 5, pp 358-66.

Jenkins, G. (1999) 'Coping with complex needs: managing competing demands', *Housing, Care & Support*, vol 2, no 3, pp 25-8.

Lund, B. and Foord, M. (1997) *Towards integrated living? Housing strategies and community care*, Bristol/York: The Policy Press/Joseph Rowntree Foundation.

Mental Health Foundation (1997) *Mental health and housing*, Briefing No 3, London: Mental Health Foundation.

NCVO (National Council for Voluntary Organisations) (2000) 'NCVO news guide to the regional agenda', *NCVO News Supplement*, April.

Poxton, R. (1999) 'Primary and community mental health and social care: making a difference at the interface', *The Mental Health Review*, vol 4, no 3, pp 24-7.

Robson, B., Peck, J. and Holden, A. (2000) *Regional Development Agencies and local regeneration*, York: Joseph Rowntree Foundation.

Sainsbury Centre for Mental Health (1998) *An Executive Briefing on the implications for mental health services of the Consultation Paper 'Partnership in Action'*, Briefing 3, London: Sainsbury Centre for Mental Health.

Taylor, M. (1997) *The best of both worlds: The voluntary sector and local government*, York: Joseph Rowntree Foundation.

Warner, L., Ford, R., Holmshaw, J. and Sathyamoorthy, G. (1998) 'Homing in on need', *Community Care*, 30 July-15 August.

Watson, L. (1997) *High hopes: Making housing and community care work*, York: Joseph Rowntree Foundation.

Wilkin, D., Gillam, S. and Leese, B. (eds) (1999) *The National Tracker Survey of Primary Care Groups and Trusts: Progress and challenges 1999/2000*, Manchester: National Primary Care Research and Development Centre, University of Manchester.

Part Two:
Partnerships in social care and health

Part Two
Partnerships in social care and health

SIX

The potential of project status to support partnerships

Valerie Williamson

Under this Labour government, while structures have been put in place to facilitate partnership, the need for incentives has also been acknowledged, as recorded in *Partnership in action* (DoH, 1998a). Traditionally, incentives have taken the form of additional targeted allocations from central government, such as the Mental Illness Specific Grant, Winter Pressures Money and the Community Care Challenge Fund. *Partnership in action* recognised that these initiatives have stimulated innovative service provision in priority areas and that important lessons have been learnt. At the same time it emphasised the need to ensure that joint working becomes part of core business rather than a peripheral activity. It therefore proposed to abolish the long-standing incentives of Joint Finance, incorporating this money in future within unified budgets.

Taken alongside the emphasis on greater organisational integration, this might be thought to imply that 'special projects' have served their purpose and will no longer have a key role to play in promoting collaborative working. On the other hand the cost-effective opportunities that project money offers to develop and demonstrate new ways of working remain politically attractive, an argument supported by recent evidence from an ADSS Report on details of 185 Winter Pressures Money partnership schemes (Healy, 1999). According to Martin and Sanderson (1999) pilot projects have an important role in evidence-based policy making which is of continuing relevance and short-term limited arrangements will inevitably retain their attraction as long as resources remain constrained (Springett, 1995). From a political perspective pilot projects also offer a relatively non-contentious opportunity to experiment with new approaches that may seem threatening to mainstream services. The introduction of the Social Services Modernisation Fund (DoH, 1998b) confirmed that there would continue to be opportunities for this kind of project-based partnership working.

The recognition of potential marginalisation, discussed in the Introduction, is an important point to note, and suggests that it is time for a critical appraisal of both the potential and the limitations of projects to promote the concept of partnership. This chapter will explore this issue through the experiences of two collaborative projects, one between the local NHS and PSS in the field of continuing care for older people (Charnley et al, 1998) and the other between the local NHS, PSS and education department concerning provision for 'cared-for' children with attachment difficulties (Williamson, 1999), both financed from short-term targeted funding. It will therefore be looking at collaboration at a local level and predominantly between health and social care agencies. This is a recognised limitation but arguably the bulk of such project-based activity has taken place in this area.

The first part of this chapter will identify from the literature the potential challenges of working collaboratively, with particular reference to project status, and the second part will relate these to the experience of the two projects, exploring the extent to which these problems have been overcome and seeking lessons for future practice. The main focus will be on the operational rather than the policy level arguing with Alter and Hage (1994) that this is where there is a need for further research in interorganisational working. It will also look at process rather than outcomes, not because the means are considered more important than the ends but because they are an essential prerequisite and have been relatively neglected in current research on change management (Pettigrew et al, 1992). For the purpose of this chapter the emphasis will be on the experience of the agency staff involved, both managers and fieldworkers. Although the projects themselves have both explored the user and carer perspective, the insights gained are addressed elsewhere in this volume (see Chapter Seven).

First however, there is a need for an initial clarification of the two key terms, 'partnership' and 'projects', as both are often used quite loosely. As suggested by Balloch and Taylor in the Introduction, joint working between agencies can be understood in terms of a continuum ranging from a formal exchange of information to the kind of integrated working implied by pooled budgets, joint commissioning and integrated service provision. Because joint working is now official policy, the concept of partnership has entered the local political rhetoric and is sometimes applied to activity right along this continuum. According to Gordon and Hanafin

(1998) the term has now become "the new cure-all and we risk a kind of partnership-itis where everything gets renamed and the term is used so indiscriminately that it becomes meaningless" (p 20). An interpretation of the term as sharing risks and profits, both 'pain' and 'gain', usefully limits the concept to joint endeavours where all parties have to surrender some element of power/resources in the expectation of subsequent mutual benefit. It also emphasises the extent to which partnership working is inherently threatening to the status quo, while at the same time lacking the benefits of full integration (Robinson and Paxton, 1998).

Project is another ambiguous term. Arguably much of any agency's activity is project based in the sense of being focused around specific objectives. A distinguishing mark of the term 'project' as used in this chapter is that it is an additional planned activity, not part of an agency's ongoing routine or 'mainstream' business, and is conducted within a limited and specific timescale. While the time-limited nature may help to minimise the threatening nature of partnership projects, it can create additional problems in respect of the potential marginalisation already identified. The partnership projects to be discussed here also involve the local implementation of central initiatives, thus reinforcing the idea that they are being used as policy devices to exemplify forms of collaboration the government is anxious to promote. Central government defines the target area and sets out the key objectives including criteria for exclusion/ inclusion, accompanied by financial inducements to local partners. This has important implications for the extent of local ownership. Although many projects across the country are funded under the same central initiative, the extent to which they form part of a coherent entity is variable. In some instances there are detailed and prescriptive guidelines and a national programme of monitoring and evaluation, for example Sure Start, but in other cases arrangements are much looser, for example, the Continuing Care Challenge Fund.

Part One: challenges facing partnership projects

There is an extensive literature on working together in the field of health and social care and many of the insights gained have been consolidated in the key texts (Hardy et al, 1992; Leathard, 1994, 1998; Ovretveit, 1997). There are generally considered to be two main domains of activity, interagency collaboration, which is concerned with strategic planning and the commissioning of services, and interprofessional working, which involves joint service delivery (Higgins et al, 1994). The terms interagency and interprofessional are deliberately chosen in preference to the terms multiagency and multiprofessional. According to the distinction made by Ovretveit (1997) *inter* implies the broader dimension concerned with cooperating to plan and run services generally, not just cooperation around meeting the needs of an individual client.

Drawing on this literature, Figure 6.1 summarises the inhibiting factors impinging on partnership working and Figure 6.2 the preconditions for success that are derived from them. They relate specifically to collaboration between health and social care agencies although many are of wider significance.

Inhibiting factors

Figure 6.1: Factors inhibiting partnership working

Concern with organisational self-preservation

Structural issues:	Geographical boundaries, management hierarchies
Procedural issues:	Different lines of accountability, different degrees of discretion
Professional issues:	Different values/culture
Financial issues:	Budgetary constraints
Policy issues:	Different priorities, overlap and gaps in service

The first thing to note about interagency collaboration is that organisations like to work as closed systems (Springett, 1995). Partnership requires the surrender of power so unless there are strong incentives to do otherwise there will be resistance to it. Stocking (1985) notes that organisational change is much more difficult to achieve than technological change because of strong vested interest in the status quo.

Structural issues also create considerable barriers. Different geographical boundaries/catchment areas present obvious difficulties for joint planning and service delivery. They can multiply the number of potential partnerships that need to be created and lead to partnerships between agencies of vastly different size and hence resources. Within overall boundaries there may also be different internal divisions both vertical and horizontal, which make it difficult for managers and professionals to link with their opposite numbers (Leathard, 1998). Where it exists, co-terminosity is obviously a great initial advantage (Rogers, 1999).

Procedures can be as varied as structures. Agencies have different lines of accountability and allow different degrees of discretion to frontline workers often depending on their status and degree of professionalisation.

Doctors in the NHS, for example, have greater autonomy in clinical decision making than social workers in PSS (Hill, 1997). The degree of democratic accountability also varies between agencies run by elected local authorities and the more centrally controlled NHS where the democratic deficit limits sensibilities to local political pressures (Leathard, 1998).

The health and social care professions are not only managed differently but have different cultural values and a tendency to stereotype each other, professional identities having been constructed on the basis of the distinction between insiders and outsiders (Leathard, 1998). These different cultures mean that users are viewed from different perspectives, which may result in conflicting priorities such as the tendency for social care workers to emphasise autonomy and nurses safety vis-à-vis the care of frail older people.

Budgets and gamesmanship

Financial constraints can make agencies fiercely protective of their individual budgets and encourage gamesmanship designed to off-load local expenditure onto potential partners (Leathard, 1998). There is a contrary argument that severe pressures facilitate the search for innovative, collaborative answers that may increase efficiency (Springett, 1995), but this is often thwarted in practice by those rigid systems of financial accountability that the government has now promised to address in Partnership No 8 in Action (DoH, 1998a).

Policy priorities also vary between agencies leading to varying degrees of commitment to specific joint initiatives and even more perniciously to different expectations of what will be achieved. Booth in his study of NHS and social services department collaboration in Calderdale showed how the priority of the latter to child care limited the pace of their response to community care initiatives concerning older people to the frustration of the health authority anxious to close continuing care beds (Booth, 1981).

Another policy-related issue is that of overlap and gaps in responsibility, which occur when there are grey areas of uncertainty about the responsibilities assigned to different agencies (Robinson and Paxton, 1998). A classic contemporary example is the responsibility for the continuing residential care for older people. Variations in practice across the country prompted the government to intervene to clarify the situation and require both agencies to draw up agreed plans for local provision (DoH, 1995).

Partnership working can also be impeded by substantial differences in power and status between partners (Hill, 1997; Pettigrew et al, 1992). As indicated earlier in this volume by Balloch and Taylor, it is difficult to establish the reciprocity on which partnership is based if one partner has much more substantial resources and/or a more professionally developed workforce. This is a particular difficulty vis-à-vis statutory and voluntary agencies but also reflects the power imbalance between the NHS and various local authority departments including personal social services.

Having identified these factors, it is possible to construct prerequisites for partnership as outlined in Figure 6.2.

Prerequisites for partnership working

The instinctive desire to maintain organisational autonomy implies the necessity for strong 'political' leadership within all potential partner organisations committed to working together (Springett, 1995). Those involved in joint endeavour must perceive that there are 'brownie points' to be won for persevering despite the difficulties.

Given the complexity of interagency relationships and the probability of different priorities, clarity of purpose is also a prime prerequisite for the success of partnership working (Robinson and Paxton, 1998). This implies a set of clear objectives that combine in a coherent and feasible programme. Hardy et al (1992) argue that, while it is sensible to avoid overprescriptive organisational procedures, allowing a certain flexibility for development over time, project objectives should be unambiguous from the outset.

Figure 6.2: Prerequisites for partnership working

Secure political legitimacy	
Clarify purpose	Clear objectives, coherence
Identify advantages and threats	Financial, service-related, professional development
Ensure equivalency	Reciprocal contribution of money and resources
Establish appropriate administrative structures	Clarification of roles and responsibilities
Establish appropriate procedures	Lines of management accountability, systems for clinical supervision, monitoring and evaluation
Ensure communication and support	Role of 'boundary spanners', stable management, communication systems
Establish internal collaborative capacity	

Closely related to the issue of objectives is the need for clear acknowledgement of the perceived advantages that the collaboration will bring, together with recognition that certain risks are being undertaken (Springett, 1995). In financial terms a clear incentive may be the access to additional funding, but partnership working may also facilitate innovative service developments that depend on the joint input of complementary professional skills. According to Thomson (1999) it is the demonstration of tangible benefits on all sides that sustains joint working. For service providers there may be exciting opportunities for professional development. A clear indication of willingness to cooperate based on a sense of the potential advantages will help to counteract the pressure to preserve organisational autonomy, but Hardy et al (1992) argue that it is also important to identify and acknowledge the potential threats to each partner so that there will be mutual sensitivity to their difficulties.

Because the concept of partnership implies equivalency (Springett, 1995), it is argued that there should be comparable levels of contribution in terms of finance and other resources and that all partners should have the same degree of involvement and management control. Alter and Hage (1994) suggest that collaborating organisations should be of a similar size. Hardy et al (1992) make clear that there should be no 'junior partners'. Where there is a significant imbalance it is reasonable to query whether there can ever be a genuine partnership.

Appropriate administrative structures imply an organisational framework that will facilitate joint planning, management and service delivery, with a clear indication of respective roles and responsibilities at each level. This should obviously be linked to relevant procedures for accountability. Several writers distinguish between the need for clear lines of management accountability back into the partnership agencies and provision for the clinical supervision of professional workers, which has been identified by Ovretveit (1997) as the most sensitive area of interprofessional working. Others stress the need to develop robust systems of monitoring and evaluation, arguing that many joint ventures are run as demonstration projects. Formative or interim feedback is seen as a key aspect of their rationale, which may also help dissipate potential isolation and mainstream hostility (Stocking, 1985; Martin and Sanderson, 1999).

Additional funding: the motivating force

Although access to additional funding is often the motivating force behind partnership working (Ayling, 1999), matching funding is usually required from the participating agencies and it is sometimes difficult to ring-fence this when there are severe pressures on mainstream services. Skilled management input is therefore a vital aspect of resourcing. Stanwick (1999), writing about social services departments' involvement in partnership projects, emphasises the key leadership role within the department linking projects into mainstream management.

Over and above these formal arrangements, the literature suggests a further range of facilitating features. Pre-eminent among these is the role of 'boundary spanners' (Alter and Hage, 1994), individuals with networking skills who can work easily across agency boundaries, facilitating and supporting joint endeavours by building up personal relationships on the basis of trust. While emphasising their importance, however, Williams (1999) argues that they are complementary to, but no substitute for, a supportive management structure. Paradoxically, change, which is implicit in almost all interagency working, is easier to bed down where there is continuity of personnel in key management positions (Pettigrew et al, 1992), a situation that is difficult to achieve in the current climate of organisational turbulence.

Good communication: ever more essential

Several writers stress the importance of effective communication systems between agency partners and often within agencies, and between the collaborative project and mainstream services (Hardy et al, 1992; Rogers, 1999, Ovretveit, 1997). Nixon (1980) links all successful policy implementation to clarity and consistency of communication, but just as the potential for misinformation, rumour and suspicion is greater in collaborative ventures, so good communication becomes ever more essential. Communication, it is argued, builds awareness, understanding and trust. Face-to-face contact in particular is an important component in the early stages of building trusting relationships. Structures and procedures can establish the preconditions but it is trust that really drives partnership working (Huxham, 1993).

Quite naturally, attention has focused on relationships between agencies when seeking to identify conditions for successful interagency working but Huxham (1993) argues that the collaborative capacity of each partner organisation depends on its own intraorganisational procedures. Alter and Hage (1994) suggest that hierarchical organisations are too rigid and inflexible to operate successfully in the current complex environment of post-industrial society, which requires new ways of thinking and managing.

They need to decentralise power and develop adaptive efficiency. Effective partnerships therefore often depend on some preliminary internal reforms.

Much of the general literature on interagency collaboration on which Figures 6.1 and 6.2 are based draws its insights from joint planning and service provision of the 'project' type, which arguably has been the main focus of joint working to date. According to Hardy et al (1992), projects are particularly vulnerable organisational forms sitting on the periphery of their respective host organisations. They describe them as "unconventional and inconvenient novelties" and argue that they need protected status if they are to survive. They believe that such projects progress best when supported by staff groups dedicated solely to working on them and that monitoring and evaluation are particularly important to secure and disseminate their early success back into the mainstream. However, Pettigrew et al (1992) argue that the success of pilot projects can itself generate hostility and rejection by the organisational mainstream. They consider that many projects fail because they are small scale and non-cumulative. Links to mainstream services are obviously an important consideration for all short-term special projects. Clearly they need a Janus-like attention to their partners across the agency divide and their colleagues within their own organisational mainstream – a difficult balancing act.

In turning to a consideration of the two case studies, it is appropriate to conclude this section with a reminder from Pettigrew et al (1992) that locally specific contextual factors are important determinants of outcome as well as the generalisable inhibiting and promotional factors identified in the literature.

Part Two: experience of two partnership projects

Background to the case studies

Both case studies relate to projects undertaken in southern England. They are sited within the same unitary local authority and relate to the same health authority and NHS community trust, although the key personnel are different in each case and there was no evidence of any transfer of learning between them; an interesting observation in itself.

Figure 6.3: Management and operational structure of the Joint Continuing Care project

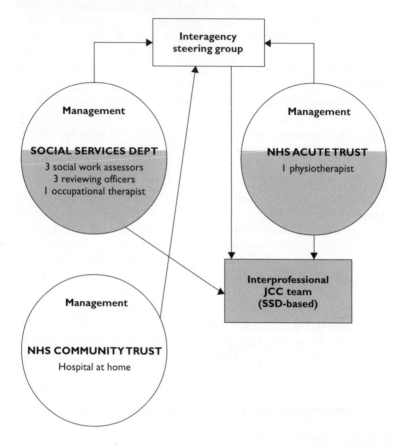

Project A (see Figure 6.3) represents one part of the Joint Continuing Care (JCC) project that is also referred to in Chapter Seven. The project, which was funded out of the Community Care Challenge Fund and matching NHS and local authority money, addressed the health and social care divide which Rogers (1999) has argued to be particularly problematic for frail older people.

The aspect of this multifaceted project which is considered in this chapter involved 'attaching' one local authority social worker (SWA) full time to each of three GP surgeries to work with older people (65-plus) who were in danger of admission to long-term residential care. All the SWAs visited their surgeries every day to collect referrals and two of them had a desk there. They aimed to work closely with all the doctors and nurses in the primary care team but their main base remained within the social services department. Here they formed part of the JCC project team together with four reviewing officers (ROs) who were working across the health authority with a remit to review the residential and domicilary services provided to older people on discharge from hospital. A physiotherapist and an occupational therapist also joined the JCC team. The team was managed and supervised within the social services. department but the project was directed by a multiagency steering group on which managers from the department, the health authority and the local NHS trusts were all represented. The two smaller parts of the JCC project, an augmentation to an existing 'hospital at home' scheme and the provision of an escort officer to offer practical help to older people on their immediate return home, were managed by the local NHS community trust and acute trust respectively. The lifetime of the JCC project was 18 months but due to a staggered start it was only effectively in operation for a little over a year.

Project B (see Figure 6.4) was financed from the Mental Illness Specific Grant together with matching funding from the NHS and local authority social services and education departments. It was set up to offer an intensive therapeutic regime to 'looked after' children who had been adopted or were in long-term foster care and were having problems with attachment. It involved a project team of eight staff, only one of whom, a social worker, worked full time on the project. The other seven sessional appointments included a consultant psychiatrist, two more social workers, two psychotherapists and one teacher and one teacher/counsellor. The team had a base within the mental health unit of the NHS community trust but no team leader or dedicated manager post.

Each collaborating agency provided line management support for their own staff but there were experiments in clinical supervision whereby a qualified social worker who was employed within the mental health unit provided supervision for the social workers and the consultant psychiatrist supervision for the teacher/counsellor. The therapists were both supervised from within their own disciplines in the trust where they worked. An additional element in this project was the provision for outside consultancy in support of the therapeutic regime being introduced. This project had a strategic steering group comprising senior managers from the three participating agencies which met six-monthly and an operational

Figure 6.4: Management and operational structure of attachment project

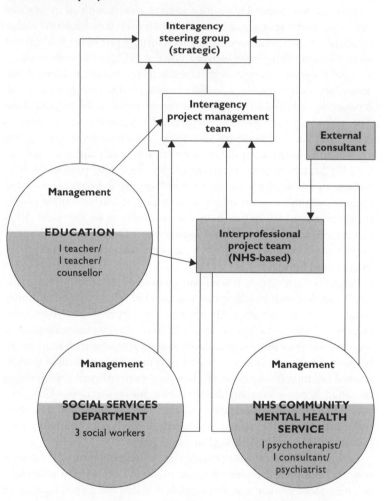

management team comprising the three line managers which met at six-weekly intervals. The lifetime of the Attachment Project was three years subject to annual review.

Evaluation design

A precondition of the funding for each project was an independent evaluation undertaken by the Health and Social Policy Research Centre (HSPRC) at the University of Brighton (Charnley et al, 1998; Williamson, 1999). In both instances this was designed as a diagnostic formative evaluation (Clarke, 1999) taking place throughout a year of the project's existence and which focused on the process as much as outcome. It was based on a multiple stakeholder approach (Smith and Cantley, 1985), the stakeholders being defined on both occasions as the service providers, their managers, users and carers and professional colleagues in mainstream services. A sample of all relevant stakeholders was interviewed face to face. In Project A, those interviewed included all three SWAs, their team leader, eight community nurses, four GPs, one practice manager and the senior health authority and social services department managers responsible for the initial project application. These were in addition to 18 users and carers. The SWAs were interviewed three times and other key interviewees twice, once near the beginning of the project and again at the end of the year. On each occasion a checklist was used that included reference to the key factors identified in the literature as promoting or inhibiting joint working.

Mindful of Pettigrew's contention that local context is significant (Pettigrew et al, 1992), respondents were also encouraged to identify local issues that they considered important. All interviews were tape-recorded with the interviewees' consent and edited transcripts sent back to them for verification. Complementary data were gathered from interim project reports and steering group minutes. After both sets of interviews were complete, a draft report was sent to the interviewees who were invited to a stakeholders' conference to discuss it.

A similar approach was pursued with regard to the Attachment Project. Eleven preliminary interviews were carried out with stakeholders representing all three groups of project workers – two social workers, one psychotherapist and one teacher, together with the consultant psychiatrist, two NHS and two social services department managers and one education department manager, and the project's external consultant. Once again interviews were based on a checklist, with opportunities for interviewees to introduce issues they considered important. They were all tape-recorded and an edited transcript sent for verification. At the time of writing the second round of interviews on this project had not taken place. Interviews were also being conducted with service users as part of a complementary evaluation of the therapeutic impact not reported on here.

It is acknowledged that both studies were small scale and heavily dependent on qualitative interviews. However, the range of views sought was comprehensive and an approach was deliberately chosen that encouraged participants to reflect on their experience. Pettigrew et al (1992) argue for research on change management that is processual, comparative, pluralistic and historical. The participants' analysis of the perceived strengths and weaknesses of the two projects vis-à-vis partnership working is presented in Figures 6.5 and 6.6, enabling comparisons to be made across them and between the two projects and findings from the literature. It is, of course, important to remember that the evaluation of Project B was still incomplete so data refers to perceptions at a comparatively early stage (about three months after the project was launched).

Perceived strengths and weaknesses of the case study project

Figure 6.5: Perceived strengths of Projects A and B

Project A

Support from the top	High political kudos, forum for launching other initiatives
Protected status	
Evidence of enhanced service provision	More holisitic services, greater continuity
Evidence of enhanced professional role	Complementary skills allowed for more specialisation, professional values modified, scope for creativity
Committed and enthusiastic staff	Boundary spanners

Project B

Support from the top	Experience of collaboration at senior levels
Independence of project	Creation of separate identity
Evidence of professional enthusiasm for new ways of working	
Links with mainstream services	

Support from the top

Looking first at the perceived strengths, those involved in both projects identified strong support for partnership working from the top of their respective organisations as a key factor. Workers spoke of a clear, top-down directive, which had stimulated a number of other successful bids. Those interviewed in Project B believed that the recent creation of a unitary local authority had renewed commitment to partnership working at a senior level. Reference was made to a number of initiatives in the child health area and to the construction of a local partnership board designed to provide an overarching structure for interagency collaborative endeavour. Senior officers in all the relevant authorities, health authority, NHS trusts, and local authority, had got to know each other well and appeared to share a collaborative culture. Project A respondents reported that the steering group meetings for their project were themselves used as an opportunity to plan future joint initiatives.

Independence/protected status

Both projects enjoyed an independent status that protected them from the everyday pressures on mainstream services. Throughout most of the life of Project A the team was sited in the social services department development unit as distinct from the operational division. The original intention had been for Project B to be sited within a proposed new day centre to be run by the child and adolescent health service and to be managed by the centre manager, but as funding for the centre did not materialise, this team also enjoyed an independent status. In both cases the teams had space and opportunity to develop a distinctive model of working, albeit at the price of some managerial isolation from the mainstream.

Enhanced service provision

From the perspective of both the team and the steering group, the new way of working in Project A had demonstrably enhanced service provision, providing a more holistic approach and greater continuity of care. This view was supported by users and carers.

Effective team building

It was also clear that working on both projects had been a very positive experience for the professional staff involved. Although health and social care professionals working in Project A recognised some initial overlap in activity, they argued that they had been able to establish complementary roles to the professional satisfaction of all. In particular, social workers and community nurses were able to utilise their respective skills more effectively. They all welcomed the chance to get to know colleagues in other professions/agencies and claimed that this established trust, which facilitated improved collaboration. There was emphasis in several interviews on the importance of communication and descriptions of how this had improved, including examples of sharing case notes, greater willingness to divulge sensitive information and better appreciation of the potential contribution colleagues could make. It was claimed that stereotypes had been revised and professional values modified.

Although Project B had only been running a few months, the representatives of the different professions working in the team were equally enthusiastic about the stimulation engendered and the extent to which they had established a common identity and shared understanding of the concept of attachment and of the therapeutic model they were following. There was a much greater degree of team working in Project B from the beginning because it was implicit in their therapeutic model.

Project A had been operational for long enough to demonstrate the capacity of workers in the team to act as 'boundary spanners' networking across a range of local and statutory agencies within the communities covered by their respective GP practices. All the SWAs demonstrated high levels of personal enthusiasm for partnership working in general and the aims of the JCC project in particular. The development of a strong project ethos around the philosophy of user choice and anti-ageist practice was developed from the bottom up within the project team itself. The workers in Project B were a similarly self-selected, highly motivated group of experienced practitioners who relished the opportunity to work in different ways with professional colleagues. Rather than feeling threatened by change, the practitioners involved in both projects had chosen to participate because they wanted an opportunity to explore new forms of practice. Their relative seniority also gave them the self-confidence to cope with uncertainty.

Links with mainstream services

All but one of the eight team members worked part time on Project B and several of them also had substantial commitments to mainstream services. Although this created some problems it was also claimed that this helped to bridge the potential divide between the project and the mainstream, keeping communication channels open and allowing workers to retain a sense of identity with their parent services.

Past experience of collaboration

While interviewees stressed a number of positive aspects within both projects, there were also factors that were seen to limit their effectiveness. Despite agreement that there was a culture of collaboration in the district,

Perceived weaknesses of Projects A and B

Figure 6.6: Perceived weaknesses of Projects A and B

Project A

Unsupportive attitudes from mainstream colleagues	Cynicism concerning projects
Project hastily constructed	
Short-term insecurity for staff and users	
Lack of effective management procedures	
Organisational turbulence	SSD restructuring, other new initiatives, financial constraints
Mounting caseloads	
Isolation from the mainstream	

Project B

Underlying anxieties	Mixed history of joint initiatives
Project hastily constructed	
Lack of clear administrative structures and procedures	
Organisational turbulence	Different agency priorities
Inadequate sessional input	
Need for closer links with mainstream	

interviewees in Project B indicated that the experience of interagency and interprofessional collaboration in the past had not always been positive. Social services department managers spoke of anxieties that social workers would be co-opted into the culture of the NHS and 'go native', a development that had led in the past to the withdrawal of social workers from child guidance clinics. A representative from Education talked of the perceived failure of earlier joint initiatives to live up to expectations, which made it very important that they succeeded this time. Respondents from Project A commented on the multiplicity of initiatives that had come and gone in recent years, with little observable long-term impact, and reported a growing mood of cynicism with the whole idea of projects.

Unrealistic timetables

There was a recognition in both instances that project bids had been compiled hastily as a result of tight deadlines for funding applications. Although the funding opportunities allowed the relevant agencies to progress plans they had already developed, the speedy response to project specifications meant that some issues such as management structures were not always fully thought through. It was difficult to get started by the appointed date and in practice there was a staggered recruitment to both projects. In Project A, social workers claimed that they had to work out what they were supposed to be doing for themselves, while in Project B the failure to realise plans for the associated day centre undermined the planned role of Education in the partnership. Although this issue was later resolved, the education department was very much the junior partner in the early stages of the project.

Potential insecurity of time-limited budget

An issue relevant to all short-term projects is the potential insecurity it engenders in both users and practitioners. While some workers in Project A were seconded, others were on short-term contracts and understandably concerned about their future employment. This, combined with uncertainty about whether the project's method of working would be retained and/or extended to mainstream services once the dedicated funding ran out, led to a period of high anxiety and considerable demoralisation within the team. All of those working on Project B were seconded so did not face the same personal insecurities and it was too early to identify similar anxieties about the long-term future of the project.

Structural and procedural issues

Management procedures created some problems in both instances although the issues are rather different. In Project A, the reporting arrangements between the team manager and the interagency steering group were not clear and as a result the steering group lacked relevant information. As the group incorporated managers from mainstream services, this was a crucial blow, which contributed to isolation from the mainstream. The front-line workers in Project A were frustrated by the fact that they had no direct contact with the steering group and so lacked an opportunity to make an informal contribution to the debates about its development. In Project B the main problem was one of sorting out administrative responsibilities within the team. The failure to develop a day centre and therefore to appoint a day centre manager, combined with the team's reluctance to designate a leadership role, created a vacuum. This led to inefficient practices such as all clinical members of the team devoting valuable sessional time to writing sections of a report that could have been more efficiently drafted by one or two individuals. The rotating chairmanship of the weekly/fortnightly team meetings was not always conducive to efficient committee procedures.

Internal organisational turbulence

As NHS trusts and social services departments appear to be in a constant state of reorganisation, organisational turbulence seems to be an ongoing problem that partnership projects must cope with (Stanwick, 1999). SSD restructuring, leading to changes in management responsibilities within mainstream services, disrupted channels of communication for project workers in Project A and diverted the attention of managers to immediate day-to-day issues. Although links at senior manager level and between fieldworkers remained robust, the weak link at middle-management level increased the isolation of the project and impaired SSD collaborative capacity in general. Project B does not appear to have been affected by organisational change in the social service department to the same extent but faced disabling turbulence within the management of the mental health division of the NHS trust where it was sited.

Budgetary constraints

Organisational changes were also linked to shifts in organisational policy and the development of new initiatives within the collaborating agencies. Increasingly severe budgetary constraints impacted on the budgets available to the SWAs in project A, which meant that a rationing system was introduced. On the basis of earlier experience with special projects, it was argued that they should not be privileged in terms of resourcing over and above mainstream services, as this would limit the scope for rolling out the initiative. However, the rationing policy created a tension between pressures to demonstrate the potential of the case management approach and the demands of equity across the service. SWAs also felt that referrals to a new rehabilitation scheme diverted occupational therapy time away from SWA referrals in the latter months of the project.

The pressures on projects from resource-starved mainstream services were compounded by those generated internally as the potential for new ways of working became apparent and case levels expanded. SWAs became trapped in service provision at the expense of wider networking opportunities. While finite resources and escalating demands are a ubiquitous fact of life in health and welfare service provision, it is a particularly difficult tension to handle in demonstration projects. In commenting on this problem, there is a need to distinguish between a possible underresourcing of the project due to a lack of clear understanding of what would be required to fulfil its objectives, as against possibly enthusiastic attempts by the workers themselves to expand the remit. Project B was at too early a stage to encounter severe problems but the team identified that limited sessional input by some workers might undermine their therapeutic model of team working.

Different priorities between agencies, a common problem identified in the introduction to this volume, also emerged in both instances. Within Project A there was a tension between the concerns of the NHS acute trust to discharge older patients and the concerns of the SSD both to cut the costs of residential care and to set up appropriate community-based packages. This tension influenced the ROs in particular but also impacted on the work of the SWAs who were tracking older people through hospital. In Project B interviewees identified the disparate concerns of the NHS trust to reduce hospital waiting lists, the concern of the SSD to prevent adoption and fostering breakdowns, and Education's interest in reducing the incidence of school exclusion. Different priorities do not necessarily lead to conflicting long-term objectives, but if budgetary or political pressures become too intense, may create short-term operational tensions.

Relationships with mainstream services

A significant problem for both projects was their uncertain relationship with mainstream services. This was particularly the case for Project A. Despite conscious attempts not to privilege it in terms of resources, it was widely viewed by mainstream colleagues as specially favoured. The steering group was aware of these potential difficulties, which have been identified as common in other social work attachment schemes (Rummery and Glendinning, 1997). The community service managers with responsibility for hospital social work services and community-based assessment services, helped to draw up and agree protocols that governed the relationship between SWAs, ROs and mainstream services. These included mapping referral rates and defining ultimate case responsibility. In addition, the project manager joined the assessment team but the difficulties remained. The SWAs did not feel any animosity directed at them personally but considered that their colleagues were 'waiting for them to fail'.

Workers in Project B were also conscious of this potential problem and hoped to pre-empt it by talking about their work to colleagues in mainstream services. They argued that the intensive service they were offering aimed to tackle some of the most intractable problems that their mainstream colleagues were unsuccessfully grappling with and that they were an asset rather than rivals 'poaching' the most interesting work.

Conclusion

This brief consideration of two small initiatives, one still incomplete, can only be indicative of the potential and limitations of using projects to promote partnerships but it does offer a number of insights into the interrelationships and relative importance of key factors. Political support from the top was widely recognised to make a significant contribution to kick-starting both these projects and was related in this instance to the unitary status of local government. Not only did this obviate some of the practical difficulties but also meant that a newly created authority was looking to establish its credentials, and partnership working was one high-profile issue through which it could do this. The senior managers were therefore strongly motivated to initiate and support examples of partnership working.

At the other extreme, those involved on the ground in service delivery within both projects were also enthusiastic supporters of the partnership concept. Despite the potential of professional jealousies outlined in the literature, the tangible benefits of a more holistic approach to care convinced them that working together enhanced rather than diminished their professional practice. There is an important proviso, already made, that those involved in project working are often the more experienced and innovative workers and that their positive perspective may be more difficult to inculcate across the board.

The main practical difficulties tended to arise in the intermediate tier of the partner organisations where middle managers were responsible for the interface between the projects and mainstream services. Arguably the responsibilities of those in these positions made them relatively more inward looking. On the one hand they were less conscious than their seniors of the political role of their organisation in the wider world, and on the other, less aware than fieldworkers of the immediate practical benefits of joint working for clients.

Middle managers are more concerned with the internal mechanics of their organisation – of living within budgets on a day-to-day basis and of sustaining administrative procedures directed to maintenance rather than innovation. To them, joint projects may well appear "unconventional and inconvenient" (Hardy et al, 1992). Yet without strong and supportive leadership at this level projects will remain isolated from the mainstream and an already demoralised workforce can easily fall into scapegoating mode, accusing special projects of taking more than their fair share of resources and interesting work. Hardy et al (1992) have argued that if projects are to fulfil their potential as catalysts for change there must be good channels of communication with the mainstream. An early exchange of experience is essential if organisational learning is to take place.

More significantly, in both cases the tight timetable involved in meeting funding deadlines did not allow for wide consultation with colleagues in mainstream services. This did not encourage a sense of supportive ownership. In Project A interviewees reported a lack of awareness and understanding of the project, which led to the development of myths that it had overgenerous resources and limited caseloads. With regard to Project B, it is unfortunate that the social services department's permanency team, which had been running an adoption support group for seven years, was not initially aware of the project proposal.

However, the two examples cited do demonstrate the potential of projects to promote close collaborative ('partnership') working between agencies and between professionals. The problem is the danger of this remaining a marginalised activity for enthusiasts unless the more fundamental issue of the collaborative capacity of the whole organisation is also addressed. Only when organisations are well integrated internally, self-confident and secure in their own purposes and processes, argues Huxham (1993), can they expect to build effective partnerships. This has implications for the lasting impact of demonstration projects but is even more important in the context of the government's current agenda for more integrated working across the board. If such capacity is lacking, demonstration projects are unlikely to have a lasting impact and the government's current agenda for making integrated working 'core business' is unlikely to succeed.

References

Alter, C. and Hage, J. (1994) *Organisations working together*, London: Sage Publications.

Ayling, R. (1999) 'The Joint Commissioning Officer's story: working across boundaries', in R. Poxton (ed) *Working across agency boundaries: Experience of primary health and social care partnerships in practice*, London: King's Fund.

Booth, T.M. (1981) 'Collaboration between health and social services', Pt 1, *Policy & Politics*, vol 9, pp 23-49.

Charnley, H., Kocher, P., Prentice, S. and Williamson, V. (1998) *The Joint Continuing Care Project: An evaluation of innovative joint working*, Brighton: Health and Social Policy Research Centre, University of Brighton.

Clarke, J. (1999) *Evaluation research: An introduction to principles, methods and practice*, London: Sage Publications.

DoH (Department of Health) (1995) *NHS responsibilities for meeting continuing health care needs*, HSG (95) 8, London: DoH.

DoH (1998a) *Partnership in action: New opportunities for joint working between health and social services*, London: The Stationery Office.

DoH (1998b) *Our healthier nation: Saving lives*, London: The Stationery Office.

Gordon, P. and Hanafin, T. (1998) 'Hands across the divide', *Health Management*, October, pp 20-1.

Hardy, B., Turrell, A. and Wistow, G. (1992) *Innovations in community care management*, Aldershot: Avebury.

Healy, P. (1999) 'Fancy brickwork', *Health Service Journal*, vol 21, January, pp 12-13.

Higgins, R., Oldman, C. and Hunter, D. (1994) 'Working together: lessons for collaboration between health and social services', *Health and Social Care*, vol 2, pp 269-77.

Hill, M. (1997) *The policy process in the modern state* (3rd edn), London: Prentice Hall/Harvester Wheatsheaf.

Huxham, C. (1993) 'Collaborative capability: an intra-organisational perspective on collaborative advantage', *Public Money and Management*, July-September, pp 21-8.

Leathard, A. (ed) (1994) *Going inter-professional: Working together for health and welfare*, London: Routledge.

Leathard, A. (1998) 'Collaborative care for health and welfare', in R. Skelton and V. Williamson (eds) *Fifty years of the National Health Service: Continuities and discontinuities in health policy*, Brighton: Health and Social Policy Research Centre, University of Brighton.

Martin, S. and Sanderson, I. (1999) 'Evaluating public policy experiments: measuring outcomes, monitoring progress and managing pilots?', *Evaluation*, vol 3, pp 245-58.

Nixon, J. (1980) 'The importance of communication in the implementation of government policy at the local level', *Policy & Politics*, vol 8, no 2, pp 127-46.

Ovretveit, J. (1997) 'Evaluating interprofessional working – a case example of a community mental health team', in J. Ovretveit, P. Mathias and T. Thompson (eds) *Interprofessional working for health and social care*, London: Macmillan.

Pettigrew, A., Ferlie, E. and McKie, L. (1992) *Shaping strategic change: Making change in large organisations*, London: Sage Publications.

Robinson, J. and Paxton, R. (1998) 'Health and social care partnerships', in R. Klein (ed) *Implementing the White Paper*, London: King's Fund.

Rogers, J. (1999) 'The social worker's story: changing roles for practitioners', in R. Poxton (ed) *Working across agency boundaries: Experience of primary health and social care partnerships in practice*, London: King's Fund.

Rummery, K. and Glendinning, C. (1997) *Working together: Primary care involvement in commissioning social care services*, Debates in Primary Care, Manchester: National Primary Care Research and Development Centre.

Smith, G. and Cantley, C. (1985) *Assessing health care: A study in organisational evaluation*, Milton Keynes: Open University Press.

Springett, J. (1995) *Intersectoral collaboration: Theory and practice*, Occasional Paper, Liverpool: Institute of Health, John Moores University.

Stanwick, S. (1999) 'The health authority commissioner's story: learning to work in partnership', in R. Poxton (ed) *Working across agency boundaries: Experience of primary health and social care partnerships in practice*, London: King's Fund.

Stocking, B. (1985) *Initiative and inertia: Case studies in the NHS*, London: National Provincial Hospitals Trust.

Thomson, A. (1999) 'The GP's story', in R. Poxton (ed) *Working across agency boundaries: Experience of primary health and social care partnerships in practice*, London: King's Fund.

Williams, C. (1999) 'The social service director's story: towards a seamless service', in R. Poxton (ed) *Working across agency boundaries: Experience of primary health and social care partnerships in practice*, London: King's Fund.

Williamson, V. (1999) 'The potential of project status to promote partnership working: Interim Report on the Attachment Project', Unpublished, Brighton: Health and Social Policy Research Centre, University of Brighton.

SEVEN

Promoting independence: a partnership approach to supporting older people in the community

Helen Charnley

This chapter examines partnership as a strategy for supporting vulnerable older people who wish to continue living in their own homes. It outlines the ways in which notions of partnership have been applied to working with older people and identifies effective strategies for achieving inclusive partnerships that focus on serving the interests of older people.

Contemporary social policy reflects the tensions created by the different ways in which older people are perceived in this society. One view, that sees them as a drain on resources, a burden on society, focuses attention on the costs of caring for older people with complex health and social care needs (DoH, 2000). A second view sees older people as undervalued and excluded victims of a discriminatory, ageist society (Harding, 1997). Responses to this view have heightened the profile of anti-discriminatory and anti-oppressive practice with older people (Age Concern, 1999; Titley, 1997). A third view that has been promoted through the campaigning activities of voluntary sector organisations and the increasingly influential voice of the user movement (Morris, 1994), sees older people as active agents of their own health and well-being, with rich potential to contribute to society (Shakespeare, 2000). New Labour has responded to this view with broad initiatives such as *Better government for older people* (Cabinet Office, 1998).

The recurrence of partnership as a theme in social policy has been outlined in the Introduction to this volume. With particular relevance for older service users, *Building partnerships for success* (DoH, 1995) argued that effective practice depends on three main elements: a commitment to the involvement and empowerment of service users and carers; a clear emphasis on outcomes as well as processes; and the importance of developing partnerships with other agencies, creating new forms of service delivery and strengthening arrangements for care management by emphasising sensitive, unbureaucratic assessments and providing services based on appropriate responses to need.

Supporting older people to maintain the degree of independence they seek requires the effective orchestration of a range of players. But, as Servian (1996) has noted, the world of community care is suffused with contradictions and tensions in power relations between carers, users, workers and managers, and the nature of partnerships is highly variable.

Inclusive or exclusive partnerships?

Inclusive partnerships are characterised by the active participation of all interested parties, including service users and carers, in goal setting, decision making and conflict resolution. Inclusive partnerships do not guarantee the achievement of desired outcomes as expressed by service users or carers. But they do imply a full hearing of user and carer views, creative responses from practitioners and managers, and clear explanations of any failure to meet particular needs or to respond to users' and carers' expressed wishes. Exclusive partnerships, on the other hand, are characterised by the centrality of narrowly perceived agency priorities and the marginalisation of service users and carers in decision-making processes. Policy rhetoric suggests that the importance of inclusive partnerships is well understood. But evidence indicates that a number of factors serve to limit the successful development of inclusive partnerships.

Legislative and policy contradictions

As the Introduction has emphasised, legislation and policy initiatives are key catalysts in defining, obliging or encouraging partnership working. But they do not address the tensions that inhibit the development of effective partnerships. Tensions between health and social services derive, in no small part, from differences in charging policies, with health services being largely free at the point of consumption while social services must be paid for in accordance with local policies (Henwood and Wistow, 1993). *A new partnership for care in old age* (DoH, 1997) argued the case for private insurance against the risks of requiring long-term care and proposed a model of partnership between individual citizens and the private sector, supported by incentives from the public sector. But research evidence suggested that strong public resistance to such a model would render this an unlikely solution to the funding of long-term care (Parker and Clarke, 1998). The Royal Commission on Long-Term Care (Sutherland, 1999) recommended that services to meet the personal care needs of those in long-term care should properly be paid for by general taxation. But the government has resisted this recommendation, arguing that new investment in improving older people's services would not be best used by making personal care universally free (DoH, 2000).

With the implementation of the 1999 Health Act (DoH, 1999), attention has shifted to the potential of joint commissioning and pooled budgets, designed to minimise opportunities for shifting budgetary responsibility from one organisation to another. The phenomenon of cost shunting and the use of eligibility criteria to control entitlement to public services have, indeed, inhibited effective joint working. But the problem is not limited to health and social services. Changing responsibilities for the care element of public services have led to the marginalisation of other potential partners.

A clear example concerns the role of housing (see Chapters Four and Five). While the 1990 NHS and Community Care Act was explicit about the active roles of health and social services in community care, the role of housing was significantly underplayed. Pressures on housing departments have served to inhibit the development of housing provision in a way that is responsive to the physical and social needs of many older people (Audit Commission, 1998). As Means (1996) argues, the history of joint working in housing, health and social welfare has been one of conflict and mistrust as organisations have sought to protect their own interests.

Interprofessional differences

A variety of mechanisms has been used to stimulate collaboration between health and social services over recent decades. But these have not led to enduring partnerships capable of responding effectively to older people whose requirements for support cross the boundaries of health and social services agencies (Bebbington and Charnley, 1990). Analyses of the failure of collaborative working have identified a number of barriers to establishing effective professional partnerships. Individuals may experience a loss of autonomy and sense of control over setting agendas and deciding priorities. There are different perceptions about the costs of joint working and misunderstandings about the statutory responsibilities of 'other' agencies. These factors, combined with differences in organisational culture, can lead to mutual stereotyping between professions and a lack of agreement about roles and responsibilities (Means et al, 1997).

Stanley, Reed and Brown (1999) suggest that interprofessional differences derive, in part, from the lack of appropriate training for practitioners from professions with different value bases. Statham (2000) has pointed to a general lack of professional training in the development and maintenance of partnerships as well as the management of changing partnerships. However, as Wilmot has argued, differences in professional values are unlikely to disappear, and could usefully be treated as "assets for clients, for whom alternatives, and therefore options, enhance autonomy" (Wilmot, 1995, p 264).

User and carer involvement: resistance to the inclusion of 'welfare subjects'

A third factor limiting the effectiveness of partnerships concerns the relationship between professionals, users and carers. There is little consensus about the meaning of user and carer involvement. It has been interpreted variously as the simple provision of information to users and carers, consultation on an individual level, consultation on a broader level, working together to address specific problems and, finally, the achievement of user and carer control (Goss and Miller, 1995; Means et al, 1997). The clearest example of user control is the use of direct payments (see Chapter Eight). But available evidence suggests that professional resistance as well as cultural expectations must be overcome before older people can effectively gain control over the purchase and pattern of the services they receive (Clark, 2000).

Morris (1994, 1997) has extended the conceptual boundaries of user involvement to embrace leadership by users. Her suggested framework for working in partnership with service users requires: (i) greater clarity in relation to user entitlements and their legitimacy; (ii) the use of a social model of disability that focuses on identifying and tackling the barriers to achieving improvements in quality of life; (iii) the use of needs-led assessments that distinguish between what is needed and what can be provided, and; (iv) the promotion of user choice and control in line with legislation and guidance on community care.

Recent analyses of user involvement, however, suggest that these four elements remain underdeveloped and continue to be resisted (Balloch et al, 1999). The use of an entitlement, or rights-based, approach is weakened by lack of knowledge on the part of service users, compounded by the inaccessibility of information and a lack of available training on legal issues and rights. The potential benefits of needs-led assessments have been compromised by the continuing focus on professional definitions of need, and constrained by eligibility criteria based on narrowly defined levels of dependency. In practice, the continuing exercise of professional power in needs-led assessments has prevailed over good intentions to follow a social model of disability and to promote user choice and control.

Distinctiveness of user and carer interests

The fourth factor limiting genuine user and carer involvement has been the failure to recognise that user and carer interests may not always be congruent. In contrast to the normative expectations surrounding familial care of dependent adults (Twigg and Atkin, 1994), the disability movement has highlighted the tensions that characterise user-carer relations. It has become clear that models of service intervention that treat users and carers as necessarily sharing the same interests fail to recognise their distinctive needs (Littlechild and Blakeney, 1996; Qureshi et al, 1998). The result is that existing tensions may increase rather than decrease, and the long-term contribution to be made by carers may be weakened rather than strengthened (Statham, 2000).

The 1995 Carers (Recognition and Services) Act introduced an entitlement to the assessment of carers' own needs. Monitoring the implementation of the Act, a Social Services Inspectorate report (SSI, 1999) demonstrated that carers' needs had been brought into sharper focus through the establishment of carers' groups and centres, and indirectly through improvements in the range and quality of services for users. But concerns about arrangements for hospital discharge, the provision of equipment and respite services, and planning for future emergencies revealed significant weaknesses in the implementation of carers' policies and the promotion of carer entitlements.

This section has reviewed four factors that limit the achievement of inclusive partnerships. The following section draws on empirical data from the qualitative evaluation of a joint continuing care project, designed to foster partnerships between health and social services professionals, older service users and their carers (Charnley et al, 1999).

A Joint Continuing Care (JCC) project

The JCC project represented a package of initiatives to meet the complex health and social care needs of older people. It focused on those at risk of hospitalisation or admission to residential care, and those being discharged from hospital to residential and nursing-home care, or to their own homes. The project reflected the emphasis placed by *Modernising social services* (DoH, 1998a) on *flexible partnership working that moves away from sterile conflict over boundaries.* It was supported by special funding from central government designed to respond to the challenges to the NHS posed by winter pressures, waiting lists, and demand for continuing care. The provision of service packages, however, continued to be funded from the main community care budget in order to prevent the development of an isolated, elitist, non-replicable model, a problem that has plagued the replication of highly effective innovations in the past (see Chapter Six).

The aims of the project reflected policy concerns to increase client choice, to maintain older people in the community and to achieve value for money. Four components operating in a loose confederation were designed to prevent unnecessary hospital admissions, facilitate hospital discharge, and provide continuing support in the community. Social work assessors were attached to GP surgeries to respond to referrals of older people by the primary care team, while reviewing officers provided regular monitoring and rapid review of the placements and packages of care for older people discharged from hospital. An existing 'hospital at home' scheme, designed to facilitate early discharge and prevent readmissions, was strengthened and an escort officer was appointed to smooth the discharge process from hospital to home for older people lacking practical support in re-establishing critical aspects of home life such as heating and food.

Management arrangements were divided between health and social services. The social work assessors and reviewing officers, together with an occupational therapist, were based in a single team with a manager. A physiotherapist was also based with the team, but was managed by the local community health services trust, as were the escort officer and 'hospital-at-home' team (Figure 7.1).

Significant numbers of older people who used the project were able to exercise choice to remain in, or return to, their own homes. The overwhelming desire of those in hospital to return to their own homes reflected wider evidence of older people's preferences (Nocon and Qureshi,

Figure 7.1: Joint Continuing Care project: key players

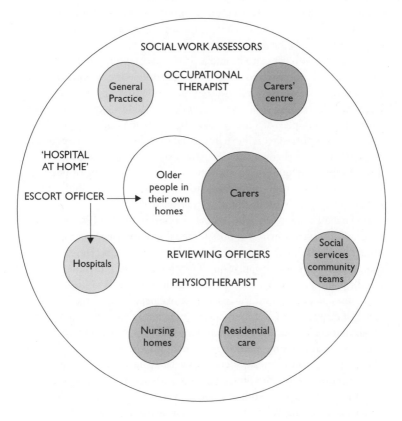

Notes:

General Practice:	GPs and community health services
Hospitals:	Limited rehabilitation facilities in hospital Hospital social work teams responsible for needs assessment prior to discharge
Nursing homes and Residential care:	Limited rehabilitation facilities – but encouraged by JCC team Residential care facilities used for respite
Social services community teams:	Responsibility for monitoring and review once older people in stable situation

1996). Of 85 project users who were discharged from hospital to residential care or nursing homes, 16 died within two months. Of the remaining 69, a third were able to return to their own homes. This was a considerably higher rate than was achieved before the introduction of proactive review of placements and service packages.

A clear focus on user choice and a clear understanding of the outcomes associated with admission to residential or nursing home care, led reviewing officers to develop new relations with residential and nursing home managers, challenging cultures of dependency and low expectation. There were clear examples of older people in residential and nursing homes who were supported to achieve improved mobility, reduced dependence, and a return to their own homes. Attention was paid to the appropriate mix of inputs including user and carer-centred assessment of needs, and a range of resources including home care, occupational therapy, physiotherapy, carer support and respite services.

Social work assessors, who received referrals from GPs, also used a range of interventions to support vulnerable older people in their own homes and to achieve a rate of admission to long-term care of three per thousand of the older population. They anticipated individual crises by building up knowledge of vulnerable individuals and fostering the development of community-based support networks. Greater use was made of respite care where providers were encouraged to focus on active rehabilitation rather than containment. Carers were offered separate support in addressing their needs through the local carers' centre. Community health practitioners found that the availability of a social work assessor led to more timely referrals and increased the level of shared information between health and social-work staff. This led to improved feedback following referral and a mutual learning process that in turn produced more appropriate referrals. Where it was not possible for project users to continue to live in the community, high value was placed on ensuring that they were fully involved in, and retained substantial control over, the decision-making process.

User and carer views

User and carer views were drawn from interviews with 28 service users and 12 carers. JCC workers were described in very positive terms by all but two of the sample of older people and their carers. Comments related to support, kindness, responsiveness, speedy arrangement of services, and the availability and accessibility of workers. These expressions of felt satisfaction contrasted sharply with the language used to describe negative experiences in hospital, residential care and in their own homes. Some home care workers were described as having a tendency to 'take over', leaving service users feeling that they were no longer in control of their own homes. Concerns were expressed about lack of privacy, rough handling, and being bossed and bullied in hospital, nursing homes and residential care. The positive experiences and outcomes associated with the JCC project were linked to resisting prevailing attitudes and practices.

Defensive practice

Defensive practice was commonplace among some GPs and family relatives. This was well illustrated by Mrs E who had been discharged from hospital to a nursing home under pressure from her GP and her son. She described the experience in her own words:

> "I'm always being nagged at by the doctor or somebody: 'You should be in a place with other people'. Yes, maybe I should, but one day if they get into that position, they'll see that it isn't as easy as that.... I said, 'I'm going home', this is my home, everything around it is mine, it's all familiar.... I just don't want to leave this.... She [the project worker] helped me right through it, and she arranged for the carers to come."

The worker had enabled Mrs E's own wishes to be heard and to be taken seriously alongside the concerns for her physical safety expressed by her GP and her son.

Lack of suitable accommodation

Another barrier preventing those in residential or nursing homes from returning home was a lack of suitable accommodation. Reduced mobility rendered some older people's homes inaccessible or inappropriate to meet their changing needs. Some owner-occupiers found that they were unable to raise sufficient funds through the sale of their home to purchase more suitable accommodation, and it has been common for housing departments to give lower priority to applicants in such circumstances, believing them to be 'in a safe place'. Negotiations between project staff and the housing department succeeded in establishing the flexibility required to recognise that a lack of accessible housing should not constitute an acceptable reason for having to live in long-term residential care. The project demonstrated success in facilitating moves from owner-occupied to local authority housing as well as between different types of rented accommodation.

Denying the agency of service users and carers

Resistance to the active involvement of users or their carers in decision-making also prevented the development of inclusive partnerships. Such resistance not only runs the risk of denying users the outcomes they wish for, but may also lead to inefficiency. Mr A had been admitted straight to a nursing home after a period of hospitalisation, but he felt strongly that he and his nephew, with whom he lived, had been excluded from the decision-making process. His project worker organised a case conference in which all interested parties were included, and this led to a successful trial period at home supported by an enlarged package of care. Mr A saw his project worker as an advocate who had "fought his case well".

Eleven of the 12 carers interviewed as part of the evaluation of the JCC project felt that they had been supported in making arrangements to care for their partners, relatives or friends at home. Mr H's wife had been admitted to a nursing home following her third stroke. He had had to fight to be allowed to bring her home. Staff at the nursing home had told him she was too ill to go home. But he felt that, with help, he could look after her. A project reviewing officer and the occupational therapist were involved in a reassessment of both Mrs and Mr H's needs that led to the provision of a package of care that supported him to care for his wife at home. He reported proudly: "Even the doctor's saying we're doing a good job. It's mainly through her [the reviewing officer] I got everything, her and the occupational therapist".

Failure to recognise the distinctive needs of carers

A further threat to successful maintenance in the community was posed by professionals' assumptions about the capacity of family carers. In Mr A's case a mistaken assumption had been made that his younger, male, carer would not play a significant role. But in other cases mistaken assumptions associated the presence of carers with adequate support. Project workers made explicit efforts to avoid such assumptions. One carer, living with her mother who had recently been discharged from hospital, had a full-time job. She described her experience before and after the involvement of a project worker:

> "I had to fight for everything, and I felt every time I spoke to the previous worker that I was being a nuisance, I felt that small. But since [project worker] has been on the case, any problems we've had, she's been on to them straight away. Never made us feel that we shouldn't be getting what we are getting, you know."

Failure to recognise conflicting interests of users and carers

A complex challenge lay in providing appropriate support where user and carer interests conflicted. Careful attention paid to the distinctive needs of older people and their carers did allow project workers to resolve what at first sight appeared to be insoluble differences. The case of Mr and Mrs P offers a clear illustration. Mr P had moved from hospital to a nursing home and then to residential care. With poor experience of previous support arrangements, Mrs P was unwilling to have her husband at home. However, by acknowledging Mrs P's sense of unreasonable obligation and her desire for privacy, a project worker was able to make arrangements that relieved her resentment and concerns. The delivery of support services was organised in a manner that met her needs as well as those of her husband, and she was offered independent support from the carers' centre.

User and carer perceptions of value for money

While value for money is a concept more commonly associated with the use of 'public money' than charges paid by individual consumers, it is important to consider the cost consequences of decisions to use particular service provider agencies. The quality of the service provided, and the outcomes achieved through the use of that service, must be taken into account, alongside its direct cost, when assessing 'value for money'.

Establishing value for money did not feature strongly in user and carer accounts of the JCC project Their responses indicated greater concern for the quality of the services received. Mr and Mrs Q commented positively on the value of the services they received. They were assessed to pay a contribution of £12 a week towards a once-a-day hourly call to help Mr Q to bathe and dress. But the value of the service went beyond this. As Mrs Q said:

> "We don't mind paying that because we think it's well worth it ... the back-up we're getting is worth a lot of money. We have had nothing but back-up and kindness and I think for your emotional side that's good, you need it, don't you, because you can go under so easily."

Negative comments about value for money were linked to efforts by private home care agencies to reduce their costs. Home care workers were not always able to spend the allocated time or carry out the allotted tasks. The important message is that user and carer perceptions of value for money focus more closely on the content, quality and effectiveness of the services they receive than the financial cost of those services to them.

Summary of user and carer experience

Maintenance in the community may be viewed as a crude measure of outcome that pays insufficient attention to the appropriateness of the setting in which an individual is living (Nocon and Qureshi, 1996). However, in the context of this project the overwhelming choice of individual service users was to remain in, or return to, the community. Concerns that the goal of maintenance in the community might have led to pressure on older people to return to their own homes, and thus erode the notion of client choice, were not borne out in the JCC project and there was no evidence of any service users returning to their own home against their wishes.

The exercise of user choice in relation to the content, timing and delivery of services was constrained by the fixed nature of service packages. Policies of using in-house services before buying in from outside agencies led, in some cases, to the use of more than one provider and a number of different home care workers visiting an older person. As well as compromising user choice, this threatened the continuity of care that could be offered.

Practitioner experiences of the JCC project

We now turn to the practitioners who formed the central JCC team and focus on the factors that they identified as being central to the achievement of the three project aims: extending user choice, maintenance in the community and value for money. All project workers agreed that including an occupational therapist and physiotherapist in the team had transformed the capacity to respond quickly to users' changing physical needs without having to face the long delays associated with referral to the community disability team.

Social work assessors

The regular presence of the social work assessors in GP surgeries created favourable conditions for making preventive interventions, building trust between professionals and developing wider partnerships in the community.

Preventive interventions

The social work assessors were able to engage in preventive interventions by offering realistic alternatives to residential care or hospital admission. Direct access to the primary care team enabled assessors to build greater knowledge of vulnerable users and to act quickly and appropriately in a crisis. They made increased use of respite care facilities to allow time for considered planning of alternatives and so avoided assumptions that admission to residential care was irrevocable.

Building trust and confidence between health and social services staff

Improved communication, the development of trust and greater clarity about respective roles led to a greater number of referrals, as well as to more appropriate referrals from members of the primary health-care team, and encouraged feedback. Having a named assessor for each practice transformed the view of one GP who described previous experiences of referral to social services as consisting of: "a gamut of phone numbers and then getting the wrong department". It had not been uncommon for older people to be admitted to hospital as a 'place of safety', the result of GPs not having sufficient confidence in the capacity of social services to respond quickly and appropriately. This new opportunity to talk through complex cases 'reduced the faceless side of it', and feedback following referral ensured that the community health practitioners did not 'lose the thread'.

Developing wider partnerships

New ways of working developed not only between social work assessors and members of the primary care teams but also with other community-based resources, including the carers' centre and a neighbourhood care scheme. The development of wider partnerships in the community strengthened the network of resources that could be called upon to support older people in their own homes.

Reviewing officers

User accounts of their experiences following discharge from hospital revealed the high value placed on the consistency and continuity offered by being linked to a single reviewing officer. The reviewing officers themselves felt that their role in influencing outcomes had been facilitated through a commitment to empowering, anti-ageist practice.

Promoting empowering practice

The ethos of the project supported by a strong team identity encouraged the reviewing officers to practice in ways that were explicitly empowering. Users were supported in expressing and realising their wishes, but where these could not be achieved, specific attention was paid to ensuring that service users remained in control of the decision-making process. This was particularly important in cases where the possibility of living at home was threatened. As Titley has argued, "many older people are frightened to ask questions at a time when they feel vulnerable, and certainly find it difficult to challenge decisions that they feel may be wrong" (Titley, 1997, p 2).

Promoting anti-ageist practice

More generally, reviewing officers expressed the view that working in the JCC team had offered them opportunities for positive anti-ageist practice, facilitating user participation and choice in decision making. They also felt that they were able to combine resources in establishing imaginative and flexible packages of care to meet user and carer needs. One reviewing officer described her experience as having been able to:

"... work in creative, more imaginative ways than usually is on offer ...
a really good opportunity for getting together new ways of working
with elderly people and improving practice in areas where people were
quite discriminated against."

Demonstrating value for money

The achievements of the reviewing officers were widely acknowledged
as representing value for money. They supported a significant number of
older people to return to their own homes from residential and nursing
homes, and succeeded in reducing the overall costs of care packages. This
demonstration of economic efficiency led to relaxation of the constraints
imposed on the provision of community-based services as a result of
general budget cuts. The reviewing officers were, therefore, able to continue
providing care packages in a flexible way, adjusting the type and amount
of services in response to the needs of service users and their carers.

The social work assessors placed in GP surgeries had less success in
demonstrating the same economic efficiency. This was largely because
the majority of users with whom they were working were living in the
community and service inputs were aimed at preventing hospital admission.
The costs of providing services in these cases fell to social services, while
preventing hospital admission represented a saving to the health service.
A clear lesson from the JCC project was that short-term investment in
supporting older people in their own homes can lead to longer-term
gains, although this message is easily blurred when costs and savings are
attributed to single organisations rather than being treated as a whole.

Promoting positive outcomes through inclusive partnerships

The JCC project demonstrated the capacity of vulnerable older people
to take an active and effective role in identifying preferred and feasible
forms of support. It also demonstrated the importance of recognising
and responding to the distinctive needs of carers. Two clear sets of factors
contributed to the achievement of choice for older people and their
maintenance in the community. One was concerned with processes of
support, the second with organisational issues.

Processes of support

Positive outcomes were associated with high levels of quality in carrying out the tasks of care management in which flexible packages of care were tailored to the changing needs of users and carers. This process was aided by a strong commitment to anti-ageist practice, embracing principles of user involvement and empowerment. Project workers operated on the basis of proactive interventions so that relationships with users, carers, and practitioners of other agencies were established before crises developed. This transformed notions of user and carer choice from rhetoric to reality.

Speedy access to rehabilitation services also transformed the ability of JCC workers to achieve the project objectives. The inclusion of an occupational therapist and a physiotherapist in the JCC team demonstrated an understanding of the importance of preserving or restoring mobility and daily living skills to avoid premature admission to long-term institutional care (Audit Commission, 2000; le Mesurier and Cumella, 1999). Their presence provided the appropriate skill mix required by many older people with complex health and social care needs.

Organisational issues

Central policy direction reflects the need to promote organisational collaboration both through incentives and through structural arrangements such as pooled budgets and integrated service provision (DoH, 1998b). The nature and importance of organisational collaboration in the JCC project is discussed at length in Chapter Six. But it is important to recognise that the achievement of positive outcomes for users was influenced both positively and negatively by the varying collaborative capabilities of individuals at different levels within, and between, organisations. In working to establish inclusive partnerships with users and carers it is vital to understand how different actors may be affected by different arrangements, and how and why certain collaborative gates are opened while others remain firmly closed. Influencing factors include the location of specialist practitioners within organisations, the status of special projects set up to develop innovative forms of working, the boundaries between partner agencies, and the collaborative capability of partner agencies.

Extending partnerships with older people to avoid unnecessary dependency

The early parts of this chapter considered four sources of influence on the development of partnerships: legislation and policy, differences in professional values, professional commitment, or resistance, to the active involvement of service users and carers, and the tendency to treat service users and carers as a single constituency of interest.

The JCC project illustrated the countervailing effects of legislation and central government policy. Government financial incentives to develop partnerships between health and social services were exploited to create the JCC project. At the same time, the aims of the project were threatened by the limiting effects of community care legislation that has marginalised the role of housing in supporting older people in the community. The promotion of carers' interests at central level was seen as instrumental to the development of inclusive partnerships through the establishment of carers' centres that focused specifically on carers' needs. Privatisation policies presented yet another constraint to the development of inclusive partnerships. Managers of private home care agencies obliged their workers to cut corners as they sought to reduce costs in the face of externally imposed financial pressures. And owners of private care homes showed initial resistance to intensive rehabilitation input for older people wishing to regain mobility and function in order to be able to return to their own homes.

Interprofessional differences between health and social services were minimised as the professional stakeholders of the JCC project focused on agreed goals, and trusting relationships were developed between GPs, community health, and social services practitioners. The common base for social work assessors, reviewing officers and the occupational therapist and physiotherapist added to a sense of common purpose, although tensions became more apparent among hospital and community social work teams who perceived the JCC project as a protected, elitist team.

Combating the barrier to partnership created by treating older people as 'welfare subjects' was a clear focus of the JCC project that adhered closely to the principles of user choice and user involvement. Evidence from the evaluation indicated that service users, carers and professionals all believed that this barrier was being successfully dismantled. So, too, was the barrier created by failing to recognise the different interests of service users and carers. This was successfully tackled by ensuring that carers received their own sources of support.

Moving from gesture involvement to genuine partnership

The very real difficulties in attaining genuinely inclusive partnerships demand a clear reminder that the value of working in partnership lies in achieving improved outcomes for service users and carers. But moving effectively from gesture involvement to achieve genuine inclusive partnerships is contingent upon a number of conditions.

Shared vision of improved outcomes

Goss and Miller (1995) have argued that the achievement of user- and carer-centred community care is associated with a clear understanding that involving users and carers is linked to improvements in outcomes, not merely processes. Changes in processes are vital, but changes in relationships between actors must be centred on users, carers *and* professional staff, not only between professionals. Relationships within partnerships must be based on a spirit of mutuality, shared risk and interdependence that focuses on the distinctive contributions of each partner. And commitment of individual actors must be matched by an organisational culture of 'listening', involving users and carers, and developing capability for collaboration, flexibility and creativity in order to maximise the opportunities for improving outcomes.

Collective action

Despite the policy rhetoric surrounding user and carer involvement, reality indicates the continuing marginalisation and isolation of service users and carers. One way of creating genuine partnerships is through the development of arrangements in which users and carers can make effective use of central policy messages to bring pressure to bear on their health and local authorities to implement policy and so bring about improvements in their lives. Collectives of current, potential, or past users and carers are one way of harnessing policy rhetoric and turning it into reality. This may be through involvement in planning and other social services and health forums, while independent, non-profit organisations represent another source of potential for advocacy and collective action.

Casting the partnership net wide

There is a clear acknowledgement that the process of empowerment requires active listening rather than making assumptions about users' and carers' wishes. Empowerment also depends upon respect for users' and carers' views, and their involvement in decision making at all levels. But it is unlikely that improvements in professional practice will be sustained in the absence of clear systems of accountability.

Partnership in action (DoH, 1998b) stressed the importance of shared information and incentives to encourage joint working and the need to introduce effective measures for monitoring and reviewing joint working. Current models of organisational accountability are commonly cited as creating tension and stress in workers whose personal and professional values are in conflict with organisational goals, and procedures that are shaped by resource constraints (Phillips and Penhale, 1996, p 48). Clearly there are trade-offs between the creation of narrow partnerships that are easier to implement, monitor and evaluate, and the creation of broader, more inclusive partnerships to ensure that the principle of user choice is complemented by a wide set of support services. Means and colleagues have done much to emphasise the central role of housing in developing partnerships and joint working to maintain or improve the quality of older people's lives (Means, 1996; Means et al, 1997). And Wilson and Charlton (1997) stress the importance of widening partnerships to include private, voluntary and community sectors and investing in the development of shared understanding between them.

Conclusion

As we have seen, the achievement of inclusive partnerships is often compromised by a lack of appropriate skills or a lack of ideological commitment to partnership ideals that involve a willingness to share power. As Thompson (1998, p 317) has argued, "working in partnership is a skilled activity. It involves communication, assertiveness and negotiation skills so that the possibilities for effective collaboration can be maximised". If genuine partnerships are so difficult to achieve it is vital we continue to remind ourselves of the logic of the partnership ideal, a logic that lies in the potential to achieve improved outcomes through changing and improving processes. The overwhelming message is that successful partnerships depend upon moving away from paternalistic, disempowering models of practice in which service users are viewed as subjects of welfare systems, to models in which users and carers are active participants, supported rather than controlled by welfare professionals.

References

Age Concern (1999) *Turning your back on us: Older people and the NHS*, London: Age Concern.

Audit Commission (1998) *Home alone: The role of housing in community care*, London: Audit Commission.

Audit Commission (2000) *The way to go home: Rehabilitation and remedial services for older people*, London: Audit Commission.

Balloch, S., Butt, J., Fisher, M. and Lindow, V. (1999) *Rights, needs and the user perspective: A review of the National Health Service and Community Care Act*, London: National Institute for Social Work.

Bebbington, A. and Charnley, H. (1990) 'Health and social care for the elderly: rhetoric and reality', *British Journal of Social Work*, vol 20, pp 409-32.

Cabinet Office (1998) *Better government for older people*, London: Cabinet Office.

Charnley, H., Kocher, P., Prentice, S. and Williamson, V. (1999) *Evaluation of a Joint Continuing Care Project*, Brighton: Health and Social Policy Research Centre, University of Brighton.

Clark, H. (2000) *Help not care: Extending the philosophy of independent living to older people*, York: Joseph Rowntree Foundation.

DoH (Department of Health) (1995) *Building partnerships for success*, London: HMSO.

DoH (1997) *A new partnership for care in old age*, Cm 3563, London: The Stationery Office.

DoH (1998a) *Modernising social services: Promoting independence, improving protection, raising standards*, Cm 4169, London: The Stationery Office.

DoH (1998b) *Partnership in action (new opportunities for joint working between health and social services)*, London: The Stationery Office.

DoH (1999) *The Health Act*, London: The Stationery Office.

DoH (2000) *The NHS Plan:The Government's response to the Royal Commission on Long Term Care*, Cm 4818-II, London:The Stationery Office.

Goss, S. and Miller, C. (1995) *From margin to mainstream: Developing user and carer-centred community care*, York: Joseph Rowntree Foundation.

Harding, T. (1997) *A life worth living: The independence and inclusion of older people*, London: Help the Aged.

Henwood, M. and Wistow, G. (1993) *Hospital discharge and community care: Early days*, London: SSI/DoH and Nuffield Institute for Health.

le Mesurier, N. and Cumella, S. (1999) 'Enhancing independence: the effectiveness of re-ablement provision in South Worcestershire', *Managing Community Care*, vol 7, no 4, pp 27-32.

Littlechild, R. and Blakeney, J. (1996) 'Risk and older people', in H. Kemshall and J. Pritchard (eds) *Good practice in risk assessment and risk management*, London: Jessica Kingsley, pp 68-79.

Means, R. (1996) 'Housing and community care for older people – joint working at the local level', *Journal of Interprofessional Care*, vol 10, no 3, pp 273-83.

Means, R., Brenton, M., Harrison, L. and Heywood, F. (1997) *Making partnerships work in community care:A guide for practitioners in housing, health and community care*, Bristol:The Policy Press.

Morris, J. (1994) *The shape of things to come? User-led social services*, London: National Institute for Social Work.

Morris, J. (1997) *Community care: Working in partnership with service users*, Birmingham:Venture Press.

Nocon, A. and Qureshi, H. (1996) *Outcomes of community care for users and carers*, Buckingham: Open University Press.

Parker, G. and Clarke, H. (1998) 'Paying for long-term care in the UK: policy, theory and evidence', in P. Taylor Gooby (ed) *Choice and public policy: The limits to welfare markets*, London: Macmillan.

Phillips, J. and Penhale, B. (1996) 'Developing care management', in J. Phillips and B. Penhale (eds) *Reviewing care management for older people*, London: Jessica Kingsley, pp 134-40.

Qureshi, H., Patmore, C., Nicholas, E. and Bamford, C. (1998) *Outcomes of social care for older people and carers*, York: Social Policy Research Unit, University of York.

Servian, R. (1996) *Theorising empowerment: Individual power and community care*, Bristol: The Policy Press.

Shakespeare, T. (2000) 'The social relations of care', in G. Lewis, S. Gewirtz and J. Clarke (eds) *Rethinking social policy*, London: Sage Publications, pp 52-65.

SSI (Social Services Inspectorate) (1999) *A matter of chance for carers? Inspection of local authority support for carers*, London: DoH.

Stanley, D., Reed, J. and Brown, S. (1999) 'Older people, care management and interprofessional practice', *Journal of Interprofessional Care*, vol 13, no 3, pp 229-37.

Statham, D. (2000) 'Guest editorial: partnership between health and social care', *Health and Social Care in the Community*, vol 8, no 2, pp 87-9.

Sutherland, S. (1999) *With respect to old age: Long term care – Rights and responsibilities: A Report by the Royal Commission on Long-Term Care*, London: The Stationery Office.

Thompson, N. (1998) 'Social work with adults', in R. Adams, L. Dominelli and M. Payne (eds) *Social work: Themes, issues and critical debates*, Basingstoke: Macmillan.

Titley, S. (1997) *Health care rights for older people: The Ageism Issue*, London: Age Concern/Nursing Times.

Twigg, J. and Atkin, K. (1994) *Carers perceived: Policy and practice in informal care*, Buckingham: Open University Press.

Wilmot. S. (1995) 'Professional values and interprofessional dialogue', *Journal of Interprofessional Care*, vol 9, no 3, pp 257-66.

Wilson, A. and Charlton, K. (1997) *Making partnerships work: A practical guide for the public, private, voluntary and community sectors*, York: Joseph Rowntree Foundation.

EIGHT

Partnership between service users and statutory social services

Michael Turner and Susan Balloch

Introduction

Central government's emphasis on best value, in conjunction with partnership working and social inclusion, requires that social services departments should work more closely with service users in planning, developing, evaluating and monitoring services and their outcomes. As illustrated in other chapters, this partnership is developing in a broader context than previously, allowing for much closer working relations between social services, health and housing. While acknowledging the broader context, this chapter focuses specifically on the progress in partnership working that has been made between service users and social services departments.

The chapter considers some of the strategies being developed to achieve user involvement, albeit patchily, around the country. These include far-reaching initiatives such as funding service users to provide their own services, either as a group or through direct payments, and more limited consultation processes such as needs audits, questionnaires to citizens' panels, postal surveys and focus groups. It discusses the extent to which professionals are prepared to share responsibility for service delivery, acknowledge users' expertise, and empower disabled people, older people, users and survivors of mental health services, people with learning difficulties and other service users, by providing the time and necessary support for their fuller involvement in decision making.

In discussing user involvement, a distinction is regularly drawn between the consumerist approach, by which best value is characterised, and user-led self-advocacy (Beresford and Croft, 1993). In the former the service users' role is limited to consultation on service planning and delivery while in the latter, far more radical, approach users seek both to change services and develop new services where the old ones are inappropriate. These approaches lead to very different conceptualisations of partnership, with the balance of power firmly held by professional purchasers and providers in the first but tipped more in favour of service users in the second.

The dichotomy is apparent even within the definition of a service user as someone who uses services. Forbes and Sashidharan (1997) suggest that such a definition is "only possible when services are presented as non-problematic commodities available in the market place, with users as consumers able to purchase and consume these commodities with a free choice". In reality, the term is problematic and complex. At its simplest level the term 'service user' can describe anyone who is assessed as in need and therefore eligible for a service, or legally obliged to receive a service to protect themselves or others. In many instances, however, the term is used more widely to encompass a broader range of disabled people, older people, people with learning difficulties and users and survivors of mental health services who, while not necessarily actually using services, do have a common experience of discrimination and a need for support or assistance. Many such people will have needs that social care services are not able to meet. They may even have opted out of the system – for example, paying for a cleaner rather than attempting to secure increasingly scarce and expensive local authority domiciliary help. In this chapter, the term service user will be employed with these caveats in mind.

The chapter looks first at examples of progress made towards user involvement and empowerment that support a more balanced partnership of equals, then at the development of direct payments, and finally at the significance of developing user defined outcomes. We will be conceptualising user involvement and empowerment on a continuum, ranging from consultation with service users to decision taking by service users on issues affecting their individual and collective well-being. David Byrne, in Chapter Twelve, sees empowerment as primarily a collective issue. We would argue, in the context of current social services policy and practice, that it is of both personal and collective importance.

Progress in partnership

A decade after the passing of the 1990 NHS and Community Care Act, even allowing for the three years it took to be implemented, there seems to have been slow progress towards user involvement in planning and delivery of services. The Caring for People White Paper that preceded the Act had explicitly addressed user involvement and outcomes in suggesting that the community care reforms would:

- enable people to live as normal a life as possible;
- help people achieve maximum possible independence;
- give people a greater say in how they live their lives and the services they need to help them do so.

But the 1998 White Paper on social services noted:

> Service users and carers often play little or no part in shaping services. Attempts at consultation can often turn out to be public relations exercises rather than genuine attempts to listen to what people want and their views of services. Genuine consultation can not only make services more responsive but also increase public confidence and trust in the services. (p 29)

Users' assessments of the situation have been even bleaker. User consultant Viv Lindow (Lindow, 1999) has concluded:

> Since there are now detailed coherent guidelines for involvement produced by service users and others, there is no excuse for the continuing failure in community care generally to involve people equally and effectively. We know how to do it properly. (p 33)

The point has also been made that,

> Against the background of cuts in services, charges for services, rationing of services, and changes to criteria for who does and does not receive service, it is almost possible to say that user involvement has continued in spite of rather than because of community care. (OVIOF, 1998, p 18)

Taking user involvement and empowerment seriously requires agencies to work in partnership with those for whom they provide services. For the majority of professionals and front-line staff with traditional training this is often a threatening and confusing experience. As noted in the Introduction, professionals may support a 'zero-sum' conception of power, in which relinquishing even partial control to an individual or group inevitably means a loss of power to the other. Meanwhile, mental health service users and survivors, who already experience a medicalised approach to many of their support needs, are particularly threatened by proposals for compulsory treatment. These are clearly contrary to user empowerment and will further disempower this group of service users.

Despite the gloomy overall picture of user involvement, there are pockets of good practice that point to a way forward. Examples include the Wiltshire and Swindon Users' Network, Surrey Users' Network and other local groups that represent service users who are resourced by their local authority and engaged in a genuine dialogue.

The Wiltshire and Swindon Users' Network

The Wiltshire and Swindon Users' Network provides a good model of how user controlled organisations can develop and best be supported. The network began after the first consultations took place on the county's first Community Care Development Plan in 1991. Participants at the meeting wanted a regular forum to discuss their concerns and to be proactive in pushing for user involvement. The network started work properly in 1993 with funding from the county council and a service agreement of, "providing a network of support for service users in Wiltshire and facilitating direct links between service users and the Social Services Department" (Evans, 1996). Further funding was obtained from Wiltshire Health Authority and through joint financing for particular projects such as advocacy and information. In 2000 the network had over 700 members; 30 staff and a turnover of around £500,000.

The core activities of this network are to promote a membership organisation of service users from all perspectives to be involved in the planning, delivery and evaluation of services and a further service agreement to employ development workers to reach out to other users to provide a safe place for them to become involved. This led to groups of older people and mental health service users coming together to monitor services in various ways. In addition the network received £20,000 to carry out user-controlled research into the Wiltshire Independent Living Fund (Wiltshire Users' Network, 1996). Building on its strong position on influencing social services and with strong allies within social services senior management, it obtained funding from the Joseph Rowntree Foundation to carry out a user-controlled best value review of Wiltshire direct payments scheme. Disabled people facilitated by a disabled researcher designed the processes to make up the review.

The Wiltshire Users' Network is a good example of collective empowerment and the work carried out by older people through it has since been held up as a model for involving users in evaluating services. The project, like the network itself, was based firmly in a community development approach. It involved making contacts with groups of older people wherever they existed, and building up others where there were none. These groups then met to discuss issues of concern to the participants, which meant, as other user-led evaluations have found, that the net was cast much more widely than immediate service provision. It meant that issues as diverse as community safety, the quality of pavements, the positioning of postboxes and reduced TV licenses were discussed, with the result of developing more integrated planning between health, social care and other service providers (Wiltshire and Swindon Users' Network, 1997).

The across-the-board approach illustrated by the Wiltshire and Swindon Users' Network is comparatively rare. In most areas user groups represent specific groups of users, for example, disabled people, older people, people with learning difficulties, and mental health service users/survivors, and, in some areas, young people in care, and in even fewer, drug and alcohol service users. However, in many areas there will be joint work and cooperation between different users groups and the wider voluntary sector.

There is evidence of growing recognition of the value of joint working amongst user organisations. For example, the Greater London Action on Disability (GLAD) set up a project called 'Common Agenda' in 1998 to build links on issues of joint concern to disabled people and mental health service users/survivors.

In many areas the process remains very difficult. Lack of funding is a problem for an ever increasing number of user organisations as local authorities cut back their funding to voluntary groups, despite the argument that user involvement can play a key part in ensuring that resources put into services are spent on services that people want. Beyond the resources issue remain questions about just how far service providers have gone, and are prepared to go, in empowering service users and their organisations. A small-scale survey of user groups' experiences of user involvement, Shaping Our Lives (see below), carried out for the Our Voice in Our Future project, found considerable experience of tokenistic consultation, where users felt they had taken part in cosmetic exercises in which there was no intention to change policies or practices.

Problems also remain around getting the process of user involvement right, despite the extensive learning that has taken place and the guidance that is available. A good example of a well-intentioned effort to develop user involvement which went wrong took place in Sheffield during the mid-1990s. The Sheffield Users' Network was set up following a decision by the joint commissioning committee (JCC) for health and social services to make funding for a user group a priority in late 1995. The network started formally in January 1997 but only worked until May of that year when the organisation was dissolved. A review of its failure (Knights and Midgley, 1998) found that a key issue had been that officers for health and social services went straight into discussion with existing groups and interested parties in the voluntary and statutory sectors to develop a funding application that would meet the requirements of the JCC. This meant that the network did not grow from the grassroots but was, in effect, forced into existence and made to grow too quickly in order to meet the needs of the authorities. This led to a range of problems for the organisation, with the people involved being put into situations with which they were not ready to deal.

The review noted that:

> From the information received from other users' networks, projects in this area that are initiated by statutory services do not work ... although support from the statutory services for their development was crucial, the initiative itself, in terms of its aims, objectives and development time had to be user initiated and user controlled to be successful. (Knights and Midgley, 1998, pp 18-19)

Direct payments

At first sight direct payments might seem to have little to do with partnership between service users and service providers. Jenny Morris has noted that direct payments only developed because traditional social services were failing to deliver the type of support that disabled people wanted (Morris, 1997), and many local authorities actually opposed the passage of the 1996 Community Care (Direct Payments) Act, which made it legal for social services to make payments in lieu of services. While this suggests that direct payments are simply about service users taking control and leaving service providers without a role, the reality is that partnership remains as important for direct payments as it is for traditional services.

The Act legalised direct payments to service users – mainly adults with physical impairments under the age of 65 – who wished to purchase their own support from agencies or employ their own personal assistants, a practice already under way in a few areas. A group of disabled people living in a residential home in the 1980s successfully persuaded Hampshire County Council to establish a direct payments scheme, with the payments being channelled through a third party voluntary organisation. Similar schemes were established in a few other areas, making it clear that some authorities were keen to pursue direct payments as part of their dialogue with service users.

The Act enables all authorities to make direct payments and removed the need to involve third party voluntary organisations. Social services departments still have a key role in direct payments, with the legislation requiring users to undergo the same community care assessments as other service users, specific assessments relating to the receipt of direct payments and monitoring of payments.

Far from removing partnership between service users and service providers, direct payments have redefined the partnership and could well be said to have made it more equitable. The partnership remains dependent on the willingness of both sides to participate. One of the limits service users have seen in the legislation is that it is enabling legislation and does not give users any rights to payments.

Reluctance to introduce direct payments

Many local authorities have been slow and reluctant to introduce direct payments. A survey of local authorities' introduction of such schemes by Hasler and Zarb (2000) found widespread but far from universal willingness to make payments available. Fifty per cent of authorities had schemes in operation at the time of the survey (July 1997), with wide regional variations; fewer authorities in the north of England, Wales and Northern Ireland having schemes than those in London, the Southwest and Scotland. In September 2000 the Department of Health estimated that 2,500 people in the United Kingdom were receiving direct payments, of whom only a tiny minority were thought to be those with learning difficulties and mental health service users (Revans, 2000).

At the time of Hasler and Zarb's survey a further 30% of authorities had plans to introduce schemes. If these plans were implemented around 80% of authorities would be offering direct payments, but the indications were that there was still a considerable delay in their introduction in some areas. There was also concern that in some areas the payments were only being made available to a very small number of users.

In their assessment of good practice in the implementation of direct payments, Hasler and Zarb identify the need to build partnerships between local authorities and organisations of disabled people as crucial. They point out that independent living should involve a fundamental change in the assessment for and delivery of services. In some – perhaps many – areas what is called independent living by service providers does not equate with the definition of independent living (often with a capital 'I' and a capital 'L') that has been developed by the disability movement. This definition involves disabled people having control over the support that they need and this cannot be achieved without a true partnership between service users and providers. Hasler and Zarb say that such partnerships need to be flexible, responsive, open and honest, and stress the need for recognition of the uneven power distribution between local authorities and disabled people.

The other key factor that Hasler and Zarb point to in areas where direct payments schemes have been successfully established is the provision of a support service for the scheme. Such support plays an important role in providing recipients of direct payments with support and training for employing their own staff and dealing with problems such as personal affairs, assistants being ill or on holiday.

Where direct payments have proved successful there is growing evidence of widespread benefits. Zarb (in Turner, 1998) begins to develop the argument that in addition to the benefits of direct payments from a perspective of civil rights and social justice, there is a case to be made for the economic benefits of direct payments. He refers to a number of studies that have shown that direct payments packages work out as much as 30% to 40% cheaper than traditional services and that people value the support that they receive through direct payments, particularly in terms of their flexibility and reliability. However, further research is needed to develop a cost-benefit analysis of direct payments that could take account of users becoming economically active, reduced demands on health and social services, and savings on social security benefits.

Savings in relation to health services have already been identified. Glendinning et al (2000) found that people receiving direct payments used their personal assistants to carry out a range of health-related tasks, giving them greater control over the process and generating savings for the health service. This makes a case for more joint funding of direct payments by health and social services, particularly where users need high levels of support.

Measuring the benefits of direct payments is at an early stage and more work is needed to develop a body of evidence on this issue. This evidence should grow as direct payments themselves become more widespread. While some local authorities do seem to remain reluctant, central government is strongly committed to the idea. This commitment has passed from the Conservative government, which passed the legislation in 1996, to the Labour government, which has extended the availability of direct payments to older people, people with learning difficulties and, most recently (summer 2000), to parents and carers of disabled children. The idea even seems to be gaining credence beyond the disability field, with plans for young people leaving the care system to receive some form of bursary.

User-defined outcomes

User-defined outcomes are central to user empowerment. As one service user has written:

> Empowerment for me then is about being in control of my life, and able to influence others. This definition involves both the individual and the opportunity as a citizen to be part of society collectively, and being able to influence decisions that society makes. Thus I want to define the outcomes of my life, and have the services that I need provided in a way which will enable me to achieve these outcomes. (Evans, 1998, p 25)

Nocon and Qureshi (1996) have provided a succinct overview and evaluation of the various measures that have been developed in relation to different types of social service users – disabled people, older people, people with learning difficulties and users/survivors of mental health services – and how these can be applied to social care. Many of these measures were initially developed to examine outcomes of medical services, and what emerges most clearly from Nocon and Qureshi's survey is that most of these measures remain rooted in a medical model. They also argue that existing statistical measures that cover issues such as mortality, or the number of people receiving domiciliary care or entering residential homes, say very little about the quality of outcome. They conclude that much more work is needed to produce effective outcome measures and that service users should be central to this.

The Shaping Our Lives project

Putting service users at the centre of the debates and discussions about outcomes was the purpose of a user-led project called Shaping Our Lives, set up in 1996 within the National Institute for Social Work with funding from the Department of Health. This project emerged from earlier discussions about standards in the process of service provision (Harding and Beresford, 1996), which had established that there was a surprising degree of consensus among service users about desired service outcomes and the need to develop user perspectives on outcomes in greater detail.

The Shaping Our Lives team spent two years looking at users' perspectives on outcomes, working with service users in a series of focus group meetings. The second phase involved the establishment of a panel representing a range of service users that met three times. The first phase of the project produced very clear evidence of the user perspective on outcomes. Users recognised the value of assessing services in terms of their outcomes and saw it as essential that users' views were primary in such assessment. Putting users first in evaluating outcomes meant working with the subjective perspectives of individual users. Although there was recognition that such work could be supported by objective measures – for example, a mental health service user suggested that effective services could be measured by reduced expenditure on drug treatment – there was also a clear view that experience of outcomes was subjective and that a way had to be found of taking this into account.

In working with users, the project found that some people had initial difficulty with the idea of looking at services in terms of outcomes or results. This was not because the issue of outcomes was beyond service users but because, in circumstances where services were inadequate and/or poorly provided, it was very difficult to determine any outcome from the user's perspective. In these circumstances some users actually experienced negative outcomes, a concept foreign to some service providers. Service users who consistently found it easier to identify outcomes were the recipients of direct payments, who were readily able to talk about the flexibility, control and independence that had resulted from using these to purchase their own services rather than relying on traditional forms of service provision.

The Shaping Our Lives project emphasised two key points about the nature of outcomes that have wide-ranging implications for the way in which issues around quality and best value are approached. Firstly, while academics and professionals tended to talk about outcomes solely in terms of the end result of a service, service users did not divorce the end product from the way in which a service was delivered. The process of service provision has a major impact on the experience of a service; it encompasses difficulties such as limited access to services, delays in service provision, poor treatment from service providers, lack of consultation, consultation which is ignored or not acted upon, and a political climate in which users are literally waiting for their services to be cut back or for charges for services to be increased beyond their means (Frazer and Glick, 2000). Such experiences have an impact on the outcome of the service and should not be treated separately.

Secondly, adopting a user perspective on outcomes means adopting the holistic perspective discussed by Peter Ambrose in Chapter One. When users think about outcomes they look at their lives as a whole and include the interface of issues such as housing, transport, employment, income and benefits, discrimination and rights, as crucial to their quality of life. Ultimately, therefore, evaluation based on outcomes should not relate to specific services, but to the overall effect of a package of services. The implications for interagency working are clear. With funding from the Joseph Rowntree Foundation, the Shaping Our Lives project has begun to translate this thinking into practice with a programme of four development projects that will work with users on outcomes over an extended period of time.

Outcomes of domiciliary care

Similar research has explored the outcomes that older people and their carers want from domiciliary care services (Henwood et al, 1998). This identified eight main components of quality: continuity, reliability, flexibility, staff attitudes, staff characteristics, training, information and communication. The research illustrated the importance of process in the delivery of home care, in particular how much users disliked seeing their home carers under such pressure of time that they were unable to offer the personal attention and empathy that was highly valued. The authors argued that the quality standards they have defined are measurable and provide a bridge between quantitative indicators which fail to measure quality and process, and qualitative indicators that are individualised and subjective.

Personal Social Services user experience survey

Little of this understanding is reflected in the Department of Health's user experience survey, which represents an effort to encourage social services departments to develop nationally comparable user satisfaction surveys (DoH, 2000a). It requires each local authority to survey individuals assessed for the first time during November 2000 and who went on to receive services, with the survey carried out two to three months after first assessment. It describes this as a first step towards an incremental approach in the future, "improving guidance, broadening the questions and expanding to cover all users and carers and client groups".

There are, however, a number of well-rehearsed problems in retrieving valid information from such satisfaction surveys. Many who receive minimal services are loath to criticise these for fear of losing what they receive; others, often unaware that they have been assessed, will remain uncertain about the nature of the services to which the assessment has judged them to be entitled (Chetwynd and Ritchie, 1996). For those with communication difficulties, completing forms handed out at first reviews or posted to them will require help from proxies. Though the Department of Health recognises this and comments that "communication difficulties may be at the heart of a slower response to meeting the needs of certain groups", it has not yet offered a constructive approach to finding a resolution, such as paying for interviewers skilled in listening to people with learning disabilities, frail elderly people, those with dementia or sensory impairments. The advice that "ultimately the only way to get a response from some users may be for the form to be completed by the person doing the review" is scarcely going to elicit independent comment.

The central problem with all this, as discussed earlier, is that the proposed survey is encompassed within a 'top-down' system of measurement that only enables service users as consumers to comment on available services. It does not enable service users to affect those policy or planning decisions on which good outcomes, as they would define them, depend, nor can it reach the thousands excluded from services. It is not a problem confined to social services but to all public services required to develop user satisfaction performance indicators under the Best Value initiative. But it is a particularly difficult problem in social services, where the services provided may be crucial to the independence of very vulnerable individuals with complex needs.

Conclusion

As reflected in this chapter, the extent to which users of social services have been sufficiently empowered to work in partnership with professionals is limited. Encouraging developments in the growth of users' networks, the extension of direct payments and the involvement of users in defining outcomes have come up against many difficulties. These include the reluctance of local authorities and professionals to share decision making, tokenistic gestures in the direction of user empowerment that fall far short of power sharing and the temptation to rely on carers and proxies to understand what users want.

Some users would go so far as to say that the word 'partnership' has become discredited and now speak in terms of alliances, with managers/ service providers working as users' allies, when defining good practice. This is in keeping with the concept of participative or facilitating management popular in management development courses, though imperfectly understood and practised by social care agencies.

These alliances may become stronger and more widespread with the increasing impetus of user involvement and empowerment evident in the establishment of the Disability Rights Commission and the implementation of the 1998 Human Rights Act. The proposed General Social Care Council also offers a major opportunity for enshrining the principle of user involvement, though it remains to be seen exactly how strong a role service users will have in this body.

While such developments are positive and promising, the immediate future is not without threat. The NHS Plan (DoH, 2000b) advises that in future it will be a requirement for the powers in the 1999 Health Act for pooled budgets, lead commissioning and integrated provision to be used in all areas. It is envisaged that there will be far greater joint working between social services, primary and community health care, often working from the same premises and with more joint assessments of patients.

Such proposals for health and social services to work more closely together promise some gains in improvements in services, but there is great concern among service user organisations that these gains may be offset by losses in relation to user involvement. While social services are far from perfect in their practice of user involvement, health services are even further behind and users are very worried that moves towards the new environment of Directorates of Health and Social Care will be a step backwards for user involvement and revert to a medicalised approach to social care. Thus the next few years will be crucial in the development of partnerships and alliances between service users and service providers and will show if these can become properly established in mainstream practice or remain a principle for which users must continue to fight.

References

Beresford, P. and Croft, S. (1993) *Citizen involvement: A practical guide for change*, Basingstoke: Macmillan.

Chetwynd, M., Ritchie, J. with Reith, L. and Howard, M. (1996) *The cost of care: The impact of charging policy on the lives of disabled people*, Bristol: The Policy Press.

DoH (Department of Health) (2000a) *PSS user experience survey: What needs doing for 2000-2001*, London: DoH, July.

DoH (2000b) *The NHS Plan*, London: The Stationery Office.

Evans, C. (1996) *From bobble hats to red jacket*, Devizes: Wiltshire and Swindon Users' Network.

Evans, C. (1998) 'User empowerment and direct payments', in S. Balloch (ed) *Outcomes of social care: A question of quality?*, London: National Institute for Social Work.

Forbes, J. and Sashidharan, SP. (1997) 'User involvement in services – incorporation or challenge?', *British Journal of Social Work*, vol 27, Issue 4, August, pp 481-98.

Frazer, R. and Glick, G. (2000) *Out of services: A survey of social service provision for elderly and disabled people in England*, London: Needs Must/RADAR (Royal Association for Disability and Rehabilitation).

Glendinning, C., Halliwell, S., Jacobs, S., Rummery, K. and Tyrer, J. (2000) *Buying independence: Using direct payments to integrate health and social services*, Bristol: The Policy Press.

Harding, T. and Beresford, P. (1996) *The standards we expect*, London: National Institute for Social Work.

Hasler, F. and Zarb, G. (2000) *Implementation of the Community Care (Direct Payments) Act – Findings*, York: Joseph Rowntree Foundation.

Henwood, M., Lewis, H. and Waddington, E. (1998) *Listening to users of domiciliary care services: Developing and monitoring quality standards*, Leeds: Nuffield Institute for Health.

Knights, D. and Midgley, R. (1998) *User involvement in community care – Where next in Sheffield?*, Sheffield: Sheffield University Press.

Lindow, V. (1999) 'Users' perspectives', in S. Balloch, J. Butt, M. Fisher and V. Lindow, *Rights, needs and the user perspective: A review of the National Health Service and Community Care Act 1990*, London: National Institute for Social Work for the Joseph Rowntree Foundation.

Morris, J. (1997) 'Care or empowerment? A disability rights perspective', *Social Policy and Administration*, vol 31, March, no1, pp 54-60.

Nocon, A. and Qureshi, H. (1996) *Outcomes of community care for users and carers*, Buckingham: Open University Press.

OVIOF (Our Voice in Our Future) (1998) *Services and support*, London: National Institute for Social Work.

Revans, L. (2000) 'Payments reform stalls', *Community Care*, 28 September–4 October, p 12.

Turner, M. (ed) (1998) 'Facing our futures', Conference report, London: National Centre for Independent Living.

Wiltshire and Swindon Users' Network (1997) *A guide to involving older people and their carers in the planning of local health and social care services: The Trowbridge Experience*, Devizes: Wiltshire and Swindon Users' Network.

Wiltshire Users' Network (1996) *I am in control*, Devizes: Wiltshire Users' Network.

NINE

Partnership working in health promotion: the potential role of social capital in health development

John Kenneth Davies

Partnerships for health will be required at different levels: international, country, regional and local. They are needed for the formulation of health policy; for increasing people's perception and understanding of health issues; for developing the potential will for action; for target-setting, carrying out policies and programmes and shaping service delivery, increasing the selection of priorities and resource allocation; and for monitoring and evaluation of outcomes. (WHO, 1999, p 156)

The aims of public health will best be achieved by agencies, organisations and individuals working together. Partnerships should be a tool for achieving an outcome and in order to achieve that outcome, there needs to be shared vision and agreement on what to do, by whom and when. (NHS Executive, 2000)

Introduction

Attempts to improve health and tackle health inequalities require new ways of working that depend on changes in working relationships and practices between all stakeholders involved in public health and health promotion. A central focus of these new working practices is partnership working as joint or interagency alliances across agencies and among communities. The development of these partnerships and networks lies at the heart of social capital production and relates to the role of social processes in health development. Active participation by people to mobilise their community resources and to involve themselves in decision-making processes, mechanisms and health improvement programmes is fundamental to building sustainable approaches to health promotion and tackling inequalities in health and well-being that are growing within and between societies:

> By capitalising upon and enhancing the value of social relationships and partnerships, social support and networks for the exchange of information, community based health promotion can help build the social resource called 'social capital' in communities, can reinforce efforts to repair the social fabric and foster cohesiveness. (Gillies and Spray, 1997, p 1)

Partnership working in the health field has grown in importance over the last 20 years. It currently constitutes one of the core principles that underpin contemporary and future developments in health and social care policy at local, national and international levels. Equal partnerships make health and social care more effective by making it more available and acceptable (Rifkin, 1990).

In this chapter, the current government's attempts in England to promote health and tackle inequality using a range of partnership initiatives will be reviewed, together with European strategies, some key issues will be highlighted for partnership working and social capital construction, and recommendations put forward to improve our understanding of the role of social processes in health development.

The English public health context

In order to understand the relevance of partnership working to social capital production and the promotion of health, we will explore its relevance in the context of contemporary English public health policy and comparative international developments.

Although the British population benefits generally from a high standard of living, which has improved radically over the past 50 years, it suffers from widening and increasing inequalities in health linked to socio-economic conditions related to income, education and employment. In addition, qualitative research has suggested that societies, such as the UK, which are highly unequal, have an unusually poor quality of social relations and lack social cohesion (Wilkinson, 1996).

The Labour government came into power in 1997 with a commitment to tackle health inequalities, and offered a 'third way' with regard to its policies on health. It borrowed many ideas from the previous Conservative administration and sought to bring in its own new initiatives. It has been suggested that the White Paper *The New NHS: Modern, dependable* (DoH, 1997) favoured 'bottom-up' approaches and a move towards partnership working, together with a desire for public consultation by persuading people that they are being empowered (Baker, 2000). The White Paper ushered in a number of new initiatives from the Department of Health that sought to embody the above principles – Health Improvement Programmes (HImPs), Health Action Zones (HAZs) and Healthy Living Centres (HLCs). All of these essentially required government to facilitate partnership working across agencies and sectors and with communities.

Health Improvement Programmes (HImPs)

Health Improvement Programmes (HImPs) constitute local health and healthcare strategies and are seen as the key way of carrying through the government's public health strategy at local level and meeting its relevant targets. The HImP establishes a framework for joint planning and coordination of action to improve the health of local people: "Its hallmark will be the way in which partners work together to deliver improvements in health" (ESBHHA, 1999).

HImPs reflect the new partnership culture towards integrated public services which is being encouraged by the government in order to raise the quality of services, improve health and reduce health inequalities. Each health authority was required to produce a three-year HImP by April 1999 that specified the health needs of their local population. They also had to specify how these needs would be met and how services should be developed to meet them, as well as the investment required. A HImP should be agreed between a number of partners, including local authorities, voluntary agencies, the NHS (the health authority, primary care groups/trusts, local NHS trusts), community health councils, and representatives from local community organisations and the public. All partners should share a common commitment to partnership working in order to understand and tackle the most important health issues in their local area.

The expectation is that HImPs will be led, coordinated and monitored by health authorities, even though a range of local 'partners' are involved in their development. In addition, *Partnerships in action* (DoH, 1998a) has proposed new mechanisms for partnership working to supersede statutory joint consultative committees. The HImP therefore requires creativity and flexibility in use and application of integrated budgets.

There is a clear expectation from government that local people should be involved in developing the HImP and should also be involved in the work of primary care groups and trusts. Even so, Baker (2000) believes that this will not necessarily increase public confidence in the NHS.

The HImP reflects the government's intention to move towards a new form of public sector partnership. This is set within the context of the local health economy, where the health authority provides the principal focus for strategic coordination of partnership action to improve health and provide effective and efficient service provision.

Health Action Zones (HAZs)

Health Action Zones (HAZs) have been established as "a framework for the NHS, local authorities and other partners to work together to achieve progress in addressing the causes of ill-health and reducing health inequalities" (DoH, 1999). Conceptually, HAZs reflect the settings approach to health promotion as reflected, for example, through the WHO Healthy Cities movement. They were established to facilitate effective partnership working to tackle local health issues and have a relatively longish life in governmental terms of seven years in the first instance. The first wave of HAZs was initiated in November 1998 and the second in April 1999.

In his review Baker (2000) regards HAZs as remaining "obscure in their uniqueness" and questions whether they offer any more than a specific multiagency model to integrate the delivery of health and social care services. It remains to be seen whether they will fulfil their aims of offering a local framework in deprived areas for tackling public health, linking with social and economic regeneration initiatives and restructuring major hospital building programmes. The problem remains that HAZs were launched prior to the White Paper *Saving lives: Our healthier nation* (DoH, 1999). The key question is whether HAZs specifically can bring about the destruction of the traditional barriers between the health service and local authorities and deliver opportunities for real and effective partnership working.

One of the problems faced by the local agencies involved in HAZ areas is whether HAZs and HImPs duplicate each other. In particular, the logistic problem arises of how to ensure that there is consistency of agreement about priorities reflected in local needs and investment plans with the various HImPs involved. For example, in the Merseyside HAZ there are four health authorities and five local authorities. The HAZ strategy needs to be reflected in the various HImPs involved, but all of the content of the HImPs need not be in the HAZ operational plan.

Healthy Living Centres (HLCs)

The basic idea of Healthy Living Centres (HLCs) originated in WHO's concept of primary health care, including the essential ingredient of public participation. A well-known example of this approach was the Peckham Pioneer Health Centre initiative, which was established in south London in the 1930s. HLCs are meant to act as a focus for health promotion and provide locally, community-based action to tackle inequalities in health.

The New Opportunities Fund, which was set up under the National Lottery in 1998, has allocated £300m to support the development of HLCs in the UK. The government plans to have HLCs covering one fifth of the population by 2002. They have a flexible format – they can be buildings or virtual centres, as long as they promote health, are targeted at deprived areas and tackle inequity. HLCs have to link clearly to HImPs and HAZ action plans, as appropriate, and have to demonstrate financial sustainability.

HImPs, HAZs and HLCs have different scope and coverage but share commonalities, primarily with regard to partnership working and the need to collaborate effectively with local people.

Saving lives: Our healthier nation

After issuing its Green Paper in 1998 (DoH, 1998b) the government, following a protracted consultation period, eventually issued its White Paper on Public Health *Saving lives: Our healthier nation* in July 1999 (DoH, 1999). It set out to emphasise the public health context of current government policy with its focus on a commitment to improve health and tackle inequalities in health. The White Paper proposed a national contract or tripartite agreement for health improvement between people, intervening agencies (employers, health authorities, schools, and so on) and the government. The government role is to establish a supportive climate for health improvement through a range of social and economic policies and also by placing requirements on statutory services, particularly the NHS. The public health strategy endorsed the views emanating from the Chief Medical Officer's *Project to strengthen the public health function* (DoH, 1998c), and supported the need for better multisectoral partnership working, with a central emphasis on community participation.

The English public health strategy also, and rather belatedly in light of the international developments discussed below, advocated a settings approach related to schools (children), workplaces (adults), and community (elderly people). Most health promotion takes place "within settings bounded by time and place that provide the social structure and context for planning, implementation, and evaluating interventions" (Green and Ottoson, 1999). Overall, to reach its goals in terms of health improvement, the strategy needs effective partnership working involving active participation by individuals, agencies and government.

The international context

In comparison with recent policy in the UK, the WHO, as long ago as the late 1970s/early 1980s, facilitated a series of initiatives at European and global levels that emphasised a new conception of public health and health promotion. The foundations of this process were based on the key principles and values of WHO's European *Health 21: Health for all in the 21st century* – participation, empowerment and equity in health (WHO, 1999). This new public health agenda reflected recognition of the limitations of biomedical, technical and individual behaviour change approaches alone being the basis for health promotion and disease prevention interventions (European Commission, 1999; DoH, 1999). A fundamental realisation dawned that many of the factors that influence health are beyond the control of the individual. Therefore a shift towards more comprehensive health promotion approaches, incorporating community-based models to influence the broader socio-economic and socio-ecological determinants of health, are being developed (DoH, 1999). Such approaches moved beyond a focus on physical capacities alone to incorporate social and personal resources, thereby expanding beyond the health-care sector and involving interagency partnerships for health with the active participation of local people.

The key sea-change in this policy shift was the increasing emphasis towards involving people themselves, as a right, in decisions about their own health and that of their families and local communities. This principle underpinned the *Ottawa Charter for Health Promotion*, which stressed the need for participation to empower people to improve their health: "People cannot achieve their fullest possible health potential unless they are able to take control of those things which determine their health" (WHO, 1986, p 1), and went on to define health promotion itself as: "The process of enabling people to increase control over, and to improve, their health". (WHO, 1986, p 1).

The active involvement of people themselves is fundamental to health promotion, which should involve "consumers and consumer ownership of the process" (Bracht and Rissel, 1999, p 86). This right to active participation by people is one of the three original Health for All values and has been endorsed more recently in *Health 21* (WHO, 1999, p 153) and stressed by the WHO executive board in its first *Resolution on health promotion*: "... people have to be at the centre of health promotion action and decision-making processes if they are to be effective" (WHO, 1998).

One of the four main strategies for action towards *Health 21*, which has been agreed by all member states of the WHO European Region including the UK, is the development of active partnerships for health, "a participatory health development process that involves relevant partners for health at home, school and work and at local community and country levels, and that promotes joint decision-making, implementation and accountability" (WHO, 1999, p 4).

Target 20 of *Health 21* specifically concerns mobilising partners for health: "By the year 2005, implementation of policies for health for all should engage individuals, groups and organisations throughout the public and private sectors, and civil society, in alliances and partnerships for health" (WHO, 1999, p 200).

WHO indicates that this can be achieved if existing partnerships for health (healthy cities, health-promoting schools and workplaces, and so on) are strengthened and new partnerships initiated at every level to create networks and alliances in order to empower people. It stresses that there are many potential players who are not fully recognised as partners for health development. Such partners are defined as "all those in society who, through their personal contribution as individuals or in their professional roles, can contribute to health improvement" (WHO, 1999, p 153).

The European Commission's public health policy also stresses the need for intersectoral collaboration and endorses the need to create partnerships for health within communities (Stein, 1996).

It is interesting that only in the last couple of years has there been a conscious movement in public health policy within the UK from an individual risk/disease-based paradigm to more holistic health promotion and healthy public policy strategies, such as the settings approach and a focus on healthy neighbourhoods, schools and workplaces. It is, however, questionable if this is a real shift in policy, when the targets established to measure progress are still firmly disease based and not related to building social capital and reducing health inequalities.

Settings-based approach to health promotion

The growth of the new public health (Ashton and Seymour, 1988) and its driving force, health promotion, has facilitated a move from a principal concern with disease categories towards social settings. This settings-based approach is fundamental to health promotion theory (Poland et al, 2000). It reflects a shift from the dominant professional/expert focus on health based around disease topic or risk factor to a focus on population and the settings in which people live, work and spend their lives in the real world.

Most health promotion activity is bounded in space and time within settings that provide the social structure and context for planning, implementing and evaluating interventions (Poland et al, 2000).

The concept of community therefore underpins much of holistic health promotion and has resulted in an emphasis on community development approaches as means of building sustainability. The term 'community development' incorporates a wide range of challenges such as encouraging citizen involvement in local politics, building partnerships to solve local problems across traditional community boundaries, improving housing, employment and health promotion (Mittelmark, 1999). A central theme of all these actions, in theory, endorses the key HFA principle discussed earlier, that is the active participation by people in their own affairs through their own abilities. A clear tension in community development work lies in the relationship between community development professionals and people at local level, particularly in terms of leadership. Nevertheless, a core principle of the community development process is community empowerment to facilitate effective local leadership (Jackson and Wright, 1989; Hawe et al, 1997).

Partnerships are at the heart of community development and the 'settings for health' approach (Kickbusch, 1997, p 433). Increasingly these include a public–private mix through community business and/or sponsorship initiatives. As Kickbusch points out, such partnerships involving organisations outside, seem to more readily understand and accept the settings approach, than those inside the traditional health sector. Such 'new partnerships' offer opportunities to move health promotion into other settings (Corti, 1997). Yet the establishment of such public/private partnerships involves major challenges to the traditional health sector culture and these are not always readily accepted.

Social capital as a resource for health improvement

Attempts to understand further the settings approach to health promotion, and its links to community development and partnership working, have recently begun to address the concept of social capital. Social capital is a resource within a society:

> It is a resource, a form of social trust produced when individuals and groups interact with organisations and social systems to produce benefits for people themselves and for society. (Gillies and Spray, 1997, p 6)

It is defined by referring to "the institutions underpinning society and the 'horizontal' and 'vertical' bonds between them – the ties within and across communities, 'those tangible substances' [that] count for most in the daily lives of people: namely goodwill, fellowship, sympathy, and social intercourse among the individuals and families who make up a social unit" (Russell, 2000). Although the term 'social capital' is used loosely by both academics and policy makers, with further investment in appropriate research and development it may provide a useful tool to help in understanding the social influences on health:

> Where you live, who else lives there, and how they live their lives – co-operatively or selfishly, responsibly or destructively – can be as important as personal resources in determining life chances. (Justice, 1994, pp 307-8)

Initial attempts have been made to investigate the relative benefit of focusing health interventions on individuals or social structural factors by using the concept of social capital (Lomas, 1998). Health promotion in particular has a key role in facilitating such interventions:

> By capitalising upon and enhancing the value of social relationships and partnerships, social support and networks for the exchange of information, community-based health promotion can help build the social resource called 'social capital' in communities, can reinforce efforts to repair the social fabric and foster cohesiveness. (Gillies and Spray, 1997, p 1)

Therefore it is important to analyse social capital and attempt to explore the processes through which it works.

Social capital was originally devised by James Coleman (1987) to describe the forms of relations that exist between and within families and communities and which were thought to exert a strong influence on educational attainment levels. It is created through "the processes between people which establish networks, norms, social trust and facilitate co-ordination and co-operation for mutual benefit" (Cox, 1996 cited in Baum, 1998, p 94), which it is acknowledged can work in both exclusive as well as inclusive ways.

Researchers internationally have stressed the need for more emphasis on seeking to understand the role of social capital in creating healthy communities (Putnam, 1993; Baum, 1997; Gillies, 1997). In reviewing the evidence, Baum concludes that people are healthier when they have supportive social linkages and networks, hierarchies are minimised and inequalities in society reduced (Baum, 1998). One aspect of social capital relevant to partnership working for health improvement involves the construction of networks to aid communication and mutual cooperation. Such networks are important facilitating mechanisms in society for promoting social cohesion and thereby promoting health.

Social capital is potentially an important factor in both the theory and practice of health promotion partnership construction and alliance building and therefore could contribute a theoretical basis to help our understanding of the settings-based approach to health promotion.

Gillies identifies four areas in which social capital progresses the development of health promotion (Gillies, 1997):

1. It focuses on the community as the unit of analysis and not the individual, as it is constructed by the interaction of individuals with their social system.
2. It incorporates the broad determinants of health and offers an opportunity thereby to cross both lay/professional and intersectoral boundaries.
3. It highlights the processes for networking between people and organisational structures – these are crucial in order to understand the barriers and facilitators that obstruct or enhance partnership working.
4. Social capital bridges disciplinary boundaries and could provide the foundation for new theoretical frameworks to aid our understanding of processes of partnership development for health promotion.

Mechanisms to facilitate the production of social capital

An important research focus lies in understanding how social capital is produced and thereby facilitating its production for health improvement. According to Gillies, there are two mechanisms to build social capital in order specifically to boost partnership and alliance working – the development of communication through information technologies and social links through family and kinship relations and support (Gillies, 1997). Gillies emphasises that the networks that carry social capital and cement partnership working (according to Putnam, 1993) could be actively facilitated through new technologies. She also identifies the role of a broad-based concept of the family and related social relationships as being a focus for the creation of social capital, and highlights the role of women in particular in partnership formation and activism for health promotion.

Before its demise in March 2000, the Health Education Authority (HEA) had begun to fund a series of research studies into the relationship between social capital and health related specifically to community networks. Initial exploratory work in Luton (Campbell et al, 1999) found linkages between health and social capital in two local communities in the city. The second phase of this study extends this work to take account of socio-economic differences and ethnic variations. Another HEA funded study in this series highlighted the key importance of gender in building and maintaining social capital (Cooper et al, 1999). This study recommended that the different roles of both women and men, from varying demographic backgrounds, in creating social capital should be explored in more depth.

As a further development in this programme of research, the HEA began working with both the health service and local authority in Salford and Nottingham to establish social action projects to influence health inequalities. Both cities are working with local people and a range of different sectors, commercial, statutory and voluntary, to develop models of community participation and partnership. One of the aims of this work is to develop partnerships across professional and lay barriers and across agencies for health improvement, especially among disadvantaged groups. A key focus will be around the processes and mechanisms of social capital construction, social cohesion and community health development.

WHO recommendations to mobilise partnerships

Moving to the international level, the WHO European *Health for all* strategy provides an important background context to the policies of individual member states. WHO (1999) emphasises that within partnership working the right to participate carries with it the duty to be accountable, and therefore it emphasises that all stakeholders have to take responsibility for the health effects of their policies and practises, as follows:

1. Governments – economic growth should be seen as only one objective to be balanced with others such as equity, environmental sustainability and improving social capital. Therefore in this process governments have to consider participation by a range of partnerships and transparency in policy development. There is a need for an interministerial group representing the wide range of key interests in health development in each member state. Within this group, the ministry responsible for health needs should take a key role, in particular to monitor implementation and health impact.
2. Politicians – have an important role and responsibility in policy formulation, target setting, monitoring and evaluation related to all public health policy. They need to be aware of the health impact of their legislation, laws and regulations, utilising findings from new approaches to health impact assessment.
3. Professionals – health professionals, in particular, also have a key role, as in their respective areas do others, such as teachers, engineers, architects, town planners, economists, and journalists.
4. Non-governmental organisations (NGOs) – have a responsibility for raising people's awareness of health issues and priorities, lobbying, acting as change advocates, providing services and self-help groups.
5. The private sector – needs to heed consumers; provide clear information on their products and services; and be aware of their health impact on people. The private and commercial sector is often forgotten in partnership working – although attempts have been made to establish a partnership dialogue, for example during the last WHO Global Conference on Health Promotion in Jakarta in 1997 held under the theme 'New Partners for a New Era'. The private sector is an important component of communities locally and nationally, the workplace being a key action setting for health promotion.
6. Individual citizens – need to identify and be aware of health as a resource and should encourage health improvement.

WHO (1999) indicates that Target 20 of its strategy to mobilise partners for health can be achieved if:

- existing partnerships networks such as healthy cities, schools, prisons, hospitals and workplaces are strengthened and new partnerships created at all levels of society;
- all participants in health take account of the mutual gains from investment in health;
- mechanisms are put in place for joint development and evaluation of policies, underpinned by *Health for all* principles;
- health professionals act as key facilitators with other professionals to achieve mutually beneficial policies;
- partnership building for health is encouraged at each level, to create networks and empower people;
- there is clear and effective public health leadership;
- international solidarity is strengthened through European intergovernmental structures and the WHO Regional Committee for Europe, the European Union and other key European and international UN agencies, and European networks, for example health promoting schools (WHO, EU, Council of Europe) and the European Environment and Health Committee.

Key issues for effective partnership working for health improvement

The current UK government's ideology is to facilitate cultural change and begin the process of shifting power to people. An aim such as this is a long-term process over at least a generation or more. The government's main method is through effective information transfer, with policies of introducing computers/Internet access into schools, promoting interactive telephone systems such NHS Direct, and disseminating effectiveness bulletins all being attempts to empower people. For example, in the planning of HImPs there is meant to be a move to encourage and facilitate effective public involvement throughout the process. But do these actions represent real and effective consultation with people as equals? Do they involve real and effective partnerships with people themselves?

One of the limitations of the Healthy Cities movement has been the inability to engage local people in active policy decision making about health. An evaluation of a pilot healthy cities scheme in Australia highlights the complexity of building effective partnerships between the community and the professionals paid to work with them (Baum, 1993).

One of the original dilemmas identified when WHO began seriously to discuss and develop its *Health Promotion Programme* in the early 1980s (WHO, 1984), was the danger that health promotion would become professionalised and hi-jacked by a specific professional group or groups. This is a contemporary dilemma with regard to the role of specialist health promotion officers in the UK. This fear of paternalism by professionals has remained, and is currently a concern with regard to the lack of community involvement in contemporary health promotion programmes.

> Does the current professionally dominated system seek to empower individuals or communities, or simply develop a new 'mask' of respectability by evolving new measures of assurance that leave the user or consumer even more confused and powerless. (Davies and Macdonald, 1998, p 214)

Real empowerment of people is only in its embryonic development. The NHS in particular has a poor record of working with the people as equal partners in matters of their own health. Its management and professional culture is founded on the expert-led biomedical/scientific paradigm, which traditionally dismisses and actively disempowers people. We therefore need clearer evidence of examples of effective partnership working for health that actively involve local people.

To develop appropriate theory

There is a dearth of research and theory building with regard to partnership working and intersectoral collaboration in health promotion (Beattie, 1995). Health promotion still tends to be dominated in industrialised countries by reductionist health education approaches, which are focused on individualised knowledge, attitude and behaviour change. Gillies has suggested that the concept of social capital may assist the development of theory to underpin partnership working. In her review of evaluation studies of partnerships and alliances for health promotion internationally, she found that the focus of these evaluations was predominantly fixed on individual health-related behaviours and rarely on broader social or contextual factors (Gillies, 1997). Little evidence was found of the extent to which partnerships for health promotion were tackling the broader determinants of health in industrialised countries.

In contrast, numerous case studies were described of such actions in the developing world in Asia, South Pacific, China, Latin America and Africa. In the majority of these studies the following recurring themes occurred and were seen as fundamental to improving social capital – cohesive social relationships, social civic action and social trust. These themes highlighted key directions to pursue to achieve social regeneration and effective community development. This raises the issue that much of our thinking and experiences are conceptualised from a Western industrial/ post-industrial perspective, and that we have a great deal to learn from experiences elsewhere with regard to social capital and partnership working.

To develop appropriate measurement indicators

There is clearly a need to develop a series of more appropriate community outcome indicators in order fully to appreciate the value and impact of the processes of partnership working and alliance building to achieve effective health promotion. One of the key problems is that traditional approaches to health promotion are locked in a medico-positivist paradigm rooted in the origins of disease. In order to understand and monitor community-based approaches to health promotion and to tackle health determinants, more appropriate indicators must be developed and evaluated. In the USA, the Centers for Disease Control (CDC) have been working on community indicators for HIV/AIDS prevention (CDC, 1997). A WHO Working Group on Evaluating Health Promotion has commissioned work on indicators for measuring social capital and community level interventions (Kreuter et al, 1996). In addition, examples of instruments related to health promotion quality and effectiveness measures are beginning to be produced and tested (Davies and Macdonald, 1998).

Emphasis needs to be given to the creation of credible intermediate indicators which see process as outcome, and are accepted by the supporters, and more importantly research funders, of the dominant positivist, medico-scientific paradigm. The Gillies review (Gillies, 1997), for example, identified the following key outcomes as relevant:

• facilitating agencies to work together;
• engaging with local people;

- capacity building (education, training of volunteers and maintaining networks);
- establishing coordination infrastructures;
- gaining political support and maintaining political visibility;
- obtaining resource investment;
- reorienting organisations;
- adopting flexible working practices;
- carrying out needs assessment and priority setting.

Conclusion

Both national attempts by the British government and international initiatives, such as the WHO *Health 21: Health for all in the 21st century*, for example, to improve health and tackle the complex and growing health inequalities within and between our societies, are to be lauded. But in order for them to be effective further research and development is urgently required, in particular to identify the social processes that enhance or obstruct health development.

Social processes lie at the core of health promotion and initiatives to involve local people in effective partnership working to improve their health and well-being (Backet-Milburn, 1998). They are particularly important in initiating and maintaining partnerships and alliances in the light of local, national or international changes.

The resource of social capital and its production, especially focused upon disadvantaged and socially excluded groups, may contribute to social cohesion, health improvement and reduction of inequalities. The concept of social capital offers great potential to health promotion theory and practice. In particular it enables further exploration of settings approaches and partnership working for health improvement. Frameworks that have been developed, such as that proposed by Gillies, need adequate testing and further development.

More research is required to develop new measurement indicators based on a more appropriate holistic paradigm of health and well-being in order to monitor and assess effectiveness of these community-based health promotion initiatives (Davies and Macdonald, 1998).

Social capital is not a panacea to solve all society's problems, but it is potentially an important concept whose absence in a community will be retrogressive to any initiatives to promote health. Further investment internationally and nationally in research and development in this key development area for health promotion will enable more careful examination of the processes through which it works. Only by clarifying our understanding of social capital through studying practical community interventions related to the production of social capital can we devise health promotion strategies that effectively empower people and improve their health.

References

Ashton,J. and Seymour, H. (1988) *The new public health: The Liverpool experience*, Milton Keynes: Open University Press.

Backet-Milburn, K.M. (1998) 'Healthy alliances depend on healthy social processes', in A. Scriven (ed) *Alliances in health promotion: Theory and practice*, London: Macmillan.

Baker, M. (2000) *Making sense of the NHS White Papers*, Abingdon: Radcliffe Medical Press.

Baum, F. (1993) 'Noarlunga Healthy Cities Pilot Project: the contribution of research and evaluation', in J.K. Davies and M.P. Kelly (eds) *Healthy cities: Research and practice*, London: Routledge.

Baum, F. (1997) 'Public health and civic society: understanding and valuing the connection', *Australian and New Zealand Journal of Public Health*, vol 21, no 7, pp 73-4.

Baum, F. (1998) *The new public health: An Australian perspective*, Melbourne, Australia: Oxford University Press.

Beattie, A. (1995) 'Healthy alliances or dangerous liaisons? The challenge of working together in health', in A. Leathard (ed) *Going inter-professional: Working together for health and welfare*, London: Routledge.

Bracht, N.K. and Rissel, C. (1999) 'A five-stage community organization model of health promotion: empowerment and partnership strategies', in N. Bracht (ed) *Health promotion at the community level 2: New advances*, Thousand Oaks, CA: Sage Publications.

Campbell, C., Wood, L. and Kelly, M. (1999) *Social capital and health*, London: Health Education Authority.

CDC (1997) *Community indicators for HIV prevention: A Delphi exercise*, Atlanta: Centers for Disease Control and Prevention.

Coleman, J.H. (1987) *Public and private high schools: The impact of communities*, New York, NY: Basic Books.

Cooper, H., Arber, S., Fee, L. and Ginn, J. (1999) *The influence of social support and social capital on health*, London: Health Education Authority.

Corti, B (1997) 'Warning: attending a sport, racing or arts venue may be beneficial to your health', *Australian and New Zealand Journal of Public Health*, vol 21, no 4, pp 371-6.

Davies, J.K. and Macdonald, G. (1998) 'Beyond certainty: leading health promotion into the twenty-first century', in J.K. Davies, and G. Macdonald (eds) *Quality, evidence and effectiveness in health promotion: Striving for certainties*, London: Routledge, pp 207-16.

DoH (Department of Health) (1997) *The New NHS: Modern, dependable*, London: The Stationery Office.

DoH (1998a) *Partnerships in action*, London: The Stationery Office.

DoH (1998b) *Our healthier nation*, Green Paper, London: The Stationery Office.

DoH (1998c) *Chief Medical Officer's project to strengthen the public health function*, London: The Stationery Office.

DoH (1999) *Saving lives: Our healthier nation*, London: The Stationery Office.

ESBHHA (East Sussex, Brighton & Hove Health Authority) (1999) *The health agenda: Developing the Health Improvement Programme*, Lewes: ESBHHA.

European Commission (1997) *Public health in Europe*, Luxembourg: European Commission.

Gillies, P. (1997) 'The effectiveness of alliances or partnerships for health promotion: a global review of progress and potential consideration of the relationship to building social capital for health', Jakarta, WHO Conference Paper.

Gillies, P. and Spray, J. (1997) *Addressing health inequalities: The practical potential of social capital*, London: Health Education Authority.

Green, L. and Ottoson, J. (1999) *Community and population health* (8th edn), Boston, MA: WCB/McGraw Hill.

Hawe, P.N., King, M. and Jordens, C. (1997) 'Multiplying health gains: the critical role of capacity-building within health promotion programmes', *Health Policy*, vol 39, pp 29-42.

Jackson, T.M. and Wright, M. (1989) 'The Community Development Continuum', *Community Health Studies*, vol 13, no 1, pp 66-73.

Justice, C. (1994) *Social justice: Strategies for national renewal*, London:Vintage.

Kickbusch, I. (1997) 'Health-promoting environments: the next steps', *Australian and New Zealand Journal of Public Health*, vol 21, no 4, pp 431-4.

Kreuter, M., Lezin, N. and Koplan, A. (1996) *National level assessments of community health promotion using indicators of social capital*, Copenhagen: WHO European Office.

Lomas, J. (1998) 'Social capital and health: implications for public health and epidemiology', *Social Science and Medicine*, vol 47, no 9, pp 1181-8.

Mittelmark, M. (1999) 'Health promotion at community level: lessons from diverse perspectives', in N. Bracht (ed) *Health promotion at the community level 2: New advances*, Thousand Oaks, CA: Sage Publications.

NHS Executive (2000) *Regional strategy for public health*, London: South East Region.

Poland, B., Green, L. and Rootman, I. (2000) *Settings for health promotion: Linking theory and practice*, Thousand Oaks, CA: Sage Publications.

Putnam, R. (1993) *Making democracy work*, Princeton, NJ: Princeton University Press.

Rifkin, S. (1990) *Community participation in maternal and child health/family planning programmes*, Geneva: WHO.

Russell, H. (2000) *Public health and regeneration: Making the links*, London: Health Education Authority/Local Government Association.

Stein, H. (1996) 'Public health and public health research: the need for concerted action at European level', *Eurohealth*, vol 2, pp 23-4.

WHO (1978) *Primary health care: A Joint Report by the Director-General of the World Health Organization and the Executive Director of the United Nations Children's Fund*, Geneva: WHO.

WHO (1984) *Health promotion: A discussion document on the concepts and principles*, Copenhagen: WHO.

WHO (1986) *Health & Welfare Canada and Canadian Public Health Association – The Ottawa Charter for Health Promotion*, Ottawa: WHO.

WHO (1998) *A resolution on health promotion*, Geneva: Executive Board of World Health Organization.

WHO (1999) *Health 21: Health for all in the 21st century: The Health for all policy framework for the WHO European region*, Copenhagen: WHO/European Office.

Wilkinson, R. (1996) *Unhealthy societies: The afflictions of inequality*, London: Routledge.

Part Three:
Power, participation and place

Partnership and power: the role of black and minority ethnic voluntary organisations in challenging racism

Jabeer Butt

Why consider issues of power when discussing partnerships? As the Introduction suggests, elements of the ideology of partnership are equality of partners, some sense of classless society and of participatory democracy. Even a cursory review of the voluntary organisations and civil society will highlight the need to understand the operation of power. For example, the funding of voluntary organisations in the United Kingdom is most often based on a very 'unequal' relationship, with voluntary organisations being 'partners' with central government or local government.

Except for a few very large organisations and a few very small organisations, the state continues to be the main funder of voluntary organisations (Kendall and Knapp, 1996). The unequal nature of this is not only that a huge bureaucracy is in a relationship with what is almost always a small(er) organisation, but that this bureaucracy has its own aims and regularly demonstrates an unwillingness to countenance any criticism or complaints of failure. At times of conflict, both national and local government cite their democratic mandate as legitimising their actions, while most voluntary organisations are only able to mobilise the people power of their users and supporters to challenge the actions of the state.

The existence of these aims and the power to implement them has been and is a constant in the relationship between voluntary organisations and the state. From time to time it may appear that there has been a shift in this balance of power; for example the publication of the Stephen Lawrence Inquiry report led to universal desire on the part of bureaucracies ('institutions' in the language of that report) to progress equality and challenge racism within their own structures. This may result in a change in the power structures between black and minority ethnic voluntary organisations and their funders. But we have been here before: the Scarman report into the aftermath of the riots of the 1980s may not have led to the soul-searching of the Lawrence inquiry, but was nevertheless hailed as a watershed in race relations in the UK. Yet as numerous reports highlight, the extent of change since 1985 has been limited (Butt and Mirza, 1997).

The purpose of this initial discussion is not to question the legitimacy (or not) of central and local government funding of voluntary organisations, but merely to highlight that investigation of issues of power is crucial if we are to understand the operation of partnership.

To explore this issue, this chapter attempts to consider the stresses and strains in maintaining partnerships that are designed to bring about change or challenge oppression. While many voluntary organisations could claim that they were established or are involved in challenging oppression, this chapter focuses on those groups that fall under the umbrella of black and minority ethnic voluntary organisations. The chapter will argue that many of these groups' *raison d'être* is to combat manifestations of direct, but more often indirect (or institutional), racism. This reason for existence may, in fact, bring them into conflict with their supposed partners. The chapter will consider whether black and minority ethnic voluntary organisations have been able to progress the aim of challenging racism and in what ways this has been supported or hindered by the state, in particular local government.

First, however, we consider some of the methodological questions that an investigation of the role of black and minority ethnic voluntary organisations raises.

Is there a black and minority ethnic voluntary sector?

A Joseph Rowntree Foundation call for bids to carry out a study of black and minority ethnic voluntary organisations posed the challenge of whether such a sector even existed. The fact that there are several national – and more local or regional umbrella or development agencies – that have been specifically established to support the development of black and minority ethnic voluntary organisations could be said to be evidence enough that this sector exists. If many hundreds, or possibly thousands of organisations, from Liverpool to Bristol, have defined themselves as being part of the black and minority ethnic voluntary sector, who are we as social scientists to question whether such a sector exists? Furthermore, if the Single Regeneration Budget, the National Lottery Charities Board and the Home Office, among others, are organising funding priorities around the existence of such groups, perhaps we should accept that this is not only a sector in itself but is a sector for itself – that there is a group of organisations that is consciously setting out to achieve a common aim.

Inevitably, however, it is important to have this discussion, as it poses other questions, particularly that of boundaries. When we speak of a black and minority ethnic voluntary organisation do we mean any organisation that works with black and minority ethnic communities, any organisation for whom the majority of 'users' are from these communities, or organisations that are run by black and minority ethnic people and are for black and minority ethnic people? While some 'black' housing associations would argue that they are servicing *all* people in their local communities, it is likely that there will be little argument with a definition of this sector as being the 'narrow definition' of an organisation run by black and minority ethnic people for black and minority ethnic people. Organisations such as the Pepperpot Club in west London, Merseyside Chinese Association in Liverpool and ASRA Housing Association in Leicester (and elsewhere) are some examples of these types of organisations.

While these boundaries are blurred at times, with, for example 'voluntary' organisations such as the NSPCC establishing Bal Raksha, a child welfare and protection project mainly staffed by black and minority ethnic staff working with black and minority ethnic users, there is sufficient coherence for us to be able to talk about a black and minority ethnic voluntary sector.

Limitations of existing source

The growth in research on voluntary organisations provides valuable guidance to the pitfalls and some of the solutions in terms of methodology. It suggests how to systematically define a voluntary organisation (Salamon and Anheier, 1997), particularly in the UK context (Kendall and Knapp, 1996), as well as what is a black and minority ethnic voluntary organisation (Lattimer and Walker, 1997); what are the possible sources of accessible information to map the sector (Pharoah, 1997, 1998) and/or act as a sampling frame; and what are the practices that may aid data collection from these organisations.

However, even with the development of this methodological sophistication, the black and minority ethnic voluntary sector in the UK continues to be underresearched. There are several studies examining one or other aspect of these groups' contribution to the provision of services (Butt, 1994, and Butt and Box, 1997, on social care providers; Royce et al, 1995, on housing associations), but there are no comprehensive investigations of the sector (Atkin, 1996). Furthermore, it is rare to see specific discussion of these groups in mainstream work (Russell et al, 1995, is one exception).

Importantly, we have only limited information on the income and wealth of this sector or whether the funds available are being managed to maximise their value (Butt and Mirza, 1997). Where information is available it is either based on surveys with comparatively poor response rates (Lattimer and Trail, 1992), or about just one source of funding (Lattimer and Walker, 1997), or has to be gleaned from a multiplicity of obscure sources (Butt and Mirza, 1997). While this limitation is being more widely recognised (Pharoah, 1998), it has not stopped major mapping exercises still failing to mention this sector (Hems and Passey, 1998), or decisions being made that subsume the contribution of these groups (Kendall and Knapp, 1996). In addition, the major study that was funded by the Joseph Rowntree Foundation to map the black and minority ethnic voluntary sector remains unpublished.

Inevitably, this causes difficulties for us in answering the questions posed at the beginning of this chapter. Mainstream and large(r)-scale studies of the black and minority ethnic voluntary sector are not available and therefore in addressing these questions we draw upon two studies (Butt et al, 1991; Butt, 1994; and Butt and Box, 1997) that provide some useful evidence.

Evidence from the Race Equality Unit survey

The goal of providing effective supportive services to Britain's black and minority ethnic communities still appears not to have been attained. However, in a survey carried out by the Race Equality Unit (REU) of agencies and individuals working in and around social care, there was universal agreement that black and minority ethnic voluntary organisations were providing appropriate supportive services. Importantly, this survey appears to provide substantial 'proof' that partnership is working, and is working in meeting the needs of communities traditionally excluded from supportive services.

The survey questioned black-led organisations, including user organisations, service providers and commissioners from the statutory, voluntary and private sector, and agencies concerned with race equality. A striking feature was that they all made reference to the important role played by black and minority ethnic voluntary organisations.

Who provides supportive services?

When asked to identify a service that they felt met the social care needs of black communities, all respondents to the REU survey identified at least one service provided by a black-led (and black-staffed) voluntary sector agency. Camden Health Authority drew attention to the grants that they have made to particular groups, such as one to support work with Somalis and people from the Horn of Africa. Bradford Social Services Department drew attention to the contracts they had with voluntary organisations working with black and minority ethnic communities for the provision of day care at community centres.

Some of the respondents drew attention to their own services. The Bibini Centre for Young People drew attention to their one service, noting:

"... [the centre] aims to provide residential care and support services primarily to young Black people of African, Asian and Caribbean heritage. The philosophy of care that underpins our services is based on a holistic approach to young people's development, central to which are issues of:

• identity – culture, religion, language, sexuality, gender, disability, heritage;
• belonging – family, groups, friends, communities, churches/temples/ mosques;
• needs – educational, health, spiritual, emotional, physical, security, safety, self-esteem."

Leeds Black Elders Association also drew attention to their own services; noting:

"All our services are aimed at improving the quality of life of the black elderly community within specific areas of Leeds:

• volunteering project – gardening, DIY, painting and decorating, befriending, shopping service;

- the joint management with Leeds social services of a day centre particularly aimed at the black community;

- an advocacy service for the clients of Leeds Black Elders."

The London Black Carers Workers Forum sent us a directory that contained a listing of 87 organisations from around London supporting carers. Many of these organisations are black led and staffed voluntary organisations. The Confederation of Indian Organisations (CIO) noted:

> "The organisations that CIO has contact with have largely been set up as a response to unmet needs or gaps in existing provision by statutory services. South Asian organisations engaged in service delivery have therefore been set up by the community and professionals within the community to make available appropriate and accessible services. There are therefore several examples of services which are meeting the needs of South Asian communities within the voluntary sector [including] Asian People with Disabilities Alliance, Apna Ghar, Ethnic Alcohol Counselling Project, Newham Asian Women's Project, Asian Women's Resource Centre (Brent), Ekta Project."

Why are these services appropriate?

Respondents to the REU survey were asked why they saw the services being provided by these voluntary organisations as appropriate. The CIO suggested that there were several reasons, including that the services are: linguistically and culturally accessible; are located in places where they are easy to access; are relevant and able to be flexible according to community need; and are holistic. The London Black Carers Workers Forum noted:

> "They are staffed by people who know the needs and social disciplines of particular communities. They speak or have access to interpreters of the various languages. And thus are able to offer services that are culturally sensitive and that respect the spiritual beliefs of the communities concerned."

Manchester Health Authority responded briefly: "All these services are provided by the voluntary sector in a sensitive and appropriate model of service delivery".

Some respondents counselled caution by pointing out the limitations of *all* service provision, but nevertheless drew attention to the 'success' of black and minority ethnic voluntary organisations. A black family centre manger stated:

> "In whatever limited way, needs are met because services are specifically targeted at sections of the black community, are provided by black people for black people, approaches and philosophies used are recognisable, relevant and appropriate, and black community, groups and individuals earn the trust that they are getting and do not need to take account of other agendas, or become entangled with attitudes or models of delivery."

Limitations of service provision

A couple of respondents pointed out that even for black and minority ethnic voluntary organisations their service provision was often responding to crisis situations, with a limit on the availability of longer-term support, and they were not in a position to support all those in need. In addition, Kente – which provides capacity-building support to black and minority ethnic voluntary organisations – suggested that some may not recognise the value of these organisations at present:

> "Local government needs to recognise that the provision of services to the black community is integral to their overall responsibility. This requires a change in the way decisions [are] made, starting with the setting of agendas all the way through to the purchasing/ commissioning/delivery of services. At the same time, there needs to be better appreciation of the work done by black and minority ethnic voluntary organisations and a need to interact with, and utilise the skills and experience of the sector as a whole."

Whether it was cheaper to provide services through black and minority ethnic voluntary organisations was not mentioned by any of the respondents to the REU survey. However, many of the responses from black-led agencies and individuals point to the unstable or short-term nature of the funding that these groups receive. This picture concurs with one identified by Butt and Mirza using data from a study carried out by Melunsky et al:

> Our calculations based on the Melunsky et al (1992) data suggest that while the average grant for all funded groups has risen from over £37,000 in 86/87 to around £41,000 in 92/93, this compares with the average grant for black-led organisations declining from over £28,000 to over £26,000. Therefore, ... black-led organisations not only started from a lower starting point than was true of the sector as a whole (a difference of £9,000) but actually declined over the period (by about £2,000) while the average grant for the sector as a whole grew (by about £4,000). (Butt and Mirza, 1997)

If this picture of smaller grants (possibly declining over time) is repeated across the country, this would make the compelling call by many respondents to the REU survey for more and longer-term funding for black and minority ethnic voluntary organisations all the more urgent.

Evidence from the Ethnic Monitoring in Social Services (EMSS) project

As part of an investigation into the development of social services for Britain's black and minority ethnic communities, the EMSS project (Butt et al, 1991; Butt, 1994) set out to explore why so many local authorities and social services departments chose to fund these organisations. In establishing these partnerships, what were departments attempting to achieve and how was this linked to their development of equality for black and minority ethnic communities? Furthermore, assuming that the objectives for this funding were articulated, did departments achieve what they had set out to do? Finally, what impact has the funding of voluntary groups to deliver a particular service had on the department's mainstream service?

The following section presents responses from some of the 38 black and white staff at various levels of seniority from a London department, a metropolitan authority and a county council.

Funding black community groups

In attempting to assess the impact of black and minority ethnic community groups in providing social services to black and minority ethnic communities, the following respondent highlights the changes in the scale of funding:

> "When we first started ethnic monitoring on the grants – and this is just in terms of grants going to black and ethnic minority groups, rather than activities with black and ethnic minority people – which is something we're getting into now, but we didn't have from the beginning – I think that, sort of, it was around 12% of the funding [that] went to black and ethnic minority groups."

> "We're now up to about 24% of funding going to black and ethnic minority groups, and that is a quite significant shift. Though we haven't, you know, in any way, shape or form got to where we feel that the funding is equitable – in the way it should be."

Though no other interviewees presented similar evidence for the level of funding of black and minority ethnic community groups, statements indicating the 'significant' scale of this funding were made by headquarters staff in all three departments. The impression of those closer to the front line appears to be different. A respondent from the same department as the senior manager quoted above referred to the yearly 'begging bowl' exercises that these groups faced. From a different department, a respondent recounted:

> "We've got a black church down the road, that has tried to get money to open up as a day care centre. And they have just been turned down at every stage. And we've advocated on their behalf quite vigorously – and it's made no difference whatsoever. And there is always really good reasons why the department is doing it somewhere else, or whatever."

> "But in terms of our relations with that black church, it's been just so embarrassing. Because we keep coming back, and saying how much we want to work with them in partnership, but don't ask for any money."

The varying perceptions of how much funding was actually directed at these community groups and whether this funding was adequate, did not mean that any workers doubted why departments were getting involved in partnerships. All saw this as an integral aspect of their department's implementation of equality for black and minority ethnic communities

Objectives of funding black community groups

In attempting to identify the objectives departments have set in the funding of black community groups, it is possible to identify two periods of funding. The first period probably lasted until the end of the 1980s. The second, which marks a significant shift in the relationship of departments and black community groups, is more recent and appears to be gaining momentum with the implementation of the new community care regime and in particular the development of the 'contract culture'.

The first phase is encapsulated by the following response to a question about how a meals-on-wheels service for black elders had been developed:

> "... I have to say I inherited what had already begun. I mean, I think in common with many authorities, the history – as I understand it from what I've read and what I've been told – essentially has been pressure and initiatives from voluntary organisations in the communities – which have typically started with something, and got premises, often of a general purpose nature."

> "And one of the early needs they flagged up in that, is to serve their old people. A gathering place for people, and so on ... a good reason for coming together is to have a midday meal together. It's a very natural progression of thinking."

> "So certainly, during the early 80s and mid-80s ... there were various requests of that kind ... which were responded to partly by the department, partly by other departments of the [authority] ... and so on. That put in place a basic infrastructure."

When discussing the development of such community group services the majority of interviewees concurred with this model of the social services department reacting to demands from community groups. These demands were often supported by pressure from black and minority ethnic councillors and/or workers. The consequence of this, however, was that the reasons for funding these groups and establishing these partnerships were pragmatic and reactive, rather than representing any planned or proactive stance. The interviewee quoted above added the following comments:

"I think to be honest with you, the department's position has been essentially ... a reactive one to community pressure – rather than a proactive one. But I don't think [this authority] is very different in that regard to many other places, and I'm not claiming any difference for me personally."

"One of the problems of being a sort of bureaucrat in a large organisation like social services, is that you do spend a lot of your time reacting to pressures, and one of the jobs is to try to disentangle the pressures, I suppose, and evaluate them."

Many of the interviewees recognised that without this pressure a number of services would not have been developed and, although the objectives for financial support were not very clear, their impact has been beneficial. The articulation of need as well as the possibility of responding to that need appropriately and 'efficiently' (this, on occasion, appears to be a euphemism for 'cheaply') was of some importance in ensuring funding. The EMSS survey also raised the possibility that if black and minority ethnic communities have been receiving any appropriate service, it has been doing so through these groups, which have at times opened the gate to other social services. A development worker who has seen a day centre grow, noted:

"Towards the last two to three years, I have seen an increased volume of people from the Asian community visiting the centre for all sorts of reasons, and part of that being that we wanted the centre to grow, and I have been able to attract funding. I have been able to attract workers there, got funding to pour in there, to say we needed a carers' group."

"And there are about 30 people from the Asian community who ... come together there once a month. In that way – just the sheer numbers of people – one gets a clear image that from there, people are then able to access other bits of social services."

Respondents to the EMSS survey suggested that the benefits of these 'reactive' developments are qualified by fears that the department was only responding to those who were most vociferous in identifying need and demanding the delivery of services. Furthermore, there was the possibility that these developments would be expected to operate with a completely different set of expectations to those of mainstream services.

In comparing the development of the mainstream meals service with that being developed for black communities, one interviewee recounts a discussion with his manager:

> "We'd had a councillor along, saying 'Now, if you know any old people who need a meal, let us know. We're really going to develop this service'. So they set it up and let the customers find it. And I said, 'Why don't you do the same thing?' But no, you had to do research before you could set it up [for black elders]."

Respondents suggested that it was hard to ensure that departments did not just jump in feet first in the development and delivery of services to black and minority ethnic communities. However, it was also the case that the requirements for the development of a service for the white majority community were not the same. It was acceptable to allow a political decision to expand a meals-on-wheels service that would only cater for white clients with little 'professional' assessment of need, but the same was not true for a meals service for black and minority ethnic communities. It would be wrong to conclude that this reflects a difference in willingness to engage in a partnership between black and white groups as what is being compared here is voluntary provision as opposed to mainstream provision. Nevertheless, it does raise another dimension of how partnerships are negotiated and agreed, with race and racism playing a part in what priorities are set and resources allocated.

Some interviewees to the EMSS study were critical of the whole system. One officer suggested that the 1980s had seen the reactive funding of black and minority ethnic community groups which allowed a number of 'corrupt practices' to operate because there was an expectation that these groups would provide a second-rate service. The officer suggested:

> "... that it almost seems there is an expectation of a lower level of quality and delivery, and standards are not specified in advance for these groups, or within the minority community – and you are encouraging that practice, and after three or four years ... you find that it is not acceptable. Then value for money considerations come in, etc – then you start saying to people, 'You are not going to get funded, because you haven't kept your books right.'"

While this respondent was one of the more critical of the funding of black and minority ethnic community groups by social services departments, he did echo some of the earlier points: the reactive nature of this funding and the consequent lack of specific objectives set for the services. He also raised the question of how the success or failure of this vehicle for change is to be measured. He highlighted the limitations of using value for money as a measurement of success or failure, when little has been done in terms of identifying what is meant to be achieved by these groups. As a consequence the only measure that appears to be possible is dependent on the financial or managerial systems that may or may not exist, rather then an assessment of whether these groups are providing an appropriate service or whether it is of a sufficiently high quality.

These concerns about the limitations of the 1980s funding of black and minority ethnic community groups have been translated into a new phase of funding, with a greater emphasis put on the quantity and quality of the service that is being delivered. The implementation of ethnic record keeping and monitoring and other management and financial information systems by these groups appears to be an integral part of this process. The senior manager quoted above said:

> "What we're requiring now is that the organisations themselves have ethnic monitoring in the way they provide their services, so that we can monitor them – and that's across all [services], and again it's patchy. Some organisations are providing it and we're not quite sure we believe it, and other organisations are spending all their time arguing how it's impossible to do it."

> "So again, we've looked at supporting the effort with some training. But at the end of the day – and our members in a sense were being rather hard-nosed about it, than perhaps we as officers were advising them to be – at the end of the day we're saying, 'Well, if you don't provide, you won't get any grant.'"

It is possible to argue that this presupposes the setting of objectives for services provided by these groups. However, departments seem to be concentrating on setting up systems that may help to measure success or failure rather than identify what success or failure means. Therefore, although social services departments are making a big break from the purely reactive and unplanned nature of the 1980s funding of black and minority ethnic community groups, they are some distance from dealing with one of the fundamental problems of the 1980s: what are social services departments trying to achieve?

The importance of clarity in what social services departments are trying to achieve is also necessitated by the many positives of funding black and minority ethnic community groups to deliver social services to these communities. The articulation of need, the development of appropriate response to this needand the cost-effective use of resources are identified as the achievements of funding these groups in the 1980s. But there appears to be little debate as to how the new structures will attempt to ensure that they foster past achievements, rather than turn these organisations into satellites of social services departments, who have all the deficiencies of these departments with few of the benefits of black and minority ethnic community groups.

The popularity of the funding of these groups by social services departments was partly dictated by the very real benefits of this funding, as the groups were able to articulate need as well as to highlight the appropriate response to it. Although this funding was reactive it did lead to the development of services that would not have existed otherwise and did ensure that some black and minority ethnic people began to receive supportive personal social services.

To this must be added the amorphous – and as a consequence more difficult to measure – impact on mainstream services, as highlighted by the following response:

> "... if there were resources for further development of meals, where should we place them? ... we wouldn't, I think, any longer, simply want to be at the opportunist level of responding to whoever happens to knock on the door. For example, we have a sense of geographic priorities, where ... there are gaps in accessible services."

However, this reactive stance also means that it is difficult to go beyond a rudimentary assessment of what social services departments were intending to achieve through this funding. It was rare that objectives were set out that went beyond the notion that this funding would allow the department to implement its equal opportunities policy. An immediate consequence was that if ever an attempt was made to assess value for money, the measure of success or failure would be dependent on the financial or managerial systems these groups had in place rather than the service they were delivering. Importantly, this occurs in the context of little articulation of the desire to establish partnerships with these groups.

Conclusion

From this evidence it appears that partnership between the 'state' and black and minority ethnic voluntary organisations has a number of plus points. In the view of respondents to both surveys, black and minority ethnic voluntary organisations appear to have some of the tools required to provide an appropriate service, such as speaking the same language as those needing the services, as well as being able to identify gaps in existing service provision. They also appear to have ideas about how to provide services so that they are acceptable, an element of this being that black and minority ethnic workers are directly involved in the delivery. In supporting these organisations the state makes these advantages available to more people than might otherwise have been possible.

These voluntary organisations appear to be able to 'earn the trust' of their users. This appears to be in part due to the values or 'philosophies' that these organisations bring to the provision of services. In so doing these organisations appear to be able to develop 'partnerships' with communities whose pattern of usage of mainstream services remains problematic.

From these surveys, it appears that there are few areas of service provision in which black and minority ethnic voluntary organisations are not involved. But there is also a recognition that this variety does not mean that all necessary services are being provided or that these services are always making up for the limitations of mainstream provision. Here, perhaps, is evidence of the limitations of these partnerships, in that state sponsorship does not appear to be accompanied by a strategy to make better services for black and minority ethnic communities part of the mainstream. As in so many other cases of partnership working, as discussed in the Introduction, the activity remains in the margin.

While a number of respondents see the continuing need for service provision through black and minority ethnic voluntary groups, there is a suggestion that this may be a stage in development, with the ultimate goal being that all mainstream services respond appropriately. Equally, there is a suggestion that the most effective way forward is for the continuation of specific provision through black and minority ethnic voluntary organisations, while mainstream providers look at how they can improve their service provision.

Interestingly, while there is considerable discussion about the funding of black and minority ethnic voluntary service providers, there is little or no mention about the cost of providing services through these groups. It may well be the case that few of those providing grants or going into service level agreements have considered the comparative costs of using black and minority ethnic voluntary organisations as opposed to other providers. Nevertheless, in this present context of ever-tighter budgets, it would be surprising if this is not done.

From the evidence discussed above, black and minority ethnic voluntary organisations involved in the social care field appear to be challenging racism. The black and minority ethnic users who use their services say so, as do the black and white staff who work in these agencies as well as those working in those agencies who fund these groups. However, there are several caveats. Firstly, these groups appear to have limited impact on mainstream provision and therefore the services that they provide are only available to some of the people who may benefit from them. Secondly, they appear to have a problematical relationship with their funders, which is often associated with short-term funding that may also be inadequate. It is also worth noting that evidence emerges (when there is continuing evidence) that mainstream voluntary organisations are still failing to meet the needs of black and minority ethnic communities (Jones and Butt, 1995; Ahmad et al, 1998).

Caution about claims

Using such a disparate set of sources of data inevitably leads us to be cautious about the claims that can be made for the validity of any conclusions. However, it appears reasonable to conclude that local government (certainly social services) is funding black and minority ethnic voluntary organisations in order to promote race equality, something called for by the Association of Directors of Social Services and the Commission for Racial Equality in 1977 (ADSS/CRE 1978). In particular, local government is doing so because there is evidence that these organisations are particularly able to meet the needs of local black and minority ethnic communities by establishing an effective partnership with them, something that social services departments still appear to be failing to do (Audit Commission/SSI, 1999).

Nevertheless the 'partnership' between black and minority ethnic voluntary organisations and their funders in local government appears to be one that remains problematic. These groups appear to have regularly to (re)prove the case for the need for the services that they provide. This appears to fly in the face of evidence, that when asked the question, Who provides supportive services to black and minority ethnic communities?, the universal response is black and minority ethnic voluntary organisations. Furthermore, these organisations have to accept that the level of funding that they will receive is likely to be lower than they need and possibly lower than other agencies (Butt and Mirza, 1997). In addition, their management of these funds is more likely to be the measure used to assess the success of funding, rather than whether they have successfully supported black and minority ethnic people in need of support. It seems legitimate to conclude that there is little evidence of equality in the relationship between these groups and their funders. In this we have the starkest demonstration of the conundrum alluded to in the introduction to this chapter: black and minority ethnic voluntary organisations are often funded because of their ability to challenge racism, but their funders continue to exert significant power over them through the manner of the support they received.

Local and central government could rightly argue that they have a democratic imperative to be accountable and to ensure that those with whom they enter into partnership are also held accountable. But at present there appears to be limited evidence that this need for accountability is placed in the context of equality between partners and the recognition that these groups are providing services to those who are still being excluded from mainstream provision – mainstream provision that receives the lion's share of funding from the state.

The implementation of partnership between local government and black and minority ethnic voluntary organisations has clearly had successes. At the same time, this partnership has been implemented in such a manner that it has left black and minority ethnic voluntary organisations in a precarious situation, with limited and short-term funding being the order of the day. While this characterisation may be applied to partnership between mainstream voluntary organisations and local government, it appears to be a particular feature of the relationship between black and minority ethnic voluntary organisation and local government. Furthermore, the public 'goodwill' that many mainstream voluntary organisations can call upon does not necessarily exist with black and minority ethnic voluntary organisations, as has been witnessed by racist reaction to the announcements of grants from the National Lottery Charities Board (even though the evidence suggested that black and minority ethnic groups were not disproportionately represented as grant recipients).

Significant agenda for change

If the analysis and evidence presented in this chapter is representative of the sector as a whole then there is a significant agenda for change. Funders of black and minority ethnic voluntary organisations need to understand their value and build this into criteria of whether funding has been successful. They need also to invest in building on the strengths of the sector (such as user involvement, participatory methods of working, detailed knowledge of local needs, effective ways of communicating) as well as dealing with their possible shortcomings. This investment has to be on a long-term basis, recognising that these organisations are having to address the long-term consequences of direct and indirect (institutional) racism. By doing so, we may start to see real partnership, rather than just talking about it.

Importantly, all this has to be done with full and frank discussion about power and how this operates in these relationships. The state has the right to expect that the funding it provides for any organisation is accountable. But equally, black and minority ethnic voluntary organisations have a right to expect that the claims about partnership are not rhetoric or a smokescreen and that a genuine attempt is made to address issues of equality in the relationship between funder and those funded. It is possible to argue that this is true for all such relationships, but it appears to be particularly relevant to the relationship between black and minority ethnic organisations and the state, because by their very nature these groups have been established to challenge the existing balance of power, which has seen many of these communities not receive the support that they need.

Final remarks

With the election of the Labour government in 1997, a new impetus appeared to be given to changing the relationship between government and the third sector. The development of 'compacts' appeared to suggest a greater emphasis on a mutually beneficial partnership.

The reality has perhaps been little different from the pre-1997 situation. For black and minority ethnic voluntary organisations there may be some signs of change with the setting up of a number of development agencies focusing on capacity building, with significant funds coming from the Single Regeneration Budget as well as the National Lottery Charities Board. Once again, however, many of these initiatives had already started or had been conceived in the period before 1997. There still appears to be little evidence of a new relationship that appreciates the work that these organisations do or the problems that they face.

References

ADSS (Association of Directors of Social Services)/CRE (Commission for Racial Equality) (1978) *Multi-racial Britain: The social services response*, London: CRE.

Ahmad, W., Darr, A., Jones, L. and Nisar, G. (1998) *Deafness and ethnicity: Services, policy and politics*, Bristol: The Policy Press.

Atkin, K. (1996) 'An opportunity for change: voluntary sector provision in a mixed economy of care', in W. Ahmad and K. Atkin (eds) *Race and Community Care*, Milton Keynes: Open University Press.

Audit Commission and SSI (Social Services Inspectorate) (1999) *Making connections: Learning the lessons from joint reviews*, London: DoH.

Butt, J., Gornach, P. and Ahmad, B. (1991) *Equally fair? A report on social services departments' development, implementation and monitoring of services for the black and minority ethnic community*, London: National Institute for Social Work (reprinted by HMSO in 1994).

Butt, J. (1994) *Same service or equal services? The second report on social services departments' development, implementation and monitoring of services for the black and minority ethnic community*, London: HMSO.

Butt, J. and Box, L. (1997) *Supportive services, effective strategies*, London: Race Equality Unit.

Butt, J. and Mirza, K. (1997) *Exploring the income of black-led voluntary organisations in dimensions of the voluntary sector*, London: Charities Aid Foundation.

Hems, L. and Passey, A. (1998) *The UK Voluntary Sector Statistical Almanac*, London: National Council for Voluntary Organisations.

Jones, A. and Butt, J. (1995) *Taking the initiative*, London: NSPCC.

Kendall, J. and Knapp, M. (1996) *The voluntary sector in the UK*, Manchester: Manchester University Press.

Lattimer, M. and Trail, P. (1992) *Funding black groups: A report into the charitable funding of ethnic minority organisations*, Directory of Social Change in association with the Urban Trust.

Lattimer, M. and Walker, D. (1997) 'Funding equality to build communities – the work of the National Lotteries Charities Board', *Dimensions of the Voluntary Sector*, London: CAF.

Melunsky, B., Ghosh, P., Mikucki, J. and Stennett, A. (1992) *Black and Asian groups: A sectoral review by the London Boroughs Grants Committee*, London: London Boroughs Grants Unit.

Pharoah, C. (ed) (1997) *Dimensions of the voluntary sector*, London: CAF.

Pharoah, C. (ed.) (1998) *Dimensions of the voluntary sector*, London: CAF.

Royce, C., Yang, J.H., Patel, G., Saw, P. and Whitehead, C. (1995) *Set up to fail? The experiences of black housing associations*, York: Joseph Rowntree Foundation.

Russell, L., Duncan, S. and Wilding, P. (1995) *Mixed fortunes: The funding of the voluntary sector*, Manchester: University of Manchester.

Salamon, L. and Anheier, H. (1997) *Defining the nonprofit sector: A cross national analysis*, Manchester: Manchester University Press.

ELEVEN

Rounding up the 'usual suspects': police approaches to multiagency policing

Peter Squires and Lynda Measor

Introduction

The phrase 'multiagency policing' emerged, ostensibly describing a new approach to policing, in the early 1980s. To some extent it reflected a development from the renewed (post-Scarman, 1981) enthusiasm for 'community policing' and a greater recognition of the need for more local consultation over policing priorities. However, despite emerging as one among a number of processes 'opening-up' policing and rendering police decision making rather more visible than in the past, multiagency policing never settled entirely comfortably alongside simple notions of greater local accountability.

Multi- or interagency policing was specifically promoted by a Home Office publication in 1990, *Partnership in crime prevention* (Home Office, 1990), and then endorsed in the paradigmatic Morgan Report of 1991 (Home Office, 1991). However, 'multiagency policing' always implied something more than just partnership or joint working and could have some potentially far-reaching implications. In this article the phrases 'multiagency' or 'interagency' policing are used fairly interchangeably as referring to the same generic forms of project management. Equally the term 'partnership' policing is sometimes referred to – and preferred – by some commentators. While there may be differences of interpretation and emphasis implied by these different phrases – which can sometimes be important – in this article we are concerned with a number of more generic issues.

This paper reflects our research into how participants in multiagency policing schemes viewed the initiatives. Interagency working is a political process in which agencies (in this case, largely the police) pursue their own interests together with those of the wider 'community'. Often, multiagency working appears to be about creating 'community interests' (to which different agencies need to respond), or legitimating certain conceptions of 'community interests' that may or may not coincide with police aims and priorities. The police enter schemes with multiple objectives, sharing (or off-loading) problems, acquiring additional resources, obtaining support, and for better management of demand for their services. Examples in this paper suggest multiagency initiatives involve calling in stakeholders and service representatives (the 'usual suspects') to achieve policing objectives ('help the police with their enquiries').

What can be involved?

Multiagency policing implies the police are no more responsible for crime problems than the fire brigade are for fires. While the police respond to crime, this may not be the defining 'service' response. A profound rethink about crime prevention and management has occurred over recent years. While things have changed, questions remain about their significance for core service priorities.

Interagency working, largely accepted by decision makers within the police service, was enshrined in the Crime and Disorder legislation of 1998. Some still regret the passing of an older ethic of policing:

> "I sometimes wonder whether we really ought to stick to what we are good at. You know, catching criminals. I'm never really sure where all this talking and planning gets us."

Non-police interviewees confirmed that older attitudes remain in lower operational ranks or CID, where the 'catching criminals' ethic prevails:

> "There can be differences between the more consensual community-type approach and the 'we're here to catch criminals and bang 'em up' type. The approach may not have filtered down to all levels of the organisation."

Equally, however, this interviewee paid tribute to the extent to which the police had begun to change its own culture and prioritise community-based policing:

> "They have made a clear commitment to community and partnership working, and taken steps to ensure that appropriately motivated officers are working in the right posts."

Another added:

> "I have noted a singular change in the attitude of the police, they want to come and talk to us about how, by working together, we can resolve some issue ... they're very willing to listen to our ideas about how we might tackle things differently."

One weakness in the 'old school' argument that "we should stick to what we are good at – catching criminals" is that, judged in terms of their case 'clear-up' rates, the police were not emerging as particularly successful on that score (Kinsey et al, 1986). Furthermore, when we turn to a rather more community-oriented set of indicators – public reassurance, tackling the fear of crime, or perhaps above all, reducing overall rates of crime and victimisation, then the assessment is equally negative:

> "Thinking police people accept policing isn't a responsibility for them alone, it's a community responsibility. You can't simply whack people over the head. Increasingly they recognise they want to sit down and see if there's a more effective way of resolving things by working together." (local authority manager)

Another interviewee, in planning work, agreed:

> "There is a recognition that policing isn't about just pounding the beat. It's about planned preventative work and helping people to 'design out' crime, creating safer communities, and they can't do that on their own."

Widening the brief, changing the culture

Significant differences exist between strategies to reduce crime and open-ended, positive ambitions promoting 'community safety' and improving quality of life. These differences are ideological but also illustrate a wider dimension of multiagency policing. 'Community safety' was originally developed by the GLC Police Committee Support Unit in the 1980s to describe local government approaches to crime prevention and related issues. In local government, 'crime prevention' was reinterpreted as the promotion of community safety by improvements in the quality of life (ADC, 1990; Coopers & Lybrand, 1994).

> Using the concept of community safety rather than crime prevention was deliberate, to set the positive agenda of emphasising people rather than property, and the roles of local authorities, community and tenants' groups rather than the police. (London Strategic Policy Unit, 1986, in Demuth, 1989)

The Morgan Report (Home Office, 1991) spelt out differences in crime prevention and community safety:

> The term 'crime prevention' is often narrowly interpreted and this reinforces the view that it is solely the responsibility of the police. The term 'community safety' is open to wider interpretation and could encourage greater participation from all sections of the community. (Home Office, 1991)

'Community safety' suggests something ambitious perhaps including addressing the causes of the social harms. The Local Government Management Board emphasised:

> Community safety is the concept of community-based action to inhibit and remedy the causes and consequences of criminal, intimidatory and other related anti-social behaviour. (LGMB, 1996)

Multiagency policing also concerns change within police organisations – opening them to wider influences, rendering police decision making more accountable to a wider series of local professional and services interests, in effect bringing local police management within the more expanded networks of "local corporatism" (Crawford, 1994).

Accountability is limited to service delivery professionals rather than communities, but multiagency policing is rarely examined as a two-way process. Proponents of multiagency policing were keen to see the beginnings of a culture shift in police management but overlooked the way police influences might travel in another direction. Later in the chapter we consider the extent to which this might have occurred in the light of the comments of multi-agency service providers.

First, however, following a description of the issues and the research upon which this paper has been based, we consider the opinions of a number of the police officers interviewed during the project concerning the significance of multiagency policing.

The research

Over the course of several years and a number of projects (the installation of CCTV cameras in Brighton, Squires and Measor, 1996a; 1996b; the 'customer' and the demand for police serevices, Squires, 1998; and the development of an integrated service strategy for young people, Measor and Squires, 1997, 2000), the authors had observed the ways local police management had adopted more broadly accountable, apparently consensual and ostensibly community-based decision-making processes.

Broader influences played their part in facilitating this process of change. These included:

1. The introduction, in section 106 of the 1984 Police and Criminal Evidence Act, of a statutory duty on the part of local police commanders to consult with local populations regarding local police priorities.
2. In Sussex, this new responsibility upon the police coincided with the appointment of a new chief constable committed to the development of a community policing strategy.
3. In Brighton these developments were given added impetus by the election, in 1986 – and for the first time ever – of a new, modernising, Labour administration. The administration initially modelled itself upon the municipal radicalism best represented by the Labour administrations in metropolitan areas, chiefly the GLC in London, and it set about establishing new policy development committees in what were, for local government, rather non-traditional areas. They included a women's committee, an economic development committee, an anti-poverty strategy committee, and a police and public safety committee, each supported by council officers to take policy initiatives forwards. For

four years in the early 1990s, one of the authors served as a member of the police and public safety committee.

In the early 1980s, the involvement of Labour local authorities in policing issues had been driven especially by concerns about police accountability. Reflecting the somewhat strained and partisan politics of policing in the 1980s, Conservative-run local councils tended not to establish 'police committees' though community groups would establish 'police monitoring groups', whose approach to the police could be overwhelmingly hostile and critical. One effect of establishing a police committee within Brighton council was a more constructive dialogue between police and other community interests. Accountability was still an issue, but not the only one. The council's police and public safety committee came to serve both local authority and police interests while allowing inputs from a diverse range of community organisations. An HM Inspectorate of Constabulary report in 1991 cited Brighton council police committee as a model of good practice for other local authorities to follow and (important for the police) the committee was taken to satisfy their section 106 statutory duty to consult about local priorities (Jones et al, 1994).

These changes exerted influence upon the culture of police management. Academic literature began to address the changing character of contemporary policing including the effectiveness of multiagency initiatives. Central here were questions about why and how multiagency initiatives worked when they did, what obstacles or conflicts might stand in their way and how they might fail (Pearson et al, 1992; Matthews, 1993; Crawford, 1994; Liddle and Gelsthorpe, 1994a, 1994b, 1994c; Gilling, 1994). Critics questioned whether multiagency policing really resolved the accountability deficits of contemporary police decision making (Blagg et al, 1988). Others saw police involvement in multiagency planning as, essentially, a legitimisation exercise designed to lend a veneer of democratic accountability to police-led decision making while allowing police priorities to come to dominate the policies of partner agencies (Kinsey et al, 1986). This could result in what came to be referred to as the 'criminalisation' of social policy, whereby the priorities of agencies were subsumed beneath a crime control agenda. Local authority housing allocation decisions might reduce the significance of housing need while emphasising crime control priorities, for example.

We interviewed 'stakeholders', decision makers and agency representatives who had had some involvement in multiagency initiatives in the Brighton area. Brighton was an ideal location: the local authority was seeking to pioneer approaches to local governance, Brighton police division was the largest and busiest in Sussex, and the town is home to a diverse array of community interests and range of conflicts.

The research examined factors that appeared to contribute towards effective multiagency policing, and those that blocked it. Resource inputs (officer time, financial investments, consultative exercises, training inputs) that the police were devoting to multiagency working were critical. Police policies, practices and decision-making processes were also scrutinised. Equally, we were interested in situations in which police priorities did not change or came to be adopted by other partner organisations.

Ultimately, these issues refer back to questions concerning the power and influence wielded by representatives of different organisations and their ability to successfully realise, defend or promote their own interests through different multiagency processes. According to Liddle and Gelsthorpe (1994a), an ability to achieve what one wants, while securing the active consent and support of others, is often one of the principal tensions surrounding multiagency working. It is not supposed to be about 'winners and losers' but where there are conflicts of interest between agencies this may be how it seems to those involved.

The fieldwork comprised in-depth, semi-structured interviews with 24 police officers with experience of multiagency working and a similar number of 'agency' representatives from the local authority, a range of voluntary and private sector agencies, organisations or community groups. A number of crime prevention or community safety projects developed through multiagency processes were studied through participant observation and unstructured interviews.

The overall aims included the attempt to identify good practice guidelines for future multiagency working. Multiagency working is an interface through which agencies pursued their objectives, rather than a rationalist policy process; any emerging 'guidelines' may well be more useful as an evaluation tool than as a recipe for future practice (Liddle and Gelsthorpe, 1994b, 1994c).

Issues, problems and tensions

One conflict is, who coordinates multiagency initiatives? The 1998 Crime and Disorder legislation addressed such issues, placing the lead responsibility for crime and disorder planning firmly with the local authorities, but this fails to remove the conflicts. Other tensions can result from different objectives, different focus or attitudes to cooperation, communication and collaboration. Questions arise about whether multiagency initiatives actually 'work' and the investment in planning pay-off for all partners. Some dilemmas concern power, control and access to resources. Which agencies invest most time and energy in multiagency initiatives and which interests are really served? One key question is the extent to which the police dominate the partnership. Local accountability is also significant; agencies will talk to other agencies and call it consultation, although the 'corporatist' processes, may exclude sections of the public.

Police perspectives on multiagency working

When researchers discussed these issues with serving police officers, many formal, positive and rational factors associated with multiagency work, forward planning, proactive intervention and effective resource utilisation were raised. In this, officers' comments reflected the 'good practice' guidance proffered by organisations such as the Audit Commission (1993). Financial constraints also were of concern to police managers. Few police respondents were willing to make the point too explicitly, but effective resource allocation often appeared to lie close to the heart of their commitment to multiagency working:

> "We have to be very performance and value-for-money driven. These days policing is a business because it has to operate within financial guidelines and tight resource allocations."

Factors driving changes in police management culture related less to police involvement in multiagency planning than financial environments. The police confronted such pressures later than other agencies and police managers sought collaboration with other agencies more accustomed to the new political and economic climate. Police managers could come to perceive advantages of alliances with other service agencies that offered different ways of achieving police objectives.

Core responsibilities

Financial constraints impacted on 'core tasks' of policing (Saulsbury et al, 1996). Police officers' concerns about the 'rubbish jobs' or even the 'social work' they undertook were sharpened by resource constraints.

Multiagency work offered alternative, perhaps more appropriate, ways of addressing these problems. Performance indicators required police to specify types and levels of service-core policing roles and tasks, implying that police managers must work proactively alongside partner agencies:

> "We have to draw up a service plan, in conjunction with other agencies, the council, probation and so on, so as to outline what our ... core functions are in the community. The idea behind this is that we become more proactive and begin to say, 'Well, hang on a minute, traditionally the police have dealt with anything and everything, but nowadays that can't go on'."

Police managers also had to liaise more effectively with communities, demonstrating commitment to policing by consent and putting responsibilities back where they should lie:

> "If you can develop some sort of structure where the community can actually begin to be a little bit more self-reliant and actually positive in the way they are dealing with things, then it can have enormous spin-offs for the police. We can't usually do this on our own, you have to work with, for instance, the housing department to tap into the tenants' associations, or schools and youth clubs, to get to young people."

Managing demands on the service

One particular value of multiagency working derived from the opportunity it offered to reduce demands upon the police. One police manager elaborated:

> "I often run into the problem on the estate where they expect every thing to be given to them. They expect Housing to provide, they expect social services to provide ... they expect the police to tackle all the problems ... they see everything as a police problem.... The children stoning the buses is 'your' problem, they say. I say to them, 'It's "our" problem. They are your children, what are you doing about it?'"

Multiagency projects could be a valuable asset to the police when they delivered policing outcomes, but they consumed a great deal of time and effort that sometimes seemed to lack strategic focus:

"This sort of work, interagency work, is extremely time-consuming. I could not tell you all the initiatives we've got going, because I still haven't found out about some of them myself. There are so many meetings ... if you looked at all the balls we've got in the air you couldn't see the sky! They're all tackling crime and crime prevention though I sometimes worry that there's no focal point to it all.... We've got so much interagency work."

Embracing the multiagency ethic was meant to be about coordinating and rationalising service inputs, not doing more of everything. To reap real benefits, interventions had to become more proactive, less reactive – although the risk was that policing might become less responsive to community needs and priorities. Moreover, new issues continued to surface. One middle-rank officer cited a couple of examples where the police felt they had had to take the initiative because other agencies had seemingly failed to do so:

"This was a problem with the truancy project.... Truancy becomes a police problem because of the offending, shoplifting and the like, that kids out of school get up to. I'd rather someone else chaired the group, Education, for instance ... but they won't take on the responsibility if we don't do it. We seem to lead and drive an awful lot. The mediation scheme, set up on the estate, has been developed primarily by our officers ... the local policemen. It seems that other agencies need our push. Why? In the last resort, we take the initiative because it helps policing ... it's in our interest to do so."

The mediation project was valuable because it involved the police sponsoring a project in which community volunteers were trained to become mediators, intervening in neighbourhood disputes and trying to bring people together before things blew up to become police problems:

"When it works and when you compare it to all the time and trouble of police and council staff just trying to resolve what is a bitch between two neighbours ... it's very valuable. If a dispute continues to develop you're going to get criminal damage, fights, threatening behaviour, whatever. Eventually one party's going to have to be moved so you've got the cost of rehousing, of removals as well. When you've added it together it's a lot of money and a lot of time. So that's the attractiveness of the mediation service just in resource terms."

In other cases a rather less honourable motive for engaging in multiagency collaboration emerged. If more than one agency was involved the responsibility for failure could be shared. Alternatively, wider 'consultation' exercises could cloak 'inaction' on any given problem. Although many police officers disliked what they called 'talking shops', others recognised that there might be some advantage to be gained in setting them up from time to time to take the heat out of an issue:

> "One direct spin-off for the police is showing the community that we are trying to help solve the problems alongside other agencies. That's the political agenda. Senior managers see it as they can say, 'We've worked with Housing on this', etc.... I think sometimes they feel that providing we can say we've met with them it doesn't always matter whether we've achieved anything or not."

Doing less by taking the lead?

The truancy project involved the police attempting to persuade other service delivery agencies to take an issue seriously. Police had their own reasons for launching the initiative but became frustrated at the reluctance of other service managers to take the lead or come on board. One of the police middle managers commented:

> "The latest initiative we started was looking at truancy and the impact of truanting on crime. We tried to get together with the schools but the schools didn't like it because they felt threatened. They don't like their dirty linen being washed in the open, so you couldn't get people talking about it for fear that one school might be compared unfavourably with another. They don't want to see you come up with any bad publicity. We had the education welfare officers involved, we had social services, we had parents' groups involved. And it didn't work because the schools weren't involved. Then we mounted an exercise in Brighton to determine within a day how many children we could sweep up truanting.... We've now changed the whole emphasis.... It's now more about looking at the vulnerability of young people in the community."

A police colleague concurred, the education service was thought to have its own reasons for not wanting to be involved. Schools were said to be on the defensive, keen to keep their truancy and exclusion problems out of the public eye. The suggestion was also made that some schools were rather less than wholly enthusiastic about the possible return of some of their more troublesome and disruptive pupils.

> "... we've still ended up picking up the ball.... Basically it's an education problem, truancy and exclusion, but we've still ended up leading it.... So we had to change tack, the whole thing is to push it in a good light. What we had to do firstly was to find research on the vulnerable side of the kids — to say to them, 'Look, these kids are at risk', and then they had no choice but to come on board."

Another officer referred to police responses to domestic violence and the issue of a women's refuge in the town:

> "What happens is that we tend to try and do everything. That's been the malaise of the police force and still is to a certain extent. If there's a problem we've traditionally been the social workers as well. Now we are more likely to say, 'That's your responsibility, this is ours', and we refer on.... Working with other agencies can be difficult but it means that you get a grasp of the bigger picture and aren't under pressure to do things that, really, you aren't equipped to do. So the establishment of a women's refuge, even though it is associated with a fair bit of criticism about how we'd been handling things in the past, actually helps us enormously. Now we can refer victims on and we don't have to try to do what we were never very good at."

Similar issues emerged in respect of a new project established in the town centre providing facilities for street drinkers. Street drinking had been a focal concern in Brighton for a number of years. Aside from the social and health needs of the street drinkers themselves, residents, traders and visitors complained about them gathering in popular tourist locations, sometimes begging, causing a nuisance or giving rise to public order problems. While a number of local authorities had begun adopting by-laws prohibiting the consumption of alcohol in certain public places, the local council (facing criticism for its inaction), in conjunction with the police, the health authority and a voluntary organisation, set about establishing a day centre for the use of street drinkers. A police sector manager responsible for the town-centre area explained how, as well as providing a better service and meeting needs more effectively, the centre provided some tangible benefits for the police:

> "Our policy towards street drinkers and anyone making a nuisance of themselves in the street, begging at bus stops, annoying traders or residents, has to be a responsive one. Most of the time we've barely got time for anything else ... we're driven by a different set of priorities. We don't look to move them on any more, we've no real power to do so anyway if they're doing nothing wrong, but we do respond to complaints and, really, we don't get that many since the centre opened.... But we have to be responsive to complaints, aggressive begging, drunk and disorderly and so on.... But I don't want my officers tied up all morning with minor nuisance work when there's better and more important things they could be doing and when there's a more appropriate and specialist service available.... There's no point in arresting drunks, locking them in a cell overnight while they sober up, and then what? The custody suite is no place to look after people; we aren't equipped or really trained to do so. It's a custody suite, not a rehab centre. A lot of this goes back to the kind of service we are being expected to provide ... we have become a much more priority-driven service these days, it's not just street drinkers, but anyone. A lot of people have quite unrealistic expectations about what we can do. Unless we've made special arrangements to run a particular operation like at Christmas, we just don't have the time to deal with drunks ... so in that sense the day centre has certainly helped free up police time and resources."

In another initiative, the police took unilateral action to prompt other agencies into responding. This involved a drugs raid on a homeless persons' day centre. The ability of the police to take such decisive action, using their legal enforcement powers, clearly gives them a valuable resource not available to other organisations:

> "Sometimes you run out of people to liaise with, or you're banging your head against the wall. Sometimes it comes back to good, old-fashioned 'let's arrest some people and shake things up' ... you can try the softly-softly approach to an extent, but in the end, sometimes, arresting people and bringing them before the court does have a salutary and 'focusing of the mind' effect. Whereas I'm an advocate of trying to resolve things amicably, that can be seen as a weakness in certain people's eyes, so you then go for hard."

The officer responsible for the raid on the day centre explained the circumstances surrounding his decision. Unilateral action was not justified in terms of the law enforcement outcomes but as the restoration of a failing service and as a way of jump-starting interagency work to tackle the issue. The use of police powers is not justified by reference to the law itself but rather by reference to a broader corporate responsibility for social problem management. As the officer explained:

"I received a fair degree of criticism for the raid but I think it was the right thing to do, despite the problems. Although they had, on paper, a very clear policy prohibiting alcohol or drugs on the premises, the vast majority of their clients were drunk or drugged up. They tried to establish a more formally controlling environment but were just losing it, the people using the centre were stealing from the staff, they hadn't got any control whatsoever, their clients were making a mockery of them. For some time we'd been trying to impress upon them the need for a more professional and effective way of working but we were getting nowhere.... When it was so obviously failing we had little option but to take action ... we were also getting complaints about the drinkers and drug dealers in the nearby streets and gardens.

"The direct outcome of the raid was that we arrested eight people, some on warrants, some for possession or 'intent to supply' and some for the possession of stolen goods.... After that the day centre was closed down. It remained closed for about four weeks and there was inevitably some displacement of the clients ... but now they've re-established a similar facility in another location, but this time they've been willing to take advice and they have established an advisory committee and an appropriate management structure. I think it's much better now, they are running a much more professional operation. We did get a lot of criticism for the raid, but it became a real problem for us when the centre, the way it was operating, caused a problem that was spilling out onto the streets ... that became a police problem and that's when we had to act."

Police officers identified a double bind when taking initiatives. Police management internalised the need for multiagency working as a way of achieving improved service delivery, conserving resources and meeting community needs more effectively. While they could recognise direct benefits for their organisation, they did not like to be seen leading from the front. Leading initiatives implied taking responsibility for them, or having to provide the lion's share of the resources. In multiagency working, a lower profile was often desired as a way to draw other agencies into shouldering more of the responsibility:

> "We often tend to be taking the lead. I'd like to be doing a bit more advice and a little less leading from the front ... because, at the end of the day, once you've put your name forward and said something you end up picking up the responsibility.... We often say, 'Are we the right people to be heading this group? Wouldn't some other group like to head it?'. Yet there's often a marked reluctance for anyone else to come forward.... It's all very well people saying you should have more multiagency approaches but this takes more resources and time and staff to get on with it."

Undoubtedly, however, leading from the front, taking initiatives and being decisive conformed to another more traditional aspect of police culture. Nevertheless, this set of attitudes or professional self-perceptions also gave rise to police criticisms of other professional service cultures. We have noted earlier how some police managers occasionally voiced rather mixed feelings about other agencies' apparent lack of commitment to multiagency initiatives. Other officers put the point more directly:

> 'Education can be very good.... Probation, on the whole, I've usually found very helpful. But social services, I do feel, drag their heels. Always late for meetings ... of all of them, I think, give the smallest input they can get away with. I think their whole image is so badly dented. It's a pretty sad state of affairs."

Other criticisms surfaced in respect of the contributions of other organisations. Often organisations were reluctant to communicate or share information with the police:

> "Confidentiality is something which is very jealously guarded by many different organisations, because we're the police and they're wary about what they might tell us. But in order to work effectively we've got to be able to pass information between organisations. There are still some barriers to overcome."

Another officer spoke of overcoming communication gaps, but in a way that sounded less like open multiagency working and information sharing than informant handling:

> "There are issues around the Data Protection Act, etc ... confidentiality and so on, where I got my fingers burnt a couple of times. Let's just say we have an understanding over certain issues. Housing tell us things that, strictly speaking they probably shouldn't tell ... but that's when it suits them, and usually on a one-to-one basis with individual housing officers."

At other times, conflicts and disagreements could emerge between different organisations, deriving from their contrasting cultures, philosophies and gender composition (Sampson et al, 1991). A community-based officer described his dismay in trying to share information with social services:

> "We're encouraged to liaise with them, for instance about kids and their families on the estate but then, when you take the trouble to find who's working on a particular case, they might not seem interested at all. You wonder why you bothered."

A more senior police manager tried to put these differences, and the conflicts they might give rise to, into perspective:

> "Even today, most police officers are not so used to different cultures in organisations, they will talk of social services as a 'let's all be happy' job. I think policemen are articulating what their fears are, because we like to be achievers and do things. Police officers get frustrated because they think social services always seem to be talking around a problem."

Conclusion

This review of police perspectives on multiagency partnerships has revealed a number of the complexities associated with this form of working. For the police, multiagency initiatives are about outcomes, but not *only* about outcomes. Questions arise about how interagency relationships can transform police management and decision making and lead to quite new conceptions of the police role. Different officers appear more or less willing or able to embrace this new role and the implications that follow.

Yet multiagency policing remains a political process. Multiagency partnerships create an interface between organisations in which factors such as power, resources, opportunities, professional culture and even personalities establish a context in which agencies seek to pursue both their own and other more generic interests. However, multiagency policing is a somewhat weak form of consensus policing; the community policed (in any event, the community is not an agency) often has the most marginal seat at the table – if they are represented at all.

Researchers attended a 'community forum' in a community centre on the estate referred to earlier in this chapter. Thirty-two people were seated around a table discussing crime prevention projects, yet all represented local service delivery agencies. Only two of the people in the room actually lived on the estate, and they were only present by virtue of their roles as part-time youth workers. Rather than seeking 'consensus', as Liddle and Gelsthorpe's (1994c) research demonstrates, agencies appear to approach multiagency negotiations in a variety of ways. They present themselves in a variety of guises and play different roles, with varying levels of commitment, overt and, invariably, covert aims and objectives, a willingness to invest more or less resources and with sometimes more, sometimes less, enthusiasm for seeing the other partners' point of view. Pragmatism and instrumentalism seem far more apt descriptions of the process.

Police officers were willing to acknowledge the important benefits that multiagency working could help to deliver in terms of crime prevention or community safety planning outcomes, more accountable decision making or better community links. It was equally clear that they recognised the benefits that new ways of working could offer the police. Responsibility for complex problems could be shared or discarded. Resources could be pooled; police decision making could achieve greater legitimacy and support or even a 'lower profile', and the police could gain better access to communities by piggybacking their initiatives on those of other organisations. From an instrumental perspective on the part of the police, effective multiagency working could be seen as a process of 'rounding up the usual suspects', all the regular members of the local multiagency panels, in order to get them to 'help the police with their enquiries'.

Note

We are grateful for the contributions of David Griffiths and Jackie Nettleton who undertook a significant portion of the fieldwork interviewing reported in this article.

References

ADC (Association of District Councils) (1990) *Promoting safer communities – A district council perspective*, ADC, November.

Audit Commission (1993) *Helping with enquiries: Tackling crime effectively*, London: HMSO.

Blagg, H., Pearson, G., Sampson, A., Smith, D. and Stubbs, P. (1988) 'Inter-agency co-operation: rhetoric or reality', in T. Hope and M. Shaw (eds) *Communities and crime reduction*, London: HMSO.

Coopers & Lybrand (1994) *Preventative strategy for young people in trouble*, ITV Telethon/Prince's Trust, September.

Crawford, A. (1994) 'The partnership approach to community crime prevention: corporatism at the local level', *Social & Legal Studies*, vol 3, no 4.

Demuth, C. (1989) *Community safety in Brighton: Report of a survey and consultation*, Brighton Council Police and Public Safety Unit, April.

Gilling, D.J. (1994) 'Multi-agency crime prevention: some barriers to collaboration', *Howard Journal of Criminal Justice*, vol 33, no 3.

Home Office (1990) 'Standing Conference on Crime Prevention', in *Partnership in crime prevention*, London: HMSO.

Home Office (1991) *Safer communities* (The Morgan Report), London: HMSO.

Kinsey, R., Lea, J. and Young, J. (1986) *Losing the fight against crime*, Oxford: Blackwell.

Jones, T., Newburn, T. and Smith, D. (1994) *Democracy and policing*, London: Policy Studies Institute.

LGMB (Local Government Management Board) (with ADC/AMA and ACC) (1996) *Survey of community safety activities in local government in England and Wales*, July.

Liddle, A.M. and Gelsthorpe, L. (1994a) *Inter-agency crime prevention*, Home Office Police Research Group, Crime Prevention Unit Series Paper no 52, London: HMSO.

Liddle, A.M. and Gelsthorpe, L. (1994b) *Crime prevention and inter-agency co-operation*, Home Office, Police Research Group, Crime Prevention Unit Series Paper no 53, London: HMSO.

Liddle, A.M. and Gelsthorpe, L. (1994c) *Inter-agency crime prevention: Further issues*, Home Office, Police Research Group, Crime Prevention Unit Series Supplementary Paper nos 52-53, London: HMSO.

Matthews, R. (1993) *Kerb-crawling, prostitution and multi-agency policing*, Home Office, Police Research Group, Crime Prevention Unit Series Paper no 43, London: HMSO.

Measor, L. and Squires, P. (1997) *Juvenile nuisance*, Brighton: Health and Social Policy Research Centre, University of Brighton.

Measor, L. and Squires, P. (2000) *Young people and community safety*, Aldershot: Ashgate.

Pearson, A. et al (1992) 'Crime, community and conflict: the multi-agency approach', in D. Downes (ed) *Unravelling criminal justice*, London: Macmillan.

Sampson, A. et al (1991) 'Gender issues in inter-agency relations: police, probation and social services', in P. Abbott and C. Wallace (eds) *Gender, power and sexuality*, London: Macmillan.

Saulsbury, W., Mott, J. and Newburn, T. (1996) *Themes in contemporary policing*, London: Policy Studies Institute.

Scarman, L. (1981) *The Brixton disorders*, London: HMSO.

Squires, P. (1998) 'Cops and customers: consumerism and the demand for police services. Is the customer always right?', *Policing and Society*, vol 8, pp 169-88.

Squires, P. and Measor, L. (1996a) *CCTV surveillance and crime prevention in Brighton: Half-yearly report*, Brighton: Health and Social Policy Research Centre, University of Brighton.

Squires, P. and Measor, L. (1996b) *CCTV and crime prevention in Brighton: Crime analysis and follow-up survey*, Brighton: Health and Social Policy Research Centre, University of Brighton.

TWELVE

Partnership – participation – power: the meaning of empowerment in post-industrial society

David Byrne

Perhaps never before has the dominant class felt so free in exercising their manipulative practice. Reactionary postmodernity has had success in proclaiming the disappearance of ideologies and the emergence of a new history without social classes, therefore without antagonistic interests, without class struggle. They preach that there is no need to continue to speak about dreams, utopia or social justice....

Weakened religiosity and the inviability of socialism have resulted in the disappearance of antagonisms, the postmodern reactionary triumphantly says, suggesting in his pragmatic discourse that it is now the duty of capitalism to create a special ethics based on the production of equal players or almost equal players. Large questions are no longer political, religious or ideological. They are ethical but in a healthy capitalist sense of ethics....

We, therefore, don't have to continue to propose a pedagogy of the oppressed that unveils the reasons behind the facts or provokes the oppressed to take up critical knowledge or transformative action. We no longer need a pedagogy that questions technical training or is indispensable to the development of a professional comprehension of how and why society functions. What we need to do now, according to this astute ideology, is focus on production without any preoccupation about what we are producing, who it benefits, or who it hurts. (Freire, 1998, pp 83-4)

In this chapter the terms 'empowerment' and 'partnership' will be compared and contrasted. 'Empowerment' will be used as a benchmark against which the claims of 'partnership' will be tested. That is to say 'partnership' will be evaluated according to whether it facilitates, is neutral towards, or has negative consequences for empowerment. The word empowerment will be used specifically in the sense given to it by the Brazilian educator and founder member of the Workers' Party, Paulo Freire. Heaney has summarised this thus:

> Empowerment – For poor and dispossessed people, strength is in numbers and social change is accomplished in unity. Power is shared, not the power of a few who improve themselves at the expense of others, but the power of the many who find strength and purpose in a common vision. Liberation achieved by individuals at the expense of others is an act of oppression. Personal freedom and the development of individuals can only occur in mutuality with others. (Heaney, 1995)

'Partnership' does not have this specific kind of intellectual origin. Mayo (1997) reviewed both the dictionary definitions of the term and its meaning in use in contexts of regeneration and community development. She notes that dictionary definitions imply shared interests and that policy makers have tended to focus on something like symbiosis in which the result of partnership is a multiplicative rather than additive outcome – the partners working together achieve more than the sum of them working alone. Mackintosh (1992) suggests a 'transformational model' in which the partners change by adapting towards each other. This is a strange use of the word 'transformation' for anyone coming fresh from reading Freire. For Freire, the purpose of social action is indeed transformation, achieved through 'conscientisation': "... a process of developing consciousness, but consciousness that is understood to have the power to transform reality" (Taylor, 1993, p 52). People act together collectively not to change each other or become like each other but because they are already like each other (Marx's classes in themselves). Through collective action (classes for themselves) they transform the oppressive social structures that block the fulfilment of their human potential.

In the long passage from Freire, which serves as epigraph to this chapter, perhaps the key phrase is 'antagonistic interests'. What are the antagonistic interests in the contexts in which 'partnership' is being proposed as the panacea for the solution of problems of urban social disorganisation and social exclusion? A neat summary runs thus:

> There is a crisis at the heart of British Democracy. Freedom and the right to dissent have been curtailed. This arises from the fact that it is in the interests of international capital to turn as many activities as possible into a commodity which can be bought and sold.... The international market is becoming the arena which determines every aspect of the nation's political decision making. (Blunkett and Jackson, 1987, p 1)

David Blunkett was then, as now, MP for a Sheffield constituency and is now Secretary of State for Education and Employment. It is therefore appropriate to conduct the evaluation of partnership as process against the benchmark of empowerment in relation to the form and content of Education Action Zones (EAZs). These are a key programme of Blunkett's department and a good example, because the issues in the selected zones are typically those of marginalisation and 'fourth world' status. Moreover, EAZs are intended specifically to address educational issues and Freire's programme has always centred on education as a key process of conscientisation.

The useful phrase 'fourth world' is an explicit analogy with 'third world' and refers to places and lives in metropolitan capitalism that are as marginalised/underdeveloped as those of the 'third world' of the South. Note that here the term 'underdeveloped' is not simply an adjective. It is used in Cleaver's sense (1979) to describe a process through which capital reconstructs metropolitan social relations by creating places and ways of living which have much in common with those of marginalised lives in the third world, and does so in order to facilitate accumulation by capitalists. The implication of this is stark. It suggests a convergence between what has conventionally been thought of as the third world and the first world, with parts of the latter becoming like the former. This is what Therborn has called 'the Brazilianisation of Advanced Capitalism' (1985). In other words, rather than São Paulo becoming like the welfare capitalist Newcastle of the 1960s, Newcastle is becoming like São Paulo.

In practice, in post-industrial capitalism the marginalised are, in fact, a crucial component of the reserve army of labour (see Byrne, 1999) but the term still has value in distinguishing a component of that reserve army by reference to the processes that created it. Freire puts it like this: "... marginality is not by choice, marginal people have been expelled from and kept outside of the social system and are therefore the object of violence" (1972, p 27). ('People' replaces 'men' in the original in accordance with Freire's own later practice.)

West Newcastle – a marginalised but partnered place

West Newcastle is a palimpsest of urban projects going back to the Community Development Project (CDP) days of the mid-1970s. Among other things it is the location of an EAZ. That project and its activities illustrate 'partnership' in practice. The four inner west wards of Newcastle have all lost more than 30% of their population since 1971 and all score highly in terms of indices of social deprivation, incidence of crime, and void housing. The schools serving the area have very low achievements in terms of public examinations.

The history of this derives from a combination of deindustrialisation and loss of unionised unskilled and semiskilled jobs, the relocation of both what is left of the old blue collar skilled, and the new white collar proletariats, to new residential areas on and beyond the urban fringe, and the particular dynamics of Newcastle's urban policy over a 40-year period, during which commercial city-centre activities have always been given priority over the provision of adequate and well-delivered public services in working-class residential areas. A key indicator is provided by house prices in this area. In much of inner west Newcastle a flat can be purchased for £3,000 or less. The same flat built from the same pattern book at the same time by the same builder will cost £75,000 just two miles away in Jesmond, a middle-class part of the city.

Education Action Zones – partnership for personal development?

An EAZ is a radical new concept based on a cluster of about twenty primary, secondary and special schools in a local area. The zone is run by a forum of business, parents, schools, the local authority and community organisations. For example:

• businesses can be involved in providing leadership, advice or services to the zone;
• parents can get involved in making sure that the schools in their area provide a high quality service, and that in return the schools get the support they need from the community. (Secretary of State, 1998)

The objective of EAZs is to raise the standards of performance, measured in terms of the conventional indicators of educational success, of children in deprived areas. The purpose is to improve the life chances of pupils by breaking a continuing cycle of intergenerational educational deprivation. In Newcastle this is operationalised thus:

- raising percentage of pupils getting five A–C GCSE passes from 16.5 to 28.5 by 2002/2003;
- reducing percentage of pupils with no GCSE passes from 25 to 5;
- raising attendance rates by 3% per year;
- significant (not defined) reduction of school exclusions by 2002/2003.

Most of the partners in this project are local and include a range of educational institutions, quangos, and Newcastle United Football Club. A major exception is the US-domiciled private corporation The Pacific Institute.

Much of the debate about EAZs has centred on the prospect that the actual delivery of educational services might be undertaken by for-profit corporations. This is not the issue with the involvement of The Pacific Institute in Newcastle. The company does not deliver educational services as such. Rather, it deals in training for personal motivation. To quote its website:

> The Pacific Institute is an international corporation specialising in personal and professional growth, change management and leadership development. The guiding principle of The Pacific Institute is that individuals have virtually unlimited capacity for growth, change and creativity, and can readily adapt to the tremendous changes taking place in this technological age.

The mission statement reads:

> We affirm the right of all individuals to achieve their God-given potential. The application of our education empowers people to recognise their ability to choose growth, freedom and personal excellence. We commit ourselves to providing this education through all means that are just and appropriate.

The intellectual foundations of the approach lie in cognitive psychology and social learning theory.

It would be inappropriate to demonise this company, which seems a perfectly straightforward and above-board operation. However, it is necessary to examine the premises on which it works and which are being imported into the Newcastle EAZ. These focus on individual achievement and social adjustment to change. Empowerment is understood as an individual process in line with the psychological foundations of The Pacific Institute's approach. There is no social analysis or collective objective. This is a profoundly Protestant approach in contrast to the continuing collectivism of the Catholic tradition that gave rise to Freire.

Social politics and policy – and the 'individualist fallacy'

The 'individualist fallacy' informing The Pacific Institute's version of empowerment is pervasive in contemporary social politics and social policy. This reflects the importance of both possessive individualism as a doctrine in Western political philosophy and the aesthetic endorsement of individual as realised self, characteristic of urban Western elites. In an otherwise excellent critique of the relationship between the 'New Labour ethic and the spirit of capitalism' Rustin asserts that under the kind of new managerialism represented by EAZs: "Education ceases to be defined as the development of the potentialities of the individual and becomes the achievement of measurable competences" (2000, pp 124-5). There is no sense, even in his radical discussion, of education as a collective activity for transformation – the essence of Freire's approach.

An examination of EAZ documentation reveals an interesting set of assumptions about how they will work. Firstly, the partnerships have only local tactical discretion. They do not have the power to specify strategic objectives. Those are laid down centrally and specified in terms of raising traditionally conceived standards through enhancing individual achievement. The discretion of local action forums is confined to modifying methods of implementation. Secondly, the vocabulary, always something to pay attention to in any analysis influenced by Freire, assigns very different statuses to business as opposed to the parents and the community. Business will lead. Its methods, obviously superior to those of the traditional public sector, may be adopted to replace current practice. Parents and the community, however, are not seen as 'leading'. Their task is to help, to facilitate, to make the process work, not to determine what the project is to be about.

The recently published *National strategy for neighbourhood renewal: A framework for consultation* (2000) does seem to recognise that issues of control matter. In the foreword to which Prime Minister Tony Blair put his name, it is noted that: "Unless the community is fully engaged in shaping and delivering regeneration, even the best plans on paper will fail to deliver in practice". However, there is no mention anywhere else in the more than one hundred pages of this document of community involvement of shaping, as opposed to facilitating, delivery of programmes developed externally. (For further discussion of the strategy, see also Chapters One and Two.)

Discussions of 'partnership' often refer to different stake- or powerholders. In their Introduction the editors of this collection distinguish between 'variable' and 'zero-sum' concepts of power and relate the former to the current fad for 'capacity building'. If there is a fundamental antagonism of interest then power is always a zero-sum game because antagonists cannot yield power to the other side without losing their own capacity to determine that outcomes serve their purpose. In an individual achievement frame of reference – in other words if everybody with a potential interest agrees that what matters is that some children will succeed – then there can be collaboration and 'capacity building'. However, if some of the participants challenge this approach, even in ways that would lie within traditional parameters of social reform, then no such accommodation is possible.

Riley and Watling in discussing EAZs remark that: "The application process induces authorities and communities into a public confession of inadequacy and, like all confessions, it first absolves the powerful of any role in the creation of the problem" (1999, p 56). Not only are the powerful 'absolved' from responsibility for the creation of the situation, they are given even more power in relation to its resolution. This is an excellent illustration of the implications of urban regime theory (see Judge et al 1995), which argues that democractic mandate and accountability are no longer the basis of the contemporary management of local affairs. Instead, urban policy is determined by the power of actors in often informal coalitions of interests. This inevitably privileges the already privileged.

It is not so surprising that partnerships are to be found in processes of physical redevelopment where large amounts of private capital, supplemented of course by massive public subsidy, are required for new construction. In EAZs, however, the private sector comes in with at best relatively trivial sums of money, but is given power because it represents what is good and progressive. Rustin considers that: "...corporate capitalism is the dominant driving force to which New Labour seeks to adapt British society, and ... it offers it a model style of political leadership for this reason" (2000, p 116). To this can be added the very real potential for long-term accumulation through the handing of public services to private capital. In the short term this is creating a new politics – the longer-term implications may involve a complete transformation of welfare provision and local administration.

Empowerment in action

In benchmarking the partnership component of EAZs against the standard of empowerment, there is a real working example to consider as a standard. Freire took on the job of Secretary of Education (equivalent to Director of Education in the UK) for the city of São Paulo under the Workers' Party administration of the early 1990s. Of course scale is different. São Paulo is the second-largest city in the world with a population half as large as that of the whole of England. However, the issues faced were in many respects the same, something which would not surprise Freire after his experience of internal division in the 'first' world in the 1970s and which reflects the real degree of "Brazilianisation of Advanced Capitalism" which has already occurred in places like Newcastle.

Harold Reynolds Jnr, former Commissioner of Education for Massachusetts, specified the problem Freire faced when he:"...confronted again the awful struggles to get the resources to make education work for all children" (Freire, 1993, p 9). Indeed Reynolds went further and argued that:

> Public schools in São Paulo and Boston [and Newcastle] also need protection from 'Education Presidents' and 'Education Governors' [and Education Prime Ministers'] who have benefited from selected expensive schools, colleges and universities designed to produce a cultivated elite to manage and govern an essentially static society. (Freire, 1993, p 11)

The flavour of Freire's approach is indicated by the following statement:

> ... to argue in favour of the active presence of pupils, pupils' fathers, pupils' mothers, security people, cooks, and custodians in program planning, content planning, for the schools, as the São Paulo administration of Luiza Erundina does, does not mean denying the indispensable need for specialists. It only means not leaving them as the exclusive 'proprietors' of a basic component of educational practice. It means democratising the power of choosing content, which is a necessary extension of the debate over the most democratic way of

dealing with content, of proposing it to the apprehension of the educands instead of merely transferring it from the educator to the educands. This is what we are doing in the São Paulo Municipal Secretariat of Education. It is impossible to democratise the choice of content without democratising the teaching of content. (1998, p 110)

This is not a proposal for free unstructured learning. On the contrary it demands enormous self-discipline and engagement from all involved in the processes of education because they have to establish both what is to be taught and how it is to be taught. Neither is Freire – a man who began teaching as an adolescent by tutoring his fellow pupils in Portuguese grammar and who was appalled by the common US practice of specifying sections of books to be read by graduate students rather than whole texts – in any way arguing for a relaxation of intellectual rigour in terms of content. What he is arguing for is a difference in purpose.

Opposition of 'banking education' and 'dialogic education'

Here it is useful to draw on Freire's opposition between 'banking education' and 'dialogic education'. Banking education deposits knowledge in the passive learner and presents a selective rather than global account of reality. The learner is an object, not only of the process of education itself but also as an object being made for purposes external to the learner and the learner's human nature; the teacher is a toolmaker – the learner is a tool being shaped for a task. Taylor (1993) identifies this as an inherently Manichean position. The Manichean doctrine of opposites is a source for dialectical reasoning in Western thought. In Freire, influenced by the young Marx, dialectical reasoning of course also becomes dialectical practice. Heaney defines Freire's conception of dialogical learning thus: "The dialogical approach to learning is characterised by co-operation and acceptance of interchangeability and mutuality in the roles of teacher and learner. In this method, all teach and all learn" (1995).

In west Newcastle the proposals are for banking education – for the development of a system that produces more people fit for work in the post-industrial economy typified by the non-unionised, panoptical call centre. Call centre staff need the level of basic education represented by five A–C grades at GCSE but they do not need to be equipped to question the organisation or objectives of the social system of which the call centre is a part.

For any given individual in west Newcastle, reaching the standard of education required for lower-middle-class employment is a real achievement and certainly enhances personal life chances. However, the personal response of such individuals – wholly rational and understandable: I would do exactly the same – is to use their comparatively better and more secure wages to depart as fast as their legs can take them from the poor locales of west Newcastle and relocate to a pleasanter and more stable residential area. In other words, people rise from their community not with it. It has to be said that the output objectives of Newcastle's EAZ are rather realistic even in terms of banking education. They propose achievement levels that are only two-thirds of the current national level. Three quarters of west Newcastle's children will still be educational failures in 'banking' terms.

Freire's programme for São Paulo is described in *Pedagogy of the city* (1993), the first part of which is entitled 'Education for liberation in a contemporary urban area'. He argues both for a relevant education that utilises the experiences of the pupils but is by no means a degraded and inferior education, and for an education that derives its purposes from the objectives of those who are engaged in it. It is plain that the actual programmes in São Paulo, in which the municipal budget was directed towards good basic primary education, were essentially and straightforwardly redistributive. They presented some educational opportunity to the children of the poor.

Back to Newcastle

West Newcastle is not São Paulo but the tendencies of globalisation are making the two places converge. West Newcastle has had formal state education for all for more than 100 years. That said, it now has a high level of functional illiteracy. Indeed observation suggests that the contemporary young poor are far more likely to be functionally illiterate than their grandparents. This is despite the existence of state primary schools funded on the same basis as everywhere in the city as a whole.

Certainly, in relative terms, west Newcastle's children are in much the same position as the poor children of São Paulo. Moreover, there is no political system that tries to engage those children and their parents in the determination of the form and objectives of educational provision. Most parents in west Newcastle, and all children, have no channel through which they can in any way influence even the 'implementation' agenda of the EAZ and, as has been pointed out, the strategic objectives are not something that have in any way been determined locally.

What is evidentially absent from partnership in Newcastle's EAZ is any notion that the system should be directed by the people who participate in it. In notable contrast with Freire's ideas, pupils are not even considered as potential partners. Parents and the community are present at least nominally. The parents on the local forum do have some representative accountability in that they are drawn from elected parental governors, even if those involved in the management of the zone are not directly elected to the action forum. There are no mechanisms through which action forum members, supposedly representing it, are even indirectly accountable to it. Local councillors are elected but turnout in the inner west Newcastle wards is below 20%, which indicates the scale of the crisis in the usual mechanisms of democratic representation.

Whether, in fact, west Newcastle is a 'community' is debatable. As in Wacquant's Parisian banlieues, (1993, p 374) we may be dealing with what he calls "an impossible community", by which he means that, rather than affirming collective identity and hence committing to collective action, people deny common status, affirm external negative views of their neighbours, and go for strategies of exit rather than solidaristic transformation. The Newcastle EAZ's methods and objectives would seem likely to reinforce rather than act against the rational pursuit of such personal strategies.

This kind of social intervention is a deeply contradictory process. On the one hand there is no doubt that the logics of contemporary business-led capitalist public policy do want good call centre fodder. On the other, the same logics also require a flexible and threatening reserve army of labour in order to discipline workers. In addition there are the problems of order posed by disorganised neighbourhoods like west Newcastle.

It is perfectly true that the injection in west Newcastle of large public order resources and some innovative, indeed rather dialogical, policing practices have led to a relative decline in burglary rates. However, the situation is still so extreme that an important part of Newcastle's 'Going for Growth' strategy involves the wholesale demolition of 4,000 social housing units in an effort to redefine the social status of the whole area. The objective is to attract middle-income households back into the area. Here we have a good old-fashioned contradiction. Banking education can lead to personal mobility but personal mobility increases the potential for anomic disorder among the residuum, among those left behind. This is the short-term problem. In the medium term there is the likelihood of other order problems consequent on the technological redundancy of the white-collar factories typified by call centres. EAZs are an explicitly short-term policy.

Is empowerment possible?

A note of caution is in order. Page reminds us that when we talk about empowerment we should remember that:

> ... social work techniques of this kind may prove to be more beneficial to facilitators and educators who wish to cling on to the vestiges of a personally rewarding form of 'radical' practice rather than to those disadvantaged members of the community for whom the promise of a better tomorrow appears to be as far away as ever. (1992, p 92)

Certainly it is easy to mount critiques of the application of Freirian ideas in practice (see Facundo, 1984). However, it is notable that such critiques precede Freire's own active engagement in social politics through the Workers' Party, with its genuinely transformative objective of social change, and relate largely to a very partial application of his approach in community projects that did not engage at all with the structural character of the societies within which they are embedded.

More seriously, any effort at collective transformation in the contemporary UK must confront the alternative programme expressed in its extreme form by Margaret Thatcher in her assertion that there is no such thing as society, only individuals and families, and endorsed in a modified form by Tony Blair and his wife when they succeeded in modifying Labour's entire educational policy in order to facilitate the educational achievement of their own children. The Blairs may well believe that there is such a thing as society but it comes a poor third after individual and family.

This is a common contemporary position for people looking at the educational prospects of their own children in the UK. The introduction of parental rights in terms of choosing the schools that their children attend means that an important part of the management of domestic life lies in facilitating access to 'good schools'. Balls et al (1995) have shown that there are two approaches to 'parental choice'. Firstly, there is an overwhelmingly working-class fatalistic localism in which people accept their local schools. Secondly, there is a middle-class cultural form to which many working-class people subscribe, of active organisation of choice in order to maximise performance potential. The third strategy, purchasing private education, requires very substantial resources. In Newcastle, private secondary education requires payments per child per year of about £8,000 from taxed income.

Parental choice is a big issue in west Newcastle. People in the western suburban fringe of the city send their children to the Northumberland schools beyond the city boundary, freeing places in their local schools that are taken in a kind of domino effect by families from the working-class inner west wards fleeing *their* local schools. Gateshead's City Technology College's catchment area extends into west Newcastle and this high-achieving institution selects part of its intake by interview from the children of the area.

In a social context dominated by these kinds of practices, one must admire parents in places like west Newcastle who make a commitment to the improvement of standards in their local schools and send their children to them. That said, the proposed achievement targets set for west Newcastle's schools are meagre. Certainly only a tiny proportion of children attending those schools will ever achieve the educational performance levels necessary for entry into the university in which I teach and which is only 20 miles from their home. What is being offered is banking education for individual mobility but for the overwhelming majority, even of the minority who 'succeed' – the target is for only two thirds of the national average level of five A–C GCSEs achievement – mobility will be very short range. Most, of course, will still 'fail' to reach even that standard.

> The social structure that generates poverty generates its own shabby educational system to serve it; and while it is useful to attack the symptom, the disease itself will continually find new manifestations if it is not understood and remedied. The solution to poverty involves, of course, the redistribution of income, but more than that, it requires the redistribution of effective social power. Self-confidence, no less than material welfare, is a crucial lack of the poor, and both can only be won by effective joint action. More contentiously, it seems to us that educational provision alone cannot solve even the problem of educational poverty, if only because in this sphere there are no purely educational problems. (Coates and Silburn, 1970)

In nominal terms, subject to the vagaries of resource allocation among local authorities, there has been very substantial change in the educational system in the UK since that passage was written. There is almost universal provision of at least nominal comprehensive secondary education. Funding on a formula basis is supposed to allocate equal resources to all children in the state system, although even at its highest level this is still less than a third of that available in the private system from fee income and charitable status. What has manifestly not been redistributed is power, other than the consumer power of individual households in exercising 'parental choice'.

A Freirian approach to the issues being confronted in EAZs would have to begin with the transfer of control of strategic objectives to the parents and children in the schools. Note that Freire's description of empowerment is prescriptive, take it or leave it. Empowerment for that social being had to be collective – it could not be about individual success while others were left to fail. That given *a priori*, then how empowerment would be achieved was up to the people concerned.

Of course Freire, like the political party he helped to found, had a view of the social order which was based on a fundamental notion of antagonism. The interests of business and poor working-class – or indeed even affluent working-class – people are not the same. The poverty of the poor working class and the general insecurity of the whole of the working class are preconditions of the prosperity of business through accumulation in flexible capitalism. Freire had learnt this himself in the process of being transformed from a liberal Christian social reformer to an adherent of liberation theology. He had no problems with this account of social reality because the exploited poor had taught it to him. He was their pupil in these matters. This means that there are no 'liberal' solutions to the issues being addressed by EAZs.

Conclusion

Is empowerment possible? The answer would seem to be: not through partnership, because that at best attempts to reconcile irreconcilables and at worst, which means usually in practice, offers the objects of policy, at the very most, some role in influencing the implementation of strategies that have already been decided on. This is incorporation, not partnership.

What might empowered education look like in west Newcastle in the early years of the 21st century? Well, it would be education for change, not for stasis. Moreover, it could not be developed in isolation from other programmes of social change and could not be developed merely in the zones of the poor and deprived without any attempt to address the character of the relationship between those zones and the areas of residence of both the middle masses and the affluent and privileged. Of course it would be education that addressed achievement, but it would also be education that addressed the realities of everyday life. This is much easier said than done! Indeed even as a teacher in a relatively privileged university, I find it difficult to raise issues of criticism with undergraduate students. It is not difficult with my MA students who are mostly employed professionals studying on a part-time basis. They have established careers. My undergraduates increasingly want banking education geared to achieving the magic 2:1 and a decent career opportunity. Insecurity is rife even at that level. Perhaps the very uselessness of banking education for most in places like west Newcastle means that a different approach might be easier, although there is no justification whatsoever for imposing segregation on the poor in the interests of their collective future.

Poor people in places like west Newcastle need no instruction in the reality of the system in which they live or in their contemporary powerlessness in the face of it. They neither need nor want tinpot Lenins arriving with a party programme to explain their degradation to them, although making available a language for describing the origins of that degradation is a valid task. What they lack above all else is a sense of capacity for achieving change.

Here the relationship with the middle masses is crucial. Transformational change is always something that is initiated by the upper sections of those suffering from domination and exploitation. Neither liberals nor Leninists have any love for those groups – the aristocracy of labour in Leninist jargon – too stroppy, independent and self-directed for real elites, but the field marshals of the revolution were always the sergeant majors of the old regime. The poor are a disciplining army for the 'middle masses' in contemporary, flexible, post-industrial capitalism. Indeed, the poor and 'middle masses' are not really separate categories because through the life course many people move back and forth between these two statuses. This means that there is really a common interest between middle people and the poor in challenging the form of the contemporary social order. This common interest is the absolutely necessary foundation of any sort of transformational politics today.

Partnership will address none of these realities. This is not merely a matter of the exclusion of the poor from any kind of determinant influence in directing the policies of partnership organisations. That is a symptom. The cause is the irreconcilable difference of interests that exists between exploitative flexible capitalism and those exploited by it.

Partnership working

References

Balls, S.J., Bowe, R. and Gerwitz, S. (1995) 'Circuits of schooling', *The Sociological Review*, vol 43, pp 52-78.

Blunkett, D. and Jackson, K. (1987) *Democracy in crisis*, London: Hogarth Press.

Byrne, D.S. (1999) *Social exclusion*, Buckingham: Open University Press.

Cleaver, H. (1979) *Reading capital politically*, Brighton: Harvester Wheatsheaf.

Coates, D. and Silburn, R. (1970) *Poverty:The forgotten Englishman*, London: Penguin.

DETR (Department of the Environment, Transport and the Regions) (2000) *National strategy for neighbourhood revival:A framework for consultation*, London:The Stationery Office.

Facundo, B. (1984) *Freire-inspired programs in the United States and Puerto Rico: A critical evaluation* (http://www.uow.edu.au/sts/bmartin/dissent/documents/Facundo/preface.html).

Freire, P. (1972) *Cultural action for freedom*, London: Penguin.

Freire, P. (1993) *Pedagogy of the city*, New York, NY: Continuum.

Freire, P. (1998) *Pedagogy of hope*, New York, NY: Continuum.

Heaney, T. (1995) *Issues in Freirean pedagogy* (http://nlu.nl.edu/ace/Resources/FreireIssues.html).

Judge, D., Stoker, G. and Wolman, H. (eds) (1995) *Theories of urban politics*, London: Sage Publications.

Mackintosh, M. (1992) 'Partnership: issues of policy and negotiation', *Local Economy*, vol 7, no 3, pp 210-24.

Mayo, M. (1997) 'Partnerships for regeneration and community development', *Critical Social Policy*, vol 17, no 3, pp 3-26.

Page, R. (1992) 'Empowerment, oppression and beyond: a coherent strategy?', *Critical Social Policy*, vol 35, pp 89-92.

Riley, K. and Watling, R. (1999) 'Education Action Zones: an initiative in the making', *Public Money and Management,* July/September, pp 51-8.

Rustin, M. (2000) 'The New Labour ethic and the spirit of capitalism', *Soundings*, vol 14, pp 127-40.

Secretary of State (1998) *'Education Action Zones – A message from the Secretary of State'* (http://www.dfee.gov.uk/edaction/foreword.htm).

Taylor, P.V. (1993) *The texts of Paulo Freire*, Buckingham: Open University Press.

Therborn, G. (1985) *Why some peoples are more unemployed than others*, London: Verso.

Wacquant, L.D. (1993) 'Urban outcasts: stigma and division in the black American ghetto and the French urban periphery', *International Journal of Urban and Regional Research*, vol 17, no 3, pp 366-83.

THIRTEEN

Spatial considerations in multiagency and multidisciplinary work

Philip Haynes

This chapter considers the spatial location of services and how spatial location difficulties can be amplified when multiagency policies and multidisciplinary teams are established. The chapter starts with a brief introduction to the relationship of space with welfare services, considering the idea that the relationship between physical space and society is important. This assumption rejects the idea that human space is entirely defined by capitalism and social relations, but instead prefers the postmodern thesis that geographical space itself can be one of the defining features of social life. This leads to a more pragmatic consideration of spatial issues. What is needed is an awareness that spatial barriers exist. Examples referred to draw on research completed by the author over the last 15 years. The names of the areas are anonymised to protect the confidentiality of the area and teams involved.

Why is space important?

It is not possible in this chapter to attempt an extensive discussion of the literature about the relationship between space and society, geography and social science, but it is necessary to indicate the sympathy that the argument in this chapter demonstrates for the reawakening of human geography in mainstream social and political science. The reader may be asking why it is important in a book about partnership working to consider spatial considerations? Surely such considerations are secondary to the obvious challenges of integrating professional cultures and organisations so as to find satisfactory solutions to complex social problems? Why consider space as one paramount part of this process?

The reason for considering space is the belief that space is a fundamental component of the construction of modern society, including the organisation and definition of social problems (Sayer, 1992; Sheppard, 1996; Byrne, 1998). This fundamental contribution of space to society can be understood by reference to two key levels.

The first level is physical. The social world is construed of physical space and physical barriers. Considerations of geographical location in relation to a wide range of social and economic variables remain pivotal to the definition of 21st-century society. The location of employment, housing, social services and neighbourhood are major factors in determining the quality of life experienced by citizens. Numerous studies have linked spatial location with social outcomes such as educational attainment and prevalence of ill health (Byrne and Rogers, 1996; Dorling, 1997; Drever and Whitehead, 1997). Finding the technology to overcome spatial barriers that allows social actors to communicate and work without crossing physical space is one of the key aspects of our new technological age. Physical space, like time, is one of the most fundamental defining characteristics of the human experience.

The second level is social. Space not only exists in the physical sense, but also exists in the social world. Physical places such as communal buildings, streets and neighbourhoods have highly complex cultural definitions attached to them, and these are powerfully associated with the quality of life we experience (Haynes, 1999, pp 26-8). In modern Britain this is illustrated by the focus on social exclusion, where concern about groups of people being excluded from a whole range of social relations is linked fairly directly to their habitation of particular streets and neighbourhoods. At least part of the solution for solving this exclusion is seen to be the improvement of these districts and streets so as make them more physically connected and similar to the other neighbourhoods and streets that surround them.

The physical and social aspects of geographical space are connected and need to be understood together. It cannot be that human society has total control of space. Space and physical geography will always set some limits on what society can achieve. Global warming and the resulting flooding is one example. Society can only continue to build on flood plains if the huge costs associated with flood prevention and flood relief are acceptable. Sheppard (1996, p 1339) summaries the theoretical link: "despite the socially constructed nature of space, it is vital to treat space as constitutive of social processes".

Having made the case that considerations of space and spatial identity are important, the chapter now progresses to consider the key elements of space that multidisciplinary teams and multiagency partnerships need to address.

There are five key elements:

1. The local prevalence and incidence of the social problem targeted by the multiagency project.
2. The relative mobility, or lack of mobility, of the target community.
3. The mobility of professional services and different perceptions of professional mobility.
4. The complex relationship between space, cultures and the subculture associated with the social problem targeted.
5. The relationship between agency culture and spatial location.

I. The local prevalence and incidence of the social problem targeted by the multiagency project

Multidisciplinary teams are often set up as a result of moral panics over specific social issues. For example, in the mid-1980s a growing number of community drug teams (CDTs) were established in response to social anxieties about the increased prevalence of heroin misuse. Similarly, following the Cleveland Inquiry in 1989, specialist assessment teams were established to cope with the new awareness of sexual abuse.

These kinds of specialist teams are usually composed of professionals who have a close proximity to the emerging problem and in this sense, multidisciplinary practice evolves from a wider generic base. Professionals seconded to CDTs often came from generic experience in mental health and criminal justice. Professionals that moved to specialist child abuse assessment teams usually had prior experience in diagnosing the physical abuse of children. Multidisciplinary work often involves professionals evolving their practice from a generic to specialist focus. In geographic terms, a specialist team frequently has to cover a wider geography than a generic team. A large number of generic teams may make referrals to a specialist multiagency team. This means that the specialist team covers a substantially bigger area than each generic team. This is particularly true in shire counties, but it can also be true in urban areas.

The emergence of 'specialist' social issues is frequently related to physical space. Certain geographical locations become associated with the emergence of the 'moral panic' of the day. This may influence the location of a multidisciplinary team, with the danger that specialist resources are focused on one geographical area at the exclusion of others. Often, new special teams are located in the geographical area labelled as 'having the problem'. In some circumstances, however, a new specialist team may find that it is located away from the apparent central hub of the social issue, because it is dependent on being located in a donated building, or cheap premises. This can have considerable influence on the nature of service development and the resulting demand that is actually expressed for the service.

The arrival of a new multiagency service is not necessarily good news for policies on social exclusion. Specialist teams that focus on the geographical location of a problem can reinforce the image that 'the problem only occurs in that area'. Newly emerging moral panics and so-called specialist problems have a particular tendency to get associated with geographical locations: drugs, HIV and youth offending, are good examples. Once new specialist teams find incidence of these problems in certain locations this can reinforce again the association between the problem and the location. Many agencies acknowledge this and attempt to undertake broader prevalence studies of larger areas, but once a service is physically located in one place, the difficulties of moving it can be considerable, given the limited funding associated with multiagency developments.

Consider the spatial dilemmas in the following real example. Western District Council is a predominantly rural part of the southeast of England that includes some small urban areas (see Figure 13.1). Near the centre of the district is a small historical market town, Weston, with a population of approximately 25,000. The town is flourishing and has a business, tourist and retail centre that supports the whole district and beyond. Some ten miles south of Weston is a larger town, Kittleworth, a coastal location that lacks the history and wealth of the small central town. Kittleworth has some large areas of social housing, originally funded by the GLC after the Second World War. The population is 70,000, but many inhabitants commute the short distance to Weston each day for their work. To the north of these two towns is a large rural area. The people here associate themselves with services at Weston and rarely travel to Kittleworth. Historically, hospital services for the whole district have been provided at Weston where there is a large general hospital, and up until recently, a psychiatric hospital that once provided a catchment for the whole shire county.

In the early 1980s drug misuse services were based around a limited

Figure 13.1: Weston District Council: sketch map of key urban and rural areas

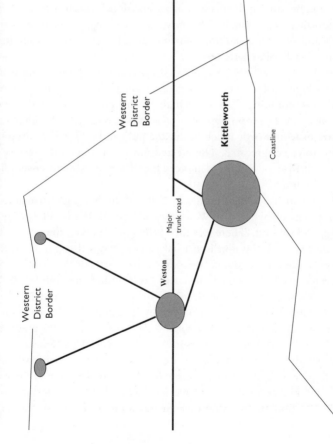

specialist sessional input from a psychiatrist and nurse at Weston psychiatric hospital. In the mid-1980s additional money became available for developing drug services. A local prevalence study suggested a significant problem in Kittleworth, but also that drugs were being misused in Weston and in some of the villages to the north. The first multiagency team was small and located in an old house belonging to the NHS, situated in a cottage hospital premise on the edge of Kittleworth. As a result of this new service location, Kittleworth was certainly better served. A prescribing psychiatrist supported the Kittleworth location and visited fortnightly, while continuing to provide a fortnightly clinic at Weston psychiatric hospital. Nevertheless, neither of the locations of these services was central to the two towns and both were culturally linked with traditional NHS sites. The team was fragmented because of having to cover a number of sites and because of the need to make occasional trips to known users in the northern rural patch. This made it harder for the team to establish itself and to gain a multidisciplinary specialist identity and reputation with other local generic services.

In the late 1980s drug use and drug-associated crime continued to have a high profile. The multiagency team grew in size and had more resources committed to it. Much of the cottage hospital site was redeveloped. The team was able to move to a community building in the centre of Kittleworth, much nearer the pubs and cafés where drug users in the town congregated. This created added demand for the service that was in danger of making it more difficult for the staff to cover all the other locations.

The team had a high profile in Kittleworth, but could it maintain a high profile elsewhere? In Weston the old psychiatric facilities were run down and sold off. There was the challenge of finding the best method for dealing with the northern rural patch. It was thought adequate to target funding to a voluntary group in that area, but they could not be expected to develop a medical service easily without a supportive GP. An emerging strategy was the decision to locate the new district alcohol services in a high-street office in Weston. The hope was that professionals from the alcohol and drug services would use each other's premises to see both drug and alcohol users in the two towns. This cemented a link between the two professional services that was good for their professional development, as well as giving more flexibility to users about where they attend. Given concerns about lowering the threshold of services to prevent HIV infection among drug users, increasingly in the 1990s the service was concerned with the spatial location of their potential service users, rather than with trying to entice them to visit the service locations.

Research shows that both drug and alcohol users have important associations with specific places, public and private places where the peer group operates, substances are brought, sold and consumed (George and Frazer, 1988). In one sense, breaking the associations attached to these locations is an important part of treatment, but on the other hand the ability of services to infiltrate these places with non-threatening invitations into treatment, and at least to give health education advice, is seen as an important service priority. There are other complicated factors to consider. The places that are important in drug and alcohol cultures are likely to change rapidly, particularly in response to the behaviour of law enforcement, and the multiagency treatment services need to be careful that they do not themselves contribute to the isolation of the user population.

The example shows how a developing team was able to be flexible in its approach to its own spatial location, while also seeking to understand the use of space by their users. Both aspects of the spatial needed to be considered and regularly reviewed, if the team were to continue to be successful in attracting its target population. Geographical dispersion of the service had to be carefully balanced with the aim of helping the new multiagency team to bond together in professional practice.

Much effort has been focused on quantitative understanding of the prevalence of social problems in recent years. This is useful, but knowing where a problem is and the extent of its coverage does not solve many of the complex challenges about how to get the relevant service delivered to those who need it. Service location is only one aspect of this problem and at worst it might be a distraction from thinking through creative methods for reaching the target population.

2. The relative mobility, or lack of mobility, of the target community

The example discussed begins to show how a multiagency service evolves from anxieties about its own spatial location in its early stages of development, to a concern with the location of its user group and potential user group. An associated issue here is the relative mobility, or lack of mobility, of the target user population.

With some social issues, the target population is relatively mobile and transient, making spatial location of services particularly difficult. This may often be the case with so-called 'deviant' groups, who have a limited access to social resources. Offenders with mental health problems, those who misuse drugs and alcohol, may change address regularly, despite the apparent existence of neighbourhoods where there is evidently a high prevalence of people with these kinds of difficulties. The point is that over a large area there may also be a large number of small neighbourhoods and peer groups that provide sanctuary and support to those excluded from the mainstream of society. Such potential service users may not be socially mobile, but they are still geographically mobile and demonstrate an ability to travel distance and change address.

This unpredictable mobility of users has an important repercussion for multiagency teams who are in danger of erroneously associating their client groups with a limited mobility of space. Experiencing a specific social problem does not necessarily mean that an individual is cemented to a specific place. Many crises in the welfare state have occurred when service users have lost contact by leaving an address, or failing to be at an address for a significant period of time. Professionals may associate home with one location and the idea of one recorded address, but those excluded by society may see their life and location differently, moving about between a complex network of peers and locations. In this sense, spatial considerations in welfare work are based on a national and regional synthesis, rather than just a local analysis of users' addresses. Multiagency law enforcement in child protection knows the need for good national awareness of the networks that exist.

In the NHS, specialist treatment centres, such as multiprofessional cancer care, may have very large geographical catchment areas that present the specialist team and its management with significant challenges about how to make the service equitable to all localities. It is important that regional specialist services are known about at the local generic referring level and that all generic professionals have a correct perception of the specialist service. In modern society, a good understanding of locality also has to be linked to people's interaction with regional and national boundaries.

When do travelling difficulties outweigh the benefits on offer?

To what extent are people in need willing to travel to access regional and national services?. At what point will an individual decide that the difficulties of travelling to a service outweigh the benefits offered? The greater the distance and the difficulties connected with travelling, the lower the threshold of rejection. This decision to reject a service can be based on individual factors, but social factors such as income and availability of transport also play a part.

For some groups, the nature of the social problem they experience may dictate that they are confined to a fixed address. Older people, those with some mental health symptoms, and those suffering from a long-term illness frequently find this to be the case. Here the ability of agency services to get to the residential location and to make it less limiting is the key, either to provide quality of life enhancing services there, or to provide transport assistance to get to services elsewhere. With this kind of service, the danger is that multiagency, multiprofessional services, based on a narrowing definition of specialism, will find themselves covering spatial areas that are much larger than those covered by generic services (such as geographical areas covered by GPs for example). If this leads to those at the spatial margins receiving less service provision, the situation is unsatisfactory. In these circumstances the consideration as to where to locate actual service provision is highly important (for example where to locate a day centre for older people). All too often, limited resources dictate that a day centre is located where a current building is already available, or where trained staff are available, rather than the mapped point where the combined needs of users, in relation to available transport networks, shows a service should be (Frost and Foley, 1994).

3. The mobility of professional services and different perceptions of professional mobility

We live in a very mobile society. It is surprising how immobile our public services sometimes are. Technology offers ways of overcoming the mobility of services, but it has a limited impact with human services. Multidisciplinary teams can face additional spatial challenges, because they usually cover larger geographical areas than generic referring services. A new team needs time to find the best way to work together and this can make them cautious about being away from a central base, but once they have established themselves, innovative thinking is needed to make the service as mobile and accessible as possible.

The co-location of professionals is not a magic and simple solution that overcomes the difficulties of interagency and multiprofessional working. The mobility of professional services – that is their ability to take services to users – rather than expecting users to come to them, is an important aspect of spatial management.

Public confidence in professional services has been reduced by the ideological and media assault on professionals in the last two decades (Clarke and Newman, 1997). Many of the social issues of the day are generational. Young drug misusers do not automatically respect middle-aged professionals. Older people with long-term limiting illness feel let down by the modern state and see no reason to be dependent on state services that apparently don't want to help them, unless they absolutely have to (Parker and Clarke, 1997). One of the contradictory messages of the early 21st century is the message of access to state services. People are taught to be hard working and independent and to look after themselves and their own, while at the same time professionals and service managers are being pressured to make their service more accessible to those who really need help and to attempt to meet more demand from fewer resources. The public reads about denied access to services because of eligibility criteria, means testing, or simply because 'I smoked' or 'it was too expensive to provide', while those working in services feel compelled to demonstrate evidence that they are providing a service for those in greatest need. It is not easy to understand this contradiction of messages, but one analysis might be to suppose that the targeting of state services is increasingly important.

This presents a challenge to service providers. How can they find those people who have the highest level of needs and how can they convince them that they need a service? It has been known for many decades that residual, means-tested welfare is often stigmatised – so that even those who are entitled to it may not want it and would rather try to go without. There seems to have been an assumption in the last 20 years that public perceptions of welfare have changed to become more based on a consumerism and the demanding of one's rights, but there is still evidence that for those most in need this is not the situation (Baldock and Ungerson, 1994). If welfare services are to be successful in targeting those in priority need they are going to have to do much better at going out and finding these people and providing for them.

A recent report on holistic and joined-up government recommended professional integration for a broad range of welfare services, not just for special projects (6, Leat, Seltzer, Stoker, 1999). The same report optimistically talks of "savings in the number of staff required through co-location" (p 19), but this seems to ignore the complexities and limitations that are faced when relying on spatial location to solve problems. Co-location does not necessarily make services more integrated in their response to social problems and social needs.

Differences in agencies' prioritisation of needs

Multiagency projects can show up the different individual agency cultures and perceptions towards the management of social problems. Some agencies have strong cultures of rationing resources and waiting for patients to persistently demand services, or letting them wait their turn on the waiting list. I remember talking to a social worker seconded to a health service project who had never experienced waiting lists before: she could not resist the temptation to see clients on demand. Different professionals react differently to the prioritisation of needs. The definition of who is most in need becomes embedded in professional judgements, conflicts and ethical priorities. Some services and professionals are much more radical than others at investigating need and recruiting those who have priorities. Multiagency working does not simplify this process, but makes it more complicated.

Voluntary agencies and their workers are often particularly innovative in terms of their approach to spatial and temporal barriers, so as to make them more accessible. Some see the potential in technology for overcoming spatial and temporal barriers. Phonelines that are answered by a helpful, informative person provide an initial service to the majority of the population regardless of their spatial location and perhaps during all hours of the day. If paid workers are not available at night, volunteers can be recruited. Statutory services are often concerned about the real quality of such provision and whether the large extra numbers can be guaranteed a continuing service of quality.

Multiagency services often appreciate the importance of providing expertise on the phone in respect of the specialist issue that they cover. Busy generic services will often tell worried users to give the specialist team a ring and thus those without a phone face an additional spatial barrier and perhaps are further excluded. Imagine the feelings of the person who finds the courage to confront their problem and negotiates to a pay phone, or a friend's phone, only to find that the thinly stretched multidisciplinary team has left the answering machine on and that its tape is already full.

One solution to the relatively wide spatial distribution of specialist multidisciplinary services is to put them on the move – in other words, to offer the service in a bus or minibus. Library services have found this an effective method for combating spatial barriers for many decades.

Drug and health services have taken this approach on a number of occasions in the last two decades. In particular, the focus on low-threshold services for HIV prevention demanded that workers take to the streets to find those at risk. Images were portrayed of nurses in hiking boots and with a rucksack full of clean injecting equipment and condoms. The Netherlands developed the idea of the methadone bus, where low-threshold drug maintenance services could be taken to many neighbourhoods, rather than based in one location. Cancer screening and other health specialist road shows are sometimes based on a similar model. If a specialism, whether in a multidisciplinary team or otherwise, results in a large geographical coverage – mobility of delivery becomes very important.

Another solution in a larger multiagency team is for each individual worker to cover a specific geographical patch, in terms of their relationship with generic referring services. The difficulty is that generic referring services often relate directly on an informal basis to their own seconded specialist, for example GPs tend to want an initial discussion with the team nurse, social services want to speak to the team social worker. If individual workers cover specific areas this can also fragment the multiagency approach. Teams can set up duty rotas, in relation to geographical patches, to try to combat professional allegiance – but it is difficult to change professional peer allegiance.

A compromise might be for one worker in a team to spend one day in a specific outlying location. For example, one of the specialist team agrees to at be a remote rural health centre on one day a week. The physical presence of a team member will help build up informal relationships with the generic professionals there, even if the visiting specialist's professional background is different. Local people can be secure in the knowledge that a member of a multidisciplinary specialist team is available.

4. The complex relationship between space, cultures and the subculture associated with the social problem targeted

It was argued at the beginning of this chapter that space is entangled with culture and local perceptions of social problems. People make comments all the time that reinforce this. "That is the estate where all the criminals live." "There are a lot of strange people who live in that street." "You don't want your children at that school, because all the people who live on Westbrook estate send their children there." "House prices are low in that street – it is not seen as a desirable place to live". Such stereotyping becomes a self-fulfilling prophecy and a cycle of exclusion continues.

If we are to combat many of the social difficulties faced by our society we need to find ways of redefining physical space and people's relationship to it. This cannot simply be done by changing attitudes to particular areas, but by making those spaces physically and culturally attractive. Put simply, there are two historical approaches to redefining social space: demolishing, rebuilding and recreation; or providing human and social resources to help people change the area themselves from the inside out. We might call these 'structure' and 'agency' (Giddens, 1984; Hay, 1995). 'Agency' here refers to the action and choice of individual people. In reality, both approaches are important, and both strategies need to be worked together. There is no point in physically recreating an area if you have not consulted with and thought about the individual needs of the people who live there. Similarly, it may be pointless just sending more social workers, health workers and youth workers into an area that is physically deprived and excluded. This will probably just reinforce the view from outside that this really is a 'place apart' that is of less value than everywhere else.

At the start of the last paragraph, the words 'social difficulties' were used instead of 'social problems'. This was deliberate. If we are to have proper understanding of the complex entanglement of space, culture and exclusion the old notion of social problems needs to be broken. The individualism of the 1980s has left a cultural legacy that excluded areas are excluded because of some pathology within – that social problems are the collation of individual problems and that individuals are somehow largely responsible for these problems. This was 'agency' in the extreme. It was perhaps something of a rebellion against the structural views of the 1960s, when policy believed that if the physical environment was transformed, so were people. Policy needs to move beyond this polemic.

What is needed is a new appreciation of the entangled 'feedback' between structure and agency. The revolutionary recreation of physical space can go a long way to recreating the culture of an area and providing opportunities to break social barriers of exclusion and spatial separation. Bricks and mortar can be a point of transformation that evolves to a steady improvement in employment statistics and crime reduction. This is the structural component. But the agency component is equally important. People living in excluded places have to believe themselves that their place is 'better' and have pride in it. If they are of low self-esteem and feel excluded from society, how can they like the place where they live? The key is allowing people to manage the transformation of their own spaces, thus giving them increased self-esteem and self-belief in the process and its possibilities (Taylor, 1998; Social Exclusion Unit, 2000).

The forgotten element: partnership

Partnership with service users may be the most important and forgotten element in multidisciplinary specialisms. There is often a danger in multidisciplinary specialisms that service users are not widely included in service planning and development. This may be because multidisciplinary specialisms are formed in response to some of what society sees as the 'most difficult social problems': mental ill health, crime committed by those with mental disorders, youth crime, drug taking and so on.

It is not only physical space that excludes these people, but the labels and processes that they have been subjected to. For some of these people it may be that their own behaviour has played some part in this exclusion. But it would be unrealistic to give them the total responsibility. Many of these behaviours could be regarded as an expression of dissatisfaction with the physical and social environment, a statement of rejecting the environment around them – that they see the quality of their life as unsatisfactory. The neighbourhood and society have to share some of the responsibility in helping the excluded find a solution. The excluded do not totally exclude themselves, but the wider community plays a part in their exclusion. Again structure and agency are entwined. As Byrne (1998, p 164) says: "exclusion is a dynamic process rather than a static one". If part of the solution lies within excluded people, part also lies in the community and streets that they inhabit and another part in the national agenda, in the politics of resource distribution and national culture and attitudes (see also Byrne's discussion in the previous chapter).

Where does this discussion of the philosophy of structure and agency leave the multidisciplinary teams that are trying to address some of our greatest social challenges? It leaves them with a sharp responsibility, not only to deal with the pathology of the person they are asked to heal, but also to explain the issue in the context of the neighbourhoods and wider community in which they live. The specialist team should not seek to carry the total responsibility for that issue, but should seek to ensure that the local community and government continues to face up to the part that they can play in solving the difficult challenges faced.

It is understood that clinical and legal responsibilities encourage professionals like psychologists and social workers to deal with individual pathology, but there should always be some part, some time, for viewing and working with the community and its response. Teams must also help local people to understand and change the spatial environment in which service users live. This is an important part of the complex process that multidisciplinary projects have become so central to. It would be counterproductive for multidisciplinary projects to ignore completely this spatial and communal responsibility, although it may well have to remain secondary to their clinical and pathological focus. Larger teams may wish to appoint a community worker, or educationalist, who can focus on this important sociological role.

5. The relationship between agency culture and spatial locations

The issue of single-agency culture and spatial locations takes us back to the issue of 'coverage' and the impact that setting up a multidisciplinary team has on addressing a social problem. At the beginning of the chapter it was mentioned that there are possibilities that 'multiagency' is associated with a certain type of 'social problem', a problem that is somehow seen as particularly serious and intractable. By setting up a specialist team of experts it is possible both for the local and national community to feel that some action has been taken. This might be a form of communal avoidance, where locality and governments then choose to forget the issue. Such multidisciplinary teams then find themselves trying to solve impossible situations and facing their own exclusion from the local community and other generic professionals. It has not been unknown, for example, for multidisciplinary teams to find that it is difficult to acquire even a building for their new service location because both the professional and local community attach so much stigma to the user group that they are hoping to help.

Professional isolation must be avoided. It is possible for a better dynamic to result where the local strategy about the social issue of concern is a shared responsibility between the specialist team and generic professionals. Generic teams continue to take some responsibility for the issue and are supported by the partnership and specialists. Generic teams and professionals often have a very detailed knowledge of particular streets and families that specialists cannot hope to have because of their wide spatial coverage. General professionals may feel marginalised if they are not given opportunities to share this local, neighbourhood-based knowledge.

An example is regional police and customs inquiries that fail to take seriously some vital local detail submitted by the community beat officer. On occasions the regional squad needs local knowledge to work effectively, so the lines of communication must be open. Single-agency professionals who have worked in the same neighbourhood for some time may become quite territorial about their work and knowledge, feeling that a particular place is their 'patch'. Generalists in some socially excluded areas may feel defensive given that such areas are often under assault from the images portrayed by outsiders. Specialists need to respect this and to try to work with the professionals concerned.

The specialist team is likely to undertake a lot of clinical work with those who are seriously suffering from a given condition, and whose needs are beyond the ability of generic services. In an ideal world the specialist team would in time put itself out of work as society changes and the local community and generic services find that they are able to cope with confidence. It is not an ideal world. Nevertheless, we can have a vision of a multidisciplinary team living in near harmony with its spatial catchment area. New technology can also be used to build stronger links between general professionals and specialists. E-mail and intranets can enhance regular communication and information exchange, but for a multiagency project this can involve the complex linking of single-agency IT systems.

This discussion shows what can be gained and lost when a new multiagency team is launched in a defined spatial location. The danger is that some local generic workers feel undermined. This can be avoided if they are included.

A story of a multidisciplinary team and its spatial approach

The chapter finishes by examining some of the issues outlined in one of the multidisciplinary service evaluations that the author has undertaken in recent years. This particular research examined the evolution of a multidisciplinary specialism in eating disorders.

Typically this social issue is one in which society communicates mixed messages. There are various important sociological explanations of eating disorders that emphasise the structural issues of advertising, patriarchy, media images and fashion capital (Lawrence, 1984), these in addition to the pathological approach of traditional psychiatric medicine. To their credit the team interviewed showed an awareness of the structural issues and expressed a frustration that there were not enough opportunities to take these further in the local community.

The story of how the team was established is a fairly typical example, in the author's experience. The issue of eating disorders had come to prominence in the locality because increasing incidence made GPs feel unable to cope. Some powerful local voices demanded a service. Generic hospital services felt that their service was inappropriate and costly and needed by other user groups. There were, however, one or two generic professionals who were enthusiastic about dealing with the issue and wanting to develop specialist skills.

The interested professionals were mainly located in one community mental health team (CMHT), there being three other similar generic teams in the health district area. The immediate location of the interested professionals resulted in the new specialist service being located in their CMHT, largely because they could not be paid to work full time with eating disorders, but only for certain sessions. Thus the additional resources of specialist counsellor, dietitian, and sessional occupational therapists were appointed to work from this CHMT base, even though there was not adequate office space. There was no money available for alternative premises.

The spatial location of the new service was not in the most populated central district, but in a district to the south (Figure 13.2, location C). While it is easy to understand this, the service was not functioning to maximum effectiveness from this point onwards – and spatial location was shown to be critical in the research evaluation, which suggested that the southern location was failing to maximise the urban coverage and was also resulting in a less effective rural service. Even the rural users, and smaller urban areas (towns A and D in Figure 13.2) would have benefited from a central location because transport routes in were generally better there. The research evaluation concluded that the authority should seriously consider relocating the service to the central urban locality (B) and that it was even possible that relocation might be financed by savings in emergency hospital admissions. If more users could access the community services, fewer emergency hospital admissions would be required.

A relocation also offered other possibilities. A building separated from generic mental health services would be less stigmatising to the young women who needed the service. It would offer better access to schools,

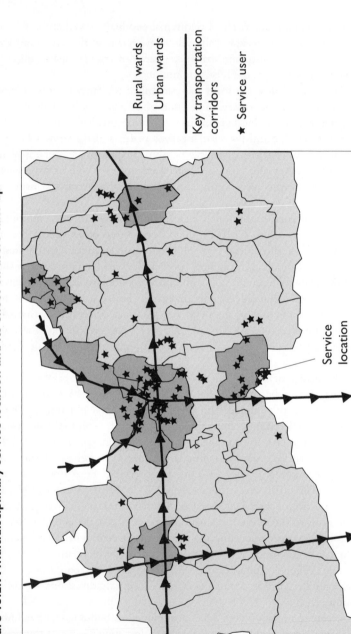

Figure 13.2: A multidisciplinary service location and its effect on users take-up

Rural wards

Urban wards

Key transportation corridors

★ Service user

Service location

colleges and the media for preventive community work. Similarly, with improved access to all areas of the district, it would become less costly for the specialists to visit rural practices and users – something that the research had also shown up as needed.

Additional research looked at the number of appointments and time spent with the multiagency team for each service user over one year. This showed that those service users living fairly near the service (in urban area C, or in the southern part of urban area B) were more likely to attend appointments and spend a longer time in treatment. It was suggested that there could be a relationship between proximity to the service location and the number of appointments successfully kept.

Conclusion

The dilemma of creating specialist multidisciplinary teams in response to moral panics and 'new' social problems is that service access moves from a low spatial threshold (where there has been a lack of confidence in dealing with the problem) to a relatively high spatial threshold (where there is a new and higher degree of confidence in dealing with the problem). Specialism often results in multiprofessionalism, because the complex nature of social problems requires a complex multiagency and integrated approach. Once a specialist multiprofessional service is created, often a minority, those who live near the specialist service, have an advantage because the spatial threshold is not raised for them. Many other members of the public will find that they live quite a long way from the specialist project. The more defined the focus of the specialism, the greater the likelihood that the spatial coverage will be larger and risk further geographical exclusions. The solutions to this spatial threshold challenge are:

- careful consideration of the main site location;
- innovative spatial and temporal approaches to actual service delivery;
- good communication and practice links between general professionals and specialists.

Good multiagency communication is vital to get these spatial issues worked out satisfactorily. Technology can play some creative part in helping overcoming spatial barriers. Once multidisciplinary teams and multiagency management groups are established to deliver joined-up solutions to the most urgent of social problems, they are to be encouraged to think through their allegiances to very specific places and to attempt to put their 'show on the road'.

References

6, P., Leat, D., Seltzer, K., Stoker, G. (1999) *Governing the round: Strategies for holistic government*, London: Demos.

Baldock, J. and Ungerson, C. (1994) *Becoming consumers of community care: Households in the mixed economy of care*, York: Joseph Rowntree Foundation.

Byrne, D. (1998) *Complexity theory and the social sciences*, London: Routledge.

Byrne, D. and Rogers, T. (1996) 'Divided spaces – divided school: an exploration of the spatial relations of social division', *Sociological Research Online*, vol 1, no 2 (http://www.socresonline.org.uk/1/2/).

Clarke, J. and Newman, J. (1997) *The managerial state*, Buckingham: Open University Press.

Dorling, D. (1997) *Death in Britain: How local mortality rates have changed*, York: Joseph Rowntree Foundation.

Drever, F. and Whitehead, M. (eds) (1997) *Health inequalities*, London: Government Statistical Service/The Stationery Office.

Frost, P. and Foley, R. (1994) *A costed model of respite care*, Brighton: Health and Social Policy Research Centre, University of Brighton.

George, M. and Frazer, A. (1988) 'Changing trends in drug use: an initial follow-up of a local heroin using community', *British Journal of Addiction*, vol 83, pp 655-63.

Giddens, A. (1984) *The constitution of society*, Cambridge: Polity Press.

Hay, C. (1995) 'Structure and agency', in D. Marsh and G. Stoker (eds) *Theory and methods in political science*, London: Macmillan.

Haynes, P. (1999) *Complex policy planning: The government strategic management of the social care market*, Aldershot: Ashgate.

Lawrence, M. (1984) *The anorexic experience*, London: The Women's Press.

Parker, G. and Clarke, H. (1997) 'Will you still need me, will you still feed me: paying for care in old age', *Social Policy and Administration*, vol 31, no 2, pp 119-32.

Sayer, A. (1992) *Method in social science: A realist approach* (2nd edn), London: Routledge.

Sheppard, E. (1996) 'Site, situation and social theory', *Environment and Planning A*, vol 28, pp 1339-44.

SEU (Social Exclusion Unit) (2000) *National strategy for neighbourhood renewal: A framework for consultation*, London: Cabinet Office.

Taylor, M. (1998) 'Combating the social exclusion of housing Estates', *Housing Studies*, vol 13, no 6, pp 819-32.

Conclusion – can partnerships work?

Susan Balloch and Marilyn Taylor

The chapters in this book have focused on a wide range of partnerships – between statutory agencies such as health, social services and housing, between communities and statutory agencies, between users and service providers and between voluntary organisations and statutory funding bodies. They have illustrated some of the advances made in theoretical and practical approaches to partnership working in the last decade in these different but closely related fields. Progress has undoubtedly been stimulated by the political commitment to combating poverty and deprivation and to "widening the policy agenda beyond issues of material poverty to address the multiple and interrelated difficulties found by people facing social exclusion" (Pearson, Chapter Three). To this must also be added the promotion of active citizenship through the empowerment of individuals and groups often excluded from the political process. This commitment has focused on partnership working as the main vehicle for policy implementation across a broad range of activities.

Partnership working has, as our contributors show, spread across the country and across policy areas. As Reid explains, for example, housing services are now expected to work in cross-functional partnerships "to tackle the more complex and intractable challenges presented by socio-economic disadvantage and 'problem' housing estates" (Chapter Four). Reid shows that such arrangements are extremely diverse, exhibiting different degrees of formality and both 'top-down' and 'bottom-up' development. At the least, a majority of local authorities in England now report that they consult with a range of organisations and interest groups when developing their housing strategies. However, the commitment to consultation demonstrated in many of our chapters is only one step along the path that can lead to defining people's needs in terms with which they agree and pursuing the outcomes that service users and communities themselves would choose.

Challenges to partnerships

Partnership and power

In the Introduction to this book we spoke of political, cultural and technical challenges to partnership. The political challenge is, ironically, the most serious at a time when partnership has become a political principle. The challenge derives from the inability of agencies involved in partnerships to address, or even be prepared to address, issues of power. If a partnership does not address issues of power it will remain symbolic rather than real. As Mayo and Taylor discuss, an apparent consensus may simply mean that the opinions of more powerful partners are dominating agendas and processes. Where this happens, only limited notions of partnership are entertained, dominated by professional providers and excluding users from decisions about strategic planning and service delivery.

This is well illustrated by Butt's chapter on black and minority ethnic voluntary organisations that come into conflict with local authority partners by challenging direct or indirect/institutional racism. In criticising the ways in which local authority social services departments fund black and minority ethnic voluntary organisations, Butt questions why black groups have regularly to prove the case for the services they need, in contrast to white groups. Because local authority funding is both limited and short term, these voluntary organisations are often left in a precarious financial situation, even though they may be the only groups able to provide the services that black communities need. Black and minority ethnic people and their communities therefore remain excluded from mainstream services and also deprived of specialist services. They are not treated as equal partners in planning and service delivery, even though their funding is directly related to the promotion of racial equality.

Another example of the failure of partnership to address empowerment is identified by Byrne in his discussion of Education Action Zones (EAZs) in deprived areas. The purpose of EAZs is to improve pupils' life chances by breaking the cycle of intergeneration educational deprivation. Using collective empowerment as a yardstick with which to evaluate the success of partnerships, Byrne has criticised 'banking education', which treats students as passive learners and imposes on them a particular version of reality. He finds no intention for the system to be directed in any sense by its participants. Thus empowerment is reduced to the limited, consumerist emphasis on parental choice and involves no element of power sharing. In this context, partnership becomes a tool of the established system for incorporation and cannot contribute either to reconciling the major conflicts between social classes or to encouraging social change.

The dangers of this happening are inevitably increased by the rapid pace of change. Although partnership is seen as a means of achieving change, the actual pace of change, the redrawing of boundaries and the turnover of personnel can prevent relationships of mutual trust from developing as well as disrupt those that previously existed. This, as Turner and Balloch have noted, is a fear expressed by those now contemplating the merger of health and social services in care trusts.

Finally, in this brief discussion of the power dynamics in partnership working, we cannot but draw attention to the importance of funding. The failure of joint finance in the early days of community care bore testament to the difficulties that could arise when agencies are asked to pool resources. The government's alternative strategy, to encourage agencies to bid for new funds in partnership, provides a halfway house, but still does not overcome the difficulties created when agencies are required to pool mainstream funding. Ambrose has pointed out the problems that may arise when agencies are working to different financial agendas with different lines of accountability.

Cultural differences and partnerships

Education and training are particularly important for challenging common-sense interpretations of the world and encouraging professionals to step beyond the confines of their own pre-qualifying training. As Davies has argued, they are important to capacity building and to the development of social capital. Northmore has shown how difficult it is for housing and mental health services managers, attempting to work in partnership to provide a better service, to appreciate each other's objectives, let alone those of service users. Charnley has emphasised, in her discussion of the empowerment of older service users, the extent to which professional resistance as well as cultural expectations have to be overcome. Professionals may experience a loss of autonomy and misunderstand the statutory responsibilities of other agencies. Such factors, combined with differences in organisational culture, can lead to mutual stereotyping between professionals and a lack of agreement about roles and responsibilities (see Charnley, Chapter Seven).

Technical and administrative challenges to partnerships

Partnership approaches need to acknowledge the technical complexities involved in bringing together disparate services. These include sharing information, joint funding arrangements and linking administrative procedures. While information confidential to one service should never be shared across services without the user's permission, shared information is important for professionals trying to work in partnership. Deciding what may be shared and, technically, how to transfer this information is fraught with difficulties. The exchange of information, as well as joint administration, becomes more complex where agencies, such as local authorities and health authorities, are not co-terminous and possibly unaware of the types of information they could more easily share at a strategic level. The development of community profiles as part of the modernisation agenda for local government may go some way to identifying and overcoming this. However, potential solutions require a long-term political commitment that can address the technical difficulties to be overcome and build the capacity and skills to make them work.

Haynes has alerted us to other complexities attached to policies relating to place and space. He argues that specialist teams may reinforce unfavourable perceptions of groups of people, or geographical areas, with special problems, fail to take account of the mobility of target populations and lose track of those they are supposed to be supporting. In contrast, they may not recognise the relative immobility of their target population who are unable to access services. In this case, one solution is to make services mobile – as library services have been for many years; another is to enlist the help and advice of local communities and to recognise that solutions to such problems must be shared; a third might depend on advances in technology to facilitate communication and service delivery.

Making partnerships work

In spite of the difficulties outlined above, there are many who argue that new policies that embrace partnership working can bring agencies and service users together in mutually beneficial and inclusive arrangements and create opportunities to be seized. Partnership has put excluded groups and communities onto the agenda in a way that they have not been before. The chapters in this book attest to this and to the champions for change who exist in the range of agencies and communities that are addressing the social exclusion agenda. Partnership working has, for example, the capacity to 'reframe' the way we tackle issues, transforming problem-based approaches into positive programmes. Thus, Squires and Measor have illustrated the significant difference between policies intended to reduce crime and those intended to promote 'community safety' through interagency collaboration. The change of emphasis implies a concentration on people rather than property and on the roles of community organisations, local authorities and others rather than just the police. In some cases it has changed police management and decision making and led to new conceptions of the police role.

There is a growing body of knowledge about what makes partnership work. Williamson points to the importance of a central government lead in strengthening the hand of those who advocate change and persuading more reluctant colleagues to the partnership table. She emphasises the perceived advantages of joint working arrangements, the equivalency of partners, appropriate administrative arrangements, limited staff turnover and additional funding. Williamson also echoes the finding of a growing number of research studies that clarity of expectations is essential to the success of partnerships. Clarity of purpose involves clarity and agreement about how success is to be defined, a definition that is too often controlled from above in a proliferation of top-down output indicators and performance targets. The need for additional funding is also a prerequisite, along with recognition that attempts to address social exclusion purely by joint working and efficiency gains are unlikely to pay off.

The chapters emphasise the importance of education and shared learning programmes in underpinning cultural change and building the capacity of professionals to respond to change, as well as that of residents and service users. Commitment and capacity are needed throughout partner agencies, from management to the front line and throughout communities and users' groups if partnership is to be built on a strong and sustainable base. The authors draw attention to the new roles that partnership requires and the skills that are needed to underpin them. The role of 'boundary spanners', individuals with networking skills who can work across agency boundaries, is of central importance. Peter Ambrose confirms the latter using the example of local community leaders, advocates and housing managers who can take up issues on behalf of residents that by their nature require a 'cross-agency' response. To the list of factors supporting partnership working he would also add retaining the benefit of 'frontline-ness', including in all job descriptions reference to the need to develop partnership working and providing the necessary training for this. The success of partnership may well depend on the extent to which innovative joint learning programmes are introduced, to break down existing stereotypes and cultural divides and develop new understandings and agendas.

Finally, we conclude that inclusive partnerships can be developed, but only if fundamental inequalities between 'partners', based on differences in income, culture, ethnicity, disability, age, education and training and other factors, are recognised, challenged and changed. This radical agenda depends on acceptance of a rights-based approach in which the rights and self-defined needs of individuals and communities provide the rationale for strategic planning and service delivery. For its implementation it will rely on the development of joint working between agencies at every organisational level, from the front line to management, with all the power sharing that this implies. The prospects are uncertain, given the degree to which organisations like to work independently and preserve their traditional territories.

Index

A

accountability 20-2, 120-1, 123, 161, 192, 193, 285
  and multiagency policing 227, 233
active learning processes 51, 52
agency characteristics 18, 19, 20-5, 36
agency culture 273-4, 275-6
agency norms 22-3, 120-1
Alter, C. 123, 124-5
anti-ageist practice 156-7, 158
anti-poverty partnerships 57-73
assessment of needs 107, 147, 270
Audit Commission 3, 100-1, 230
audit processes 52-3

B

Baker, M. 184
Balls, S.J. 254-5
'banking education' 251-2, 253-4, 255, 257, 284
Baum, F. 190
'benchmarking and baselining' project 18
best value approach to user involvement 165-6, 168, 176
Bibini Centre for Young People 207
black community groups 203-21, 284
  marginalisation of 49, 70, 71, 110
Blair family: impact on education 254
Blunkett, David, MP 245
Booth, T.M. 121
'bottom-up' approaches 30-1, 82, 91, 183
'boundary spanners' 124, 132, 287
Bourdieu, Pierre 43
Bramley, G. 28
Brazil 245, 250-1, 252
Brighton: multiagency policing project 227-9
bureaucracy 106, 203
business community see private sector partners
Butt, J. 210
Byrne, D. 274

C

capacity building 42, 43-4, 249, 285
capitalism 245, 249-50
care in the community see community care
Care Trusts 5
cared-for children project 125-37
carer involvement 146-7, 150-4, 160
Central Stepney Single Regeneration Budget (SRB) 18, 32
chairmanship of partnerships 7, 68
Charlton, K. 161
children
  access to participation 41, 253
  cared-for children project 125-37
Cleaver, H. 245
Coates, D. 255
Cole, I. 88
Coleman, James 190
collaborative networks 6, 93, 145-6, 168-70
co-location of services 269-70
communication channels 47, 104, 105, 106-7, 124-5
community care
  for mentally ill people 99, 100-1, 168
  for older people 143-62, 168, 175
community development approaches to health 188-90
Community Development Projects 2-3, 58
community initiatives 2-3
community organisation partners 109-11
community participation 21
  anti-poverty strategies 69-71
  Education Action Zones 248-9, 252-3, 284-5
  knowledge and power 50-1
  in multiagency policing 239
  in regeneration partnerships 39, 41, 45-50, 70
  social housing tenants 80, 87-9
community safety 226, 287
competitive networks 6

Confederation of Indian Organisations (CIO) 208
confidential information 105, 237-8, 286
consumerist approach 165-6, 176
contract culture 3
cost-effectiveness
  of black and ethnic minority organisations 216, 217-18
  in community care for older people 153-4, 157
  of direct payments 172
  and lack of holism 26-9
  see also funding regimes
Cost-effectiveness in Housing Investment (CEHI) programme 18, 27, 32
crime prevention 226, 287
culture
  agency norms 22-3
  contract culture 3
  for multiagency policing 226-7, 228
  for partnerships 6, 9, 31, 121, 271, 285

D

data collection 24-5, 129, 205-6
'delivery vehicles' 20-1
development of partnerships 65-6, 84-7
'dialogic education' 251
direct payments schemes 168, 170-3
disabled people
  direct payments to 170-3
  user involvement 168, 169
domiciliary care 175
drug use 264-7, 271-2

E

Early Years partnerships 3-4
eating disorders specialist team 276-9
education
  and empowerment 245-57, 284-5
  parental choice 254-5, 256, 284-5
  truancy projects 232, 233-4
  see also training regimes

Education Action Zones (EAZs) 3-4, 245, 246-50, 251-4, 255, 256-7, 284-5
elderly people *see* older people
electoral accountability 20, 21, 36, 121
empowerment 42-4, 69, 156, 161, 169, 243-4
  direct payments schemes 168, 170-3
  and education 245-57, 284-5
  meaning of term 244
  practicalities of 254-7
  user-defined outcomes 173-6
  see also participation processes; user involvement
energy diversion effect 29
ethnic minority groups
  marginalisation of 49, 70, 71, 110
  voluntary organisations 203-21, 284
Ethnic Monitoring in Social Services (EMSS) project 210-16
evaluation processes 44-5, 52-3, 107, 123, 129-30, 161
  by users 168, 169, 173-6
  of health promotion partnerships 194, 195-6
exclusive partnerships 144, 152, 239, 248-9, 252-3
  marginalisation of minority groups 49, 70, 71, 110
expertise diversion effect 26, 29, 36
exported costs 27, 28, 32-3, 36

F

financial accountability 22, 121, 285
'flat' spending programmes 28
FLD agencies 20, 21, 36
Forbes 166
fragmentation of services 105-6
Freire, Paulo 50-1, 243-4, 245, 248, 250-1, 252, 254, 256
frictional costs 28-9, 36
'frontline' approach 30, 287
funding regimes 22, 27-8, 285
  anti-poverty strategies 68-9
  black and ethnic minority groups 203, 204-5, 210-16, 217-19, 284
  direct payments schemes 168, 170-3

Education Action Zones 249-50
financial gamesmanship 121-2
health partnerships 185
incentives 117-18, 123-4
short-term projects 134, 136-7
user-controlled organisations 168,
    169
see also cost-effectiveness

G

gamesmanship 121-2
Gelsthorpe, L. 229, 239
geographical space 261-80, 286
    jurisdiction of services 23-4, 120
Gillies, P. 182, 189, 190, 191, 194-6
Glendinning, C. 172
Gordon, P. 118-19
Goss, S. 160
Greater London Action on Disability
    (GLAD) 169

H

Hage, J. 123, 124-5
Hanafin, T. 118-19
Hardy, B. 122, 123, 125, 138
Hasler, F. 171-2
Hastings, A. 6-7
Health Act (1999) 5, 6, 100, 145, 177
Health Action Zones (HAZs) 3-4,
    184-5
Health Education Authority (HEA)
    191
Health Improvement Programmes
    (HImPs) 183-4, 193
health services
    health promotion partnerships
        181-97
    'hospital at home' scheme 148-50
    inequalities in 182-3
    international context 186-8
    mental health care 97-112
    partnership policy for 5-6, 185-6
    partnership projects 125-37
    partnerships with local authorities
        5-6, 63

partnerships with social services
    99-101, 155-6
pilot projects 125-37
settings approach to health promotion
    186, 188-9
social capital and health 181, 189-91,
    194-5, 196-7
user experience survey 176
Healthy Cities movement (WHO)
    184, 193-4
Healthy Living Centres (HLCs) 185
Heaney, T. 244, 251
holism 17-35, 36
    approach to health promotion 187-8
    and cost-effectiveness 26-9
    in practice 25-6
    user perspective 175
Holly Street renewal scheme 18, 32
home care delivery 175
homeless people 101-2
'hospital at home' scheme 148-50
housing association partners 84-5
housing conditions and exported costs
    27
housing policy 21, 47-8, 283
    impact on older people in the
        community 145, 151-2
    see also social housing
Huxham, C. 124, 139

I

'impossible communities' 253
incentives 117-18, 123-4
inclusive partnerships 144-7, 152,
    157-8, 159, 160
independent living
    direct payments enable 172
    support in community for older people
        143-62, 168, 175
indicators of progress 25, 52
'individualist fallacy' 248-50
inequalities in health 182-3
information
    collection 24-5, 129, 205-6
    confidentiality 105, 237-8, 286
    sharing 105-6, 107, 286

interagency policing *see* multiagency policing
interorganisational networks 93
Iqbal, B. 6

J

Jackson, K. 245
job descriptions 31-2
Johnson, H. 44
Joint Continuing Care (JCC) project 125-37, 148-59
Joseph Rowntree Foundation 52, 97, 100, 102, 204, 206
jurisdiction of partners 23-4, 120
Justice, C. 189

K

Kickbusch, I. 188
King's Fund 110
Kingston workshops 102-8, 111
knowledge 50-1, 104, 105-6

L

lack of holism costs 29, 36
Leadbeater, C. 50
Leeds Black Elders Association 207-8
legislative frameworks 20, 104
  for direct payments 170-1
  for multiagency policing 223, 224
  for user involvement 144-5, 159, 166-8
Liddle, A.M. 229, 239
Lindow, Viv 167
local democracy 4, 20, 21, 253
local government
  anti-poverty strategies 57-73
  direct payments schemes 171-2
  partnership policy for 4
  partnerships with health authorities 5-6, 63, 183
  service delivery systems 18-25
Local Government Association 4
Local Government Management Board 226
Local Strategic Partnerships 4

London Black Carers Workers Forum 208
long-term care policy 144-5
'looked after' children project 125-37
Lowndes, V. 6
Lukes, S. 40

M

Mackintosh, M. 6, 244
Malpass, P. 77
management of partnerships 66-9, 123, 124, 135
marginalisation
  of minority groups 49, 70, 71, 110
  in post-industrial capitalism 245
Martin, S. 117
Mayo, M. 244
Means, R. 145, 161
mental health
  policy for 5, 97-112, 168
  staff perspective 103-4
Miller, C. 160
minority groups
  challenge racism 203-21, 284
  marginalisation 49, 70, 71, 110
Mirza, K. 210
mobility
  of services 269-72, 286
  of users 267-9, 286
monitoring partnerships 44-5, 52-3, 107, 123, 129-30, 161
  with black and ethnic minority groups 215-16
moral panics 263-4
Morgan report (1991) 223, 226
Morris, J. 146, 170
multiagency policing 223-39, 287

N

National Lotteries Charities Board 204-5, 219, 220
National Service Framework for Mental Health 98, 99
National Strategy for Neighbourhood Renewal 4, 8, 60, 61
needs-led assessments 147, 270

Neighbourhood plc exercise 33-5
New Commitment to Regeneration
    Programme 4
New Deal for Communities 18, 24-5
New Opportunities Fund 185
new urban left 58-9
Newcastle
    Education Action Zone (Newcastle
        West) 246-8, 251-4, 255, 256-7
    Going for Growth strategy 253
    parental choice in education 255
NHS Plan (2000) 5, 177
Nixon, J. 124
Nocon, A. 173

O

older people
    Joint Continuing Care project
        125-37, 148-59
    policy for care of 5
    services for black and ethnic minority
        communities 207-8, 212, 214
    support in community 143-62, 168,
        175
organisation of partnerships 66-9, 123,
    135, 158
'osmosis' 31, 36
outcomes
    of health promotion 195-6
    user-defined 173-6
Ovretveit, J. 120, 123

P

Pacific Institute 247-8
Page, R. 254
'parallel action' partnerships 90
parental choice in education 254-5, 256,
    284-5
participation processes 21, 39
    anti-poverty strategies 69-71
    Education Action Zones 248-9,
        252-3, 284-5
    evaluation of 44-5, 52-3
    exclusive processes 144, 152, 239,
        248-9, 252-3

marginalisation of minority groups
    49, 70, 71, 110
housing partnerships 79-80
inclusive processes 144-7, 152,
    157-8, 159, 160, 168, 169, 175
multiagency policing 239
power relations 41, 42, 44-50, 68-9,
    70-1, 284
tenant participation 80, 87-9
see also empowerment; user
    involvement
partnership projects 117-39
partnership working
    advantages 1-2, 123
    background on 2-3, 58-9
    challenges facing 119-22, 145-6,
        284-6
    cost considerations 26-9
    coverage of term 6, 118-19, 244
    culture for 6, 9, 31, 121, 271, 285
    current initiatives 3-6
    debatable issues 7-9
    imprecise terminology 17-18
    prerequisites for 122-5, 286-8
    staff perspective 103-4, 132
    strategies to improve 29-33
    types of partnerships 6-7, 64-5, 82-4
performance indicators 31, 195-6
personal development 246-8
Pettigrew, A. 125
pilot projects 117, 118, 125-37
police partnerships 223-39, 287
policy 3-6, 78-80, 121, 144-5, 159
    see also housing policy
political change 69, 91
poverty
    anti-poverty strategies 57-73
    and education 255, 257
power mapping 51-2
power relations 8, 39-53, 121-2, 284
    in anti-poverty partnerships 68-9,
        70-1
    challenging imbalances 50-3
    dimensions of power 40-2
    empowerment and partnership
        243-57
    practical experiences 44-50

role of black and ethnic minority groups 203-21, 284
practitioners' perspective
black and ethnic minority groups 207-8, 209, 211, 212-16
of community care project 154-7
interprofessional differences 145-6, 159, 285
of multiagency policing 230-8
of partnership working 103-4, 132, 167-8
Pratt, J. 6
private sector partners
in Education Action Zones 247-8, 249-50
financial accountability 22
in health promotion 188-9, 192
low level of involvement 64
professional differences 145-6, 159, 285
'progressive' spending programmes 28
project status 117-39
case studies 125-37
use of term 119
public expenditure *see* funding regimes
public participation *see* community participation; participation processes

Q

Qureshi, H. 173

R

Race Equality Unit survey 206-10
racism and race relations 203-21, 284
regeneration partnerships 4, 70
early initiatives 2-3, 59
holistic approach 17-35
housing partnerships 85-7
power relations 39-53, 70-1
Reid, B. 6
resource constraints 106, 136-7, 230
responsibility allocation 121
see also accountability
Reynolds, Harold, Jr 250
Riley, K. 249
Rogers, J. 126

Royal College of Psychiatrists 101
Rustin, M. 248

S

Sainsbury Centre for Mental Health 99-100, 102
Sanderson, I. 117
Sao Paulo, Brazil 245, 250-1, 252
Sashidharan 166
Saving Lives White Paper 185-6
Scottish Community Development Centre 52
Seebohm report 3
self-advocacy approach 165, 166
service delivery systems 18-25
user evaluation 174-5
service users *see* user involvement
settings approach to health promotion 186, 188-9
Shaping Our Lives project 174-5
Sheffield Users' Network 170
Silburn, R. 255
simulation situations 33-5
Single Regeneration Budget programme 18, 32, 86, 204-5, 220
Skeffington report 3
Skelcher, C. 6
social capital 42, 43-4, 285
in health development 181, 189-91, 194-5, 196-7
social exclusion
and spatial location 262, 264, 272-4
see also social inclusion partnerships
Social Exclusion Unit 79-80
social housing 21, 47-8, 77-93
and mental health care 100-112
social inclusion partnerships 57-73, 61-2
social services
partnership policy for 4-5, 9
partnerships with health services 99-101, 155-6
pilot projects 125-37
police view of 237, 238
support for black and ethnic minority communities 206-16, 284

support in community for older people 150, 155, 168, 175
user involvement strategies 165-78
Social Services Inspectorate report 147
Social Services Modernisation Fund 117-18
society and space 261-2
spatial location 261-80, 286
mobility of services 269-72, 286
mobility of users 267-9, 286
and social problems 263-7
specialist teams and spatial location 263-4, 275-9
Spray, J. 182, 189
staff *see* practitioners' perspective
Stanley, D. 146
Stanwick, S. 124
Statham, D. 146
Stepney Housing and Development Agency (SHADA) 21
Stepney Single Regeneration Budget (SRB) 18, 32
Stocking, B. 120
strategy
anti-poverty strategies 57-73
design and development 84
for mental health 98-9
for partnership working 29-33
street drinkers' centre 234-5
structural costs 27-8, 36
structure and agency 273-5
support in community
for black and ethnic minority groups 206-10, 284
for older people 143-62, 168, 175
supported housing schemes 101
Supporting People initiative 89-90

T

Taylor, P.V. 251
tenant participation 80, 87-9
Therborn, G. 245
Thompson, N. 161
Thomson, A. 123
Titley, S. 156
training regimes

for community participants 46, 47-8, 50
for holism 32
for practitioners 107, 146
training for 107, 146
travelling difficulties 268-9
truancy projects 232, 233-4

U

unitary authorities' jurisdiction 23, 24
Urban Programme 2-3, 58
urban regime theory 249
Urban Task Force 85-6
user involvement
community care for older people 146-7, 150-4, 157-8, 159, 160, 168, 169, 175
Education Action Zones 248-9, 252-3, 284-5
in health services 186-7, 194
in mental health care 110-11, 112
multiagency policing 239
social services strategies for 165-78
user-controlled organisations 168, 169-70
user-defined outcomes 173-6
view of community care practitioners 150-1, 152-3
see also empowerment

V

value for money 153-4, 157, 165-6
voluntary organisation partners 108-10, 112
black and ethnic minority groups 203-21, 284
coverage of term 205-6
spatial management 271
vulnerable people 89-90, 105
see also children; mental health; older people

W

Watling, R. 249
West Newcastle Education Action Zone
   246–8, 251–4, 255, 256–7
WHO 181, 184, 185, 186–7, 192–4
Williams, C. 124
Wilmot, S. 146
Wilson, A. 161
Wilson, G. 44
Wiltshire and Swindon Users'
   Network 168–70

Y

young people
  as participants 41
  services for 207

Z

Zarb, G. 171–2

60 4077409 0